Slavery, Capitalism and the Industrial Revolution

SLAVERY, CAPITALISM AND THE INDUSTRIAL REVOLUTION

Maxine Berg and Pat Hudson

polity

First published in 2023 by Polity Press

Polity Press
65 Bridge Street
Cambridge CB2 1UR, UK

Polity Press
111 River Street
Hoboken, NJ 07030, USA

ISBN-13: 978-1-5095-5268-9

A catalogue record for this book is available from the British Library.

Library of Congress Control Number: 2022948165

Typeset in 11.5 on 14pt Adobe Garamond
by Fakenham Prepress Solutions, Fakenham, Norfolk NR21 8NL

The publisher has used its best endeavours to ensure that the URLs for external websites referred to in this book are correct and active at the time of going to press. However, the publisher has no responsibility for the websites and can make no guarantee that a site will remain live or that the content is or will remain appropriate.

Every effort has been made to trace all copyright holders, but if any have been overlooked the publisher will be pleased to include any necessary credits in any subsequent reprint or edition.

For further information on Polity, visit our website:
politybooks.com

Contents

Maps and tables

Maps

Tables

Acknowledgements

Our main research interest is the history of industrialization, particularly in Britain. Between us, in the past, we have written about artisan manufacture and technological change; shifts in consumption and product innovation; the impact of commodities imported from Asia; and the globalization of Britain's overseas trade. We have researched the metal trades and the textile industries; regional and structural shifts; demographic changes; the advantages and the limits of quantitative assessments; and the importance of changes in business organization, finance and banking. Although we have considered slavery from time to time in our work, it is only in recent years that we have begun fully to explore the ways in which slavery links to all of these topics.

We have written this book in order to examine those links in detail and to provide an accessible account of the place of slavery in British industrialization. Work on the volume has involved a steep learning curve and a recognition of the immense debt that we owe to a small group of colleagues past and present who have produced excellent studies of Atlantic slavery, the operation of Britain's trade in enslaved people and the wider impact of slavery on capitalist society. From the classic *Capitalism and Slavery* thesis of Eric Williams, published in 1944, key works influencing our approach range from the analyses of Richard B. Sheridan and Richard Pares, the demographic work of B. W. Higman, the commercial and financial studies of S. G. Checkland and Jacob Price, to Joseph Inikori's account of the contribution of Africans to the industrial revolution. These authors led the way in keeping the role of slavery in British economic development alive over many decades when mainstream economic history marginalized its importance. A number of UK, European and US scholars writing since the 1970s and 1980s have added further detail to our knowledge of the operation of the slave trade, the history of slave ports, the wealth produced by slavery and its distribution. In addition to others mentioned below, we must especially acknowledge the research we have drawn upon in the works of David Alston, William Darity, Tom Devine, David Eltis, Stanley Engerman, Douglas J. Hamilton, Kenneth Morgan, Nicholas Radburn, David Richardson, S. D. Smith, Barbara Solow, James Walvin and Gavin Wright.

Adding to this list, we are directly indebted to colleagues, with expertise in different aspects of industrialization, slavery and Atlantic trade, who selflessly read and made valuable comments on earlier versions of various chapters and encouraged us in our efforts. We thank them all: Jeremy Adelman, Kristine Bruland, Trevor Burnard, Jan de Vries, Nick Draper, Chris Evans, Miriam Goodall, Aaron Graham, Catherine Hall, Jane Humphries, Mina Ishizu, Philip John, Sebastian Keibek, Tony Lane, Patrick O'Brien, David Ormrod, Mary O'Sullivan, Dexnell Peters, James Poskett, Giorgio Riello, Carolyn Sissoko, Keith Smith, John Styles, Keith Tribe and Nuala Zahedieh.

Our sincere thanks go to Helen Clifford for her work on the references and her reading of the text. We are also grateful to Sebastian Keibek and Leigh Shaw Taylor for providing the mapping data and maps for chapters 5, 6 and 7, and to Karolina Hutkova, Giorgio Riello and John Styles for the data assembled in table 7.2. We alone are responsible for the interpretation of these maps and the table.

Finally, we have had the good fortune of helpful advice from four anonymous readers engaged by the publisher as well as the thoughtful assistance, sequentially, of George Owers, Pascal Porcheron and, above all, Julia Davies and Lindsey Wimpenny at Polity. We own all the faults and errors that remain.

This book includes a number of passages from eighteenth-century primary sources that describe people of African descent in language which is now unacceptable. They also contain negative portrayals of people and cultures. The terms 'Negro'/'negro' and 'negroes' were in common usage during the eighteenth century. We retain these and other pejorative expressions within quotations from contemporary primary sources in order to call them out and to convey the racial divisions at the heart of early industrial capitalism.

Maxine Berg and Pat Hudson
October 2022

Introduction

Edward Colston (1636–1721) became the public face of the British slave trade when his statue was thrown into Bristol harbour during the Black Lives Matter protests of June 2020. Colston had been a member of the Society of Merchant Venturers in Bristol and deputy governor of the Royal African Company (RAC). Slave trading was his main source of wealth from the 1680s. He later became MP for Bristol and a noted philanthropist, giving more than £70,000 to educational and social causes. In the nineteenth century he was a Bristol legend, celebrated in statuary and stained glass, in landmarks and street names, in the (charitable) Colston Society (disbanded in 2020 after 275 years) and even in a regional bread roll, the 'Colston bun'.[1] 'The Colston Four', charged with criminal damage to the statue, were acquitted in a Bristol jury trial on 5 January 2022 to applause from the public gallery. Britain's leading public historian, echoing their legal defence, suggested that the Four were 'on the right side of history'.[2]

Two days after Colston was toppled, the statue of Robert Milligan (1746–1809), a Scottish West India merchant, ship owner and slave factor, was covered with a calico shroud and placard by protesters in London. Mulligan, the main instigator of the West India Docks, had also made his fortune from slavery and plantations. A week later, the statue was quietly removed as part of a wider drive to review all London's statues with links to slavery.[3]

At the same time, heated debates about the memorialization of individuals involved in slavery were underway in Scotland, above all in calls for the 46-metre-high Melville Monument in St Andrew's Square, Edinburgh, to be 're-interpreted' or removed. The statue is

[1] Morgan (2004a).
[2] See Olusoga (2022a; 2022b).
[3] https://www.museumoflondon.org.uk/application/files/2915/9827/8333/lr-misc-docks-milligan-statue.pdf; Dresser (2007).

1

dedicated to Henry Dundas (1742–1811), the statesman whose advocacy (against William Wilberforce) of 'gradual' rather than immediate abolition probably delayed the ending of the British slave trade by fifteen years.[4] In south Wales, another area of Britain that benefitted markedly from Atlantic slavery, the 23-metre Picton Monument in Carmarthen became a focus of protest generating a petition, with 20,000 signatories, calling for its removal. Sir Thomas Picton was a British lieutenant general notorious for the ill treatment and torture of enslaved people during his period as governor of Trinidad (1797–1803).[5] A marble statue in the 'Heroes of Wales Gallery' and a portrait of Picton at Cardiff City Hall were removed in 2020.[6]

Many British cities, universities, museums, public and private institutions and commercial and financial houses of long standing have, in the last few years, carried out or completed reviews of their connections to slavery. A report by the National Trust, which has in its care many of the fine country houses connected with wealth from slavery, created much controversy.[7] Many Oxford and Cambridge colleges and several universities, especially Bristol and Glasgow, have committed resources and made appointments to investigate their connections to the profits of slavery and empire.[8] Glasgow University pledged to raise £20 million for a joint Glasgow–Caribbean Centre for Development Research. The Church of England initiated a review of its slave-related statuary in 2021, yet an application to the Church from Jesus College Cambridge to remove a chapel memorial to seventeenth-century slave trader Tobias Rustat was controversially declined by a consistory church

---

[4] His legal advocacy had earlier resulted in the abolition of slave holding within Scotland: https://www.historyofparliamentonline.org/volume/1790–1820/member/dundas-henry-1742–1811.

[5] Picton's horrific reign as governor of Trinidad was immortalized by Naipaul (1969). In a notorious case Picton was put on trial in London for approving the torture of a fourteen-year-old girl, Luisa Calderón. He had the conviction overturned by arguing that Trinidad was still subject to Spanish law, which permitted torture: Havard (2004).

[6] The latter was 're-interpreted' and returned to display in a travel case at Cardiff Museum in 2022.

[7] https://www.nationaltrust.org.uk/features/addressing-the-histories-of-slavery-and-colonialism-at-the-national-trust.

[8] See report by Cambridge University, for example: https://www.cam.ac.uk/stories/legacies-of-enslavement-inquiry.

court.[9] The Bank of England has apologized for its role in the slave trade and for the twenty-five governors and directors who owned slaves. It has removed eight paintings and two busts from public display.[10] Reviews by several banks and businesses in the City of London have led to a number of secretive 'restorative justice grants' intended to benefit the Afro-Caribbean population in Britain.[11]

Protest and debate over the commemoration and activities of slave traders and plantation owners operating centuries ago highlight major questions about the origins of Britain's wealth as well as the foundations of deep-seated racial disparities and racial injustice in Britain and elsewhere. Britain's early industrial revolution, which has defined her economic, political and cultural identity ever since, was inextricably bound up with the slave trade and colonial plantations. But this has received less attention from historians than has Britain's celebrated, pioneering role in the abolition of her transatlantic trade in enslaved people (in 1807) and in ending slavery in most British territories (in the 1830s). The extent of Britain's trade in enslaved peoples, her brutal exploitation of plantation labour and the wealth that these activities brought to British families and wider society have been obscured in favour of a more heroic island story of early economic improvement and cultural benevolence. This has been reflected in school curricula and in the treatment of slavery as a minor subject in the range and sweep of British domestic and imperial history as taught in universities.

In 2022 an engaging popular history of the 1823 slave rebellion in Demerara was published with the title *White Debt: the Demerara*

[9] *The Guardian*, 22 March 2022: https://www.theguardian.com/uk-news/2022/mar/23/church-court-rejects-cambridge-college-bid-to-move-tobias-rustat-slave-trader-memorial.

[10] From the 1770s to 1790 the Bank itself owned 599 slaves in Grenada after a defaulted loan made to Alexander and Sons: *The Guardian*, 16 April 2022. https://www.theguardian.com/world/2022/apr/15/bank-of-england-owned-599-slaves-in-1770s-new-exhibition-reveals.

[11] The secret grants have been governed by non-disclosure agreements: Rawlinson (2020); https://www.theguardian.com/world/2020/jun/18/lloyds-of-london-and-greene-king-to-make-slave-trade-reparations; Hannah Capella, 'Glasgow University's Bold Move to Pay Back Slave Trade Profits', *BBC News*, 23 August 2019: https://www.bbc.co.uk/news/uk-scotland-glasgow-west-49435041.

Uprising and Britain's Legacy of Slavery. Despite graduating from elite British educational institutions, the author, as he began his research, was 'quickly shocked' at how little he knew:

> That it had been British captains commanding British boats operated by British sailors who had transported around 2.8 million captive Africans to the British Caribbean, that it was British families who owned plantations in the Caribbean run by British managers and overseers where hundreds of thousands of enslaved men, women and children were forced to live and die. That it had been British businesses that had transported the cotton, tobacco, sugar and other crops cultivated by the enslaved people to the consumers back in Britain. How was it possible I didn't know any of this? It was like a national amnesia.[12]

The bulk of professional historians of Britain were partly to blame for this amnesia, although the history of slavery did gain increasing prominence as part of the rise of social and labour history in the 1970s and 1980s, and as a response to the growing historiography of slavery in the United States at that time. With a few notable exceptions, however, it was largely treated as an aspect of the history of the Americas rather than as a vital element of Britain's history. In *Capitalism and Slavery* (1944), the Trinidadian scholar Eric Williams stood alone in placing the slave trade and plantations centrally among explanations of Britain's industrial revolution.[13] His work was initially largely dismissed, but discussion resurfaced in the 1970s and 1980s with debate over profit rates in the slave trade and plantation businesses, and the degree to which those profits directly financed Britain's industrial infrastructure. Such partial assessments of Williams' thesis, which were also constrained by the data available at the time, led most historians to give slavery a minimum role, if any, in the economic history of Britain. The gains from slavery accrued not only to elite merchants and wealthy plantation owners but also, by providing incomes and livelihoods, to many others throughout British society. But the widespread connections between the exploitation of enslaved Africans and mainstream

---

[12] Harding (2022: 5).
[13] Williams (1944/1994).

British economic history have been avoided by the bulk of historians. The separation of British history from wider colonial and global history sidelined the history of slavery in British research, education and popular consciousness.

Most major works on the industrial revolution since the 1980s have ignored slavery and plantations altogether. Textbooks that currently lead the field concentrate on changes in resource use, capital and labour, internal to Britain, or on the economic benefits derived from favourable 'inclusive' politics and institutions. They devote scarcely a sentence to slavery or West Indian plantations.[14] Slavery has, however, returned to wider historians' interests in recent years with the heightened political consciousness of racial inequality in Britain. Historians are also now addressing this subject as part of fresh conceptual frameworks: new histories of consumption and commodity flows; new forms of global history; studies of globalized coercive labour regimes, including modern slavery; and moves, in the USA in particular, to write new histories of capitalism that give central significance to slavery and race.

Apart from new historical frameworks, we also now have a wealth of digitized and searchable primary sources that were unavailable to earlier scholars. In particular, the Legacies of British Slavery database makes it possible not only to trace many British owners of plantations and the enslaved, but their links with other businesses, industries and investments. 'Slave Voyages', the Transatlantic Slave Trade Database, details all recorded slave ships and their human cargoes travelling from Europe to the Americas via Africa.[15] Other online data, such as the Cambridge Group's occupational statistics, make it easier to consider the impact of slave-based Atlantic trade upon Britain's pioneering industrial regions

---

[14] Allen (2009b); Mokyr (2009; 2017); Wrigley (2016); Acemoglu and Robinson (2012). The stand-out exception to these texts about the industrial revolution, one that emphasizes the role of both slavery and the mercantilist policies of the state, is Ashworth (2017). The only detailed account of the industrial revolution giving a principal place to Africans and slavery is Inikori (2002). Findlay and O'Rourke (2007: 227–364) give slavery prominence in a volume covering the last millennium of world trade, but a recent textbook that includes a consideration of slavery and Britain's industrial revolution relegates it to a 'background condition': Koyama and Rubin (2022: 158–60).
[15] Legacies of British Slavery: https://www.ucl.ac.uk/lbs/. See also Hall et al. (2014). Trans-Atlantic Slave Trade Database: https://www.slavevoyages.org/voyage/database.

and sectors.[16] New historical frameworks, new sources and the political moment make this the time for a broadly focused book setting out the connections between slavery and the British economy.

We are not experts on the institution or experiences of slavery or on the history of the Caribbean, colonial America or Africa. This is not a book that aims to examine any of those subjects in detail. The economic, social and cultural history of slavery and the inhumane practices of slavery are vitally important subjects but are well beyond the scope of our study. Our approach is that of two historians of Britain's industrial revolution and of her longer trajectory as an economic power. Our question is: where does slavery fit into this story? This of course requires us to consider aspects of the slave trade within Africa, the operation of chattel slavery, the exploitation of the enslaved and the ways in which the trade in enslaved people and plantation agriculture were organized to maximize and to direct profits, but fuller studies of all these topics must be left to other scholars.

Our approach

Although it had much longer roots, the 'industrial revolution' in Britain took place most obviously in the half century following the 1760s. It was marked by (slow) acceleration in the rate of increase of national income and output; by structural and regional shifts in the economy; by urbanization; and by technological and organizational innovation, all of which contributed to increased productivity. New technologies were introduced; steam power was gradually diffused throughout industry; internal transportation was transformed with road improvements, canal construction and railways; manufacturing and commercial organization grew more efficient; new forms of investment and financial intermediation were put in place; and there was a revolution in consumption. The build-up to these changes from the later seventeenth century, and the changes themselves, took place at the same time that Britain became the world's primary slave trader and a leading exploiter

---

[16] Cambridge Group for the History of Population and Social Structure, Occupational datasets: https://www.campop.geog.cam.ac.uk/research/occupations/datasets/catalogues /occupationspopulation/.

of colonial slave-plantation systems of production. The big question, addressed in this book, is the degree to which these developments were connected.

We do not argue that slavery caused the industrial revolution. Neither do we suggest that slavery was necessary for the development of industrial capitalism in Britain. Even less does our study attempt to estimate that the gains from slavery contributed a particular percentage to Britain's economic growth, GDP or capital formation in the eighteenth century, as earlier studies have attempted. That is not our purpose, partly because many aspects of the impact of slavery are not measurable in quantitative terms. What we do say is that the role of slavery in the process of industrialization and economic transformation in the eighteenth and early nineteenth centuries has been generally underestimated by historians, and that it is time for a rounded examination in the light of accumulated research. The slave and plantation trades were the hub around which many other dynamic and innovatory sectors of the economy pivoted. Slavery, directly and indirectly, set in motion innovations in manufacturing, agriculture, wholesaling, retailing, shipping, banking, international trade, finance and investment, insurance, as well as in the organization and intensi-fication of work, record keeping and the application of scientific and useful knowledge. Slavery certainly was formative in the timing and nature of Britain's industrial transition.

In our analysis we survey a wide range of literatures that are too often generated and read separately from one another. They include studies of consumption habits and tastes; Atlantic science; regional transforma-tions; industrial skills; the impulse to innovate; accounting; business management; and changes in national and international finance. Bringing these subjects together creates a new view of the industrial revolution and of capitalism in Britain.

Structure of the volume

Our first chapter provides a chronology of Britain's involvement with African slavery over more than three centuries. We follow with a series of themed chapters that represent different areas of connection between the slave trade, plantations and the industrialization of the economy. In the two final chapters, we discuss the longer-term impact of slavery on the British economy and society and on the nature of British capitalism, beyond the abolition of the slave trade and of slavery in most British territories in the 1830s.

We start with an overview of how the trade in enslaved people was organized and developed; why and how plantations producing valuable and desirable consumer crops to satisfy European tastes came to use enslaved African labour. Trade, shipping and finance in the Atlantic included the African and Iberian trades and extended beyond to the re-export of textiles imported from Asia and of manufactured goods originating on the European continent. These trades created innovations in international payment and credit systems and in manufacturing, across a whole range of new goods destined for new markets. A central role was played by the state: aggressive mercantilism and warfare extended colonial possessions and trading influence. Here as elsewhere we use the term mercantilism to convey a range of state policies, especially fiscal and military policies (most not unique to Britain) aimed at the extension of trade at the expense of rivals; the maintenance of favourable trade balances; protectionism; and a focus upon colonies as markets for exports and to supply raw materials.[17]

Eighteenth-century commentary about the Africa trade, slavery and plantations emphasized their vital contribution to the British economy. This, however, got lost, along with historians' interest in slavery during the nineteenth century, when free trade and the exercise of imperial power in new forms came to dominate the historical imagination. The breakthrough work of Eric Williams in the 1940s might have led to a widespread reappraisal of the role of slavery in Britain's industrial revolution, but historians of the time were more concerned with the history of abolition and with other factors in the rise of industrial capitalism in Britain. Our second chapter confronts this history and sketches out the broad approach necessary fully to comprehend how slavery impacted upon the nature of the British economy and its industrial transition.

---

[17] State policies of the period are often viewed as holding back the development of markets and capitalist society but they can equally be seen as an integral part of their evolution. See Pincus (2012); Rössner (2020: 1–49, 137–68); Ashworth (2017: 105–44).

Trade and consumption drove the early British industrial revolution, much of it underpinned by the growing taste, and escalating demand, for sugar as well as other tropical 'groceries'. Our third chapter surveys how sugar, tobacco, cacao and coffee joined tea from Asia to become the key commodities shifting European consumer taste and culture. These new drinks and foods stimulated new British refining and manufacturing industries. The rituals and equipage surrounding their consumption also brought increased imports of porcelain from China and glass, ceramics and silverware from Europe, which prompted imitative innovation in British industries producing such tablewares for consumers across the social scale. Demand for colonial groceries and for the receptacles used in their consumption hastened a move from household self-sufficiency to wage labour.

West Indian and southern mainland American plantations combined enslaved labour exploitation with agri-business, capital intensity and organizational capability. Our fourth chapter shows how plantation economies utilized seeds and plants, labour, capital, skills and knowledge from across the globe, and made innovations in wind, water and steam power as well as in refining and distilling. The plantation system was part and parcel of the organizational and technological innovations of the industrial revolution.

Britain's Atlantic ports and their industrial hinterlands are studied in chapter 5. This demonstrates how the increasing power of Atlantic trading caused a geographical reorientation of the country's industrial focus. The key manufacturing regions of the industrial revolution relied on access to Atlantic port cities, principally Liverpool, London, Glasgow and Bristol, and to the capital and credit that they generated. Most investigations into the causes of the Industrial Revolution focus on the national level and miss the causes and impact of industrial agglomeration in the dynamic industrial regions of the northwest, the midlands, the Scottish lowlands and south Wales that benefitted most from Atlantic orientation.

Regional dynamics were a feature of the heavy, capital-intensive industries of mining, iron and copper smelting, as well as the lighter metal trades, the subject of chapter 6. London and Bristol merchants and banks financed investment in the south Wales coalfield, in Cornish copper mines, in copper refining in the Swansea Valley, in iron refining in south Wales and the west midlands and in coal mining in the northeast for the London market. The metalwares trades from copper vessels to agricultural implements and guns became more diversified and specialized in response to Atlantic markets.

It is to cotton textiles that we usually look to explore connections between slavery and industrialization, but Scottish, Irish and Lancashire linens, west Yorkshire woollens, midlands hosiery and even London's silks were also important parts of Britain's textile revolution. Chapter 7 explores links between slavery and the textile sector. New Atlantic demands helped to drive changes in the weight, patterns and quality of cloth, and in the mixing of different fibres. Plantation-produced indigo together with other Atlantic dyestuffs and Senegalese gum (used in printing) were instrumental in creating more colourful patterns and designs. Above all, the qualities of raw cotton from Caribbean plantations aided the product revolution and hastened the great spinning inventions of the jenny, the water frame and the mule. These developments long pre-dated the better-known connection between Lancashire cotton factories and the slave plantations of the American South.

During the process of state-supported Atlantic trade expansion and industrial transformation London became the leading global financial centre, and it is to finance that we turn in chapter 8. The expectation and realization of profits from the trade in enslaved peoples and from the cultivation and importation of plantation products, particularly sugar, underpinned aspects of the early eighteenth-century evolution of the national debt, taxation, the formation of Bank of England policy and the trade in government stock. Plantation investment and shipping also brought innovation in the mortgage and insurance markets, in multiplex financial transfers and in the expansion of commercial credit that linked provincial merchants, manufacturers and banks with the resources of the London money market.

When chattel slavery was ended in British territories (with the exception of the East India Company's possessions, St Helena and Ceylon) in 1833, compensation of £20 million was paid to slave owners. We address this further financial legacy of slavery in chapter 9. The debts taken on by the British state to pay compensation to slave holders were only finally repaid in 2015. From the records of compensation payments we can see how deeply embedded relationships with slavery and plantations were at many of levels of society and right across the country.[18]

The ending of the British slave trade and slavery did not mark the end of Britain's involvement. The inter-colonial slave trade continued, and British investors had interests in plantations and mining operations employing enslaved people in the Americas and Asia throughout the nineteenth century. The plantation system, rather than declining in the wake of abolition, burgeoned globally, based on other sorts of racially based coerced labour, often indentured labour, much of it brought from British and European colonies in the global South in British ships that dominated the trade. Racial capitalism was the other face of European modernization during the nineteenth and early twentieth centuries.

The legacies of slavery continue in great inequalities of wealth and income both within Britain and between Britain, the Caribbean and West Africa. There is also a great divide between London and its 'home counties' and Britain's former industrial regions, which were created in the time of slavery but which have in the past half century experienced deindustrialization. Overlaying this income and wealth divide are deep racial divisions with their roots in slavery and later imperialism. Labour for the factories, infrastructures and hospitals of Britain's years of expansion from the 1950s to the 1970s was drawn from her former colonies, notably the Caribbean. These minority workforces, particularly in Britain's former industrial regions, have faced an unreceptive and often aggressive environment and are now among the poorest in the country.

The relationship between slavery and capitalism has been foundational in US history and historiography since the end of the Civil War. This has been endorsed in recent years by the 1619 Project, which reaches back to the arrival in Virginia of the first enslaved Africans, and by New Histories of Capitalism (NHC), in which slavery is placed at the heart of both US and global capitalist development. We turn in our final chapter to consider Britain's story in parallel with these North American narratives. We mark out the distinctive connections between slavery and the economy in Britain and within the wider history of a global capitalism

[18] https://www.ucl.ac.uk/lbs/; https://taxjustice.net/2020/06/09/slavery-compensation -uk-questions/.

that grew out of the west European colonial project and Britain's role within it.

A common question asked of those who emphasize the impact of slavery on the industrial precocity of Britain is why industrial revolutions did not occur earlier in Spain, Portugal, France or the Netherlands, countries that were also deeply engaged in transatlantic slavery. We address this question in a number of chapters that consider the other factors that Britain had in her favour, though few were unique and many had a close synergy with the development of Britain's slave-based Atlantic trading system. We argue that Britain was in a position to benefit disproportionately from slavery in the eighteenth century during the period when she dominated the slave trade. The advantage was firmly endorsed by the Atlantic territorial and trading gains of the Seven Years War and the Napoleonic War period, which came at the expense of French and Dutch rivals.

This is an economic history of industrializing Britain with its slave roots examined and acknowledged. State policy, colonial ambitions and slavery brought Europe, the African continent, North America and a group of small islands in the West Indies into a dynamic of capitalist development that proved crucial to the making of the industrial revolution and that also influenced the nature of British capitalism in the longer term. It is the story of Scotland and Wales as much as England, and of regional development alongside the emergence of London as a world financial and trading centre. We 'follow the money' generated by the enslavement of Africans and the development of plantations but we also highlight their wider impact on institutions, culture and practices in the making of the modern economy. Plantation output, above all sugar and cotton, shifted consumer tastes and encouraged new manufactures and methods of production. Atlantic demands, underpinned by slavery and plantations, were important to the transformation of manufactures and technologies that drove the industrial revolution. The slave trade, plantations and Atlantic colonialism also brought a revolution in financial services that set the scene for Britain's future global role. By emphasizing these aspects, our book challenges established views of the role of slavery in Britain's economic history and in the making of Western capitalism.

CHAPTER 1

Slavery and the British economy: how the slave and plantation trades worked and how they changed

In one of history's greatest crimes against humanity at least 12.5 million enslaved Africans were trafficked across the Atlantic over the course of three centuries.[1] Around 11 million reached their initial destinations. Many died during the brutalities of capture, trade and detention on the West African coast and even more from disease, ill-treatment and suicide during the transatlantic passage and in the early weeks after arrival. The trade was initiated in the fifteenth century but accelerated, for Britain especially, after the Restoration. It peaked in the 1780s with the transport of more than 80,000 annually, most to the Caribbean. And it remained high into the 1860s, well beyond the abolition of the British trade in 1807.[2] British traders were leading players in the Atlantic trade in enslaved people as early as the 1670s; they dominated the trade between the 1740s and 1807, when they accounted for around 40% of total shipments from Africa.[3]

Labour shortages, alongside profitable opportunities for mining in South America and an abundance of fertile land for agricultural crops, encouraged a growing use of enslaved labour in the Americas. Expansion of the slave trade meant that enslaved labour became a cheaper option than wage labour or indentured servants.[4] Rapidly escalating European demands for tropical produce, particularly sugar, in the eighteenth century lay behind the accelerating growth of the slave trade after the Peace of Utrecht (1713). Meeting such demands required new forms of specialized labour-intensive plantation agri-business. Sparse indigenous

---

[1] Phrase used by David Brion Davis (2010: xvii). 12.5 million are recorded on over 36,000 voyages on the Slave Voyages database: https://www.slavevoyages.org/.
[2] See also Eltis and Richardson (2010).
[3] See table 1.1; Richardson (2022: 24–5); Morgan (2016: 7–30); Zahedieh (2014: 403).
[4] Zahedieh (2023).

Table 1.1: The growth of the Atlantic trade in enslaved people (numbers taken from Africa by nationality of vessel to nearest %, with totals) 1676–1850.

Date	Great Britain	France	Netherlands	Spain Uruguay	Portugal Brazil	Northern colonies/ United States	Baltic states	Total
1676–1700	38%	4%	12%	<1%	41%	<1%	3%	718,200
1701–25	38%	11%	7%	0	43%	<1%	<1%	1,089,100
1726–50	38%	18%	6%	0	36%	2%	<1%	1,471,800
1751–75	43%	17%	7%	<1%	27%	4%	1%	1,926,200
1776–1800	37%	22%	2%	<1%	34%	3%	2%	2,008,400
1801–25	15%	7%	<1%	9%	62%	6%	<1%	1,877,700
1826–50	0	4%	<1%	23%	73%	<1%	0	1,771,300
Totals	3,102,000	1,372,000	419,100	585,500	4,971,000	304,500	108,600	10,862,700

Source: Adapted from Eltis and Richardson (2010: 23) and https://www.slavevoyages.org/.

populations were heavily depleted by disease and extermination after the arrival of Europeans, and neither settler populations nor indentured servants and transported convicts satisfied the prodigious demand for arduous manual labour in disease-ridden tropical conditions. Enslaved workers were preferred by planters because they were cheaper and could be more harshly exploited. By the end of the seventeenth century, slavery and the plantation system of production were key to developing the resources of the Americas.[5]

Although enslaved domestic workers were common in urban and rural locations, in North America the enslaved worked mainly on tobacco plantations in Virginia and Maryland (the Chesapeake region) and on rice and indigo plantations in South Carolina and Georgia. In the Caribbean they laboured on sugar, coffee and cocoa plantations, but sugar was by far the most important crop. Barbados (settled from 1627) was initially the foremost sugar colony alongside Saint Kitts (from 1624), Nevis (from 1627), Montserrat and Antigua (both from 1632). But Jamaica (captured from Spain in 1655) became Britain's largest and most valuable West Indian sugar colony in the eighteenth century. From the 1730s Jamaica was at the forefront of the development of large sugar estates and plantations.

[5] Solow (1991: 21–42; 1987: 51–78); Morgan (2016: 59–63); Johnston (2020: 262–3, 279–86).

Map 1.1: The British Transatlantic Slave Trade 1563–1810.

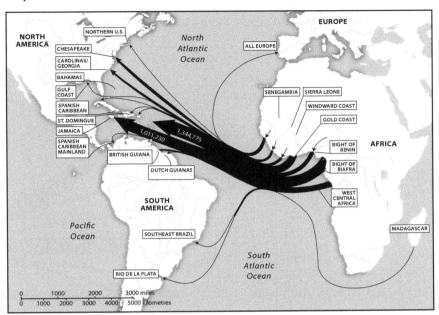

Source: Based on Eltis and Richardson (2010: 32). Figures of embarkations from Africa destined for Jamaica and the rest of the Caribbean are from the Transatlantic Slave Trade Database (slavevoyages.org). Proportions of enslaved African peoples embarked from different parts of Africa and destined for different areas across the Atlantic are indicated by the thickness of the arrows.

Most of the enslaved aboard British vessels were absorbed by British colonies, but a high proportion was sold on to the Spanish colonies. By the 1680s between a third and a half of slaves arriving in Jamaica was trans-shipped from the slave entrepôt in Kingston to Spanish America largely in exchange for silver. At the Peace of Utrecht Britain gained the right under the *Asiento* legally to supply slaves to Spanish America. The South Sea Company alone supplied 65,000 Africans to Spanish America between 1714 and 1739, with 70% passing through Jamaica. Although the *Asiento* expired in 1739, slave supply to Spanish and to other non-British territories in the Americas remained a large component of the British trade. Between 1702 and 1775, 2,090 ships discharged 497,736 slaves at Kingston, of which around 28% went on to foreign colonies in exchange for draught cattle, indigo, cacao and

Map 1.2: The British trade to individual colonies of the Lesser Antilles, 1563–1810.

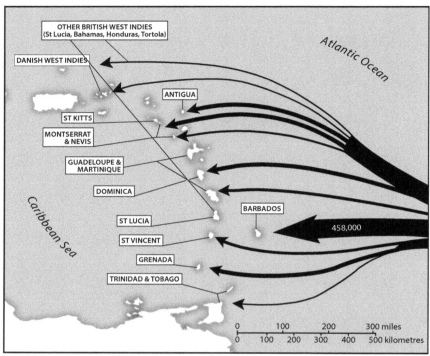

Source: Based on Eltis and Richardson (2010: 32). Proportions of enslaved African peoples destined for different islands of the Lesser Antilles are indicated by the thickness of the arrows.

bullion. Bullion worth £3 million was sent to the Bank of England from Jamaica and other islands between 1748 and 1765 alone: a significant element of the trade.[6] The slave trade between Jamaica and Spanish America as a whole may have contributed as much as £1 million annually to Britain's national income between 1692 and 1775. By 1795–7 a third of the enslaved peoples landed in Kingston were shipped on to Cuba and Saint-Domingue (then under British occupation).[7]

---

[6] https://www.slavevoyages.org/voyage/database; Sheridan (1969: 18–19, 24); Sheridan (1974: 506); Morgan (2016: 7–30); Pearce (2007: 67–8, 230–41).
[7] McNeill (1985: 169); Pares (1936: 84, 113–27); Radburn (2015a: 275); Pearce (2007: 89).

By the mid-eighteenth century the supply of enslaved labour in Britain's North American colonies was sustained by natural increase and internal trading. Most slave shipments in the eighteenth century, and particularly at the height of the trade in the second half of the century, thus went to the expanding plantation systems of the Caribbean and Brazil, where high and increasing rates of slave mortality, especially on sugar plantations, demanded constant replacement.[8]

The Royal African Company and the rise of private slave traders

The policy of the British state after the Commonwealth was to ensure that the proceeds of British colonies accrued only to citizens of the British Empire. The Company of Royal Adventurers Trading to Africa was granted a monopoly of the British slave trade in 1663 which transferred to its successor the Royal African Company (RAC) after 1672. This monopoly gradually removed the Dutch as large-scale suppliers of slaves to the British colonies. The RAC alone transported an estimated 84,000 enslaved Africans to the Americas between 1680 and 1692. From the start, however, the Company was unable to meet the demand for slaves and lacked the power to enforce its monopoly. It was forced to share the trade with licensed private traders and with 'interlopers'. Private trading grew markedly from the 1690s: between 1698 and 1707 independent merchants sent 376 vessels to Africa from London alone, compared with 128 from the RAC. In Jamaica in the same period they landed 35,718 enslaved African people compared with the Company's 6,854.[9] In 1698 the RAC's monopoly was rescinded.[10]

The British slave trade from an early stage was a credit trade based upon trust, personal bonds and bills of exchange. These all favoured wealthier private traders who had taken over the bulk of the trade by the 1720s.[11] It was they who developed credit and trading practices into a credit system that benefitted the British trade over that of its European rivals.[12] Although

---

[8] Richardson (2022: 33); Morgan (2016a: 21–7); Solow (1991: 199).

[9] Figures estimated by Price (1991: 293–339).

[10] The trade was opened to all private merchants subject to a 10% toll on their exports to Africa, though this condition lapsed after 1710.

[11] Sheridan (1958: 249–63); Price (1991); Morgan (2016a: 32–7).

[12] See chapter 8.

not wound up until 1752, the RAC struggled to compete with private traders largely because it failed efficiently to collect debts arising from slave sales.[13] Fluctuations in the prices received for plantation products, together with gluts and shortages of slave supply caused by wars, weather and seasonal factors, affected the prices received for slaves and the need for credit. The RAC commonly extended credit for two or three years.[14] Merchants trading on their own account and employing trusted ships' captains and resident middlemen to conduct credit sales in the Caribbean generally proved better than the RAC at managing their liquidity.[15]

The Navigation Acts and the politics of the slave trade

Monopoly was central for merchants in the commerce of the Atlantic. The British Navigation Acts (1651–96) enabled traders and the state to gain a disproportionate stimulus from foreign trade. Under an Act of 1660 all trade to and from the colonies was restricted to English or colonial ships, and at least three-quarters of the crew, including the captain, had to be English. This encouraged a huge expansion of the merchant navy over the course of the following century and a half. By the 1780s Britain had roughly 50,000 merchant seamen and a million tons of shipping.[16] In addition, the most valuable colonial imports, almost all from the Caribbean, were 'enumerated'. This required them to be landed first at an English or colonial port even if destined for a foreign market. An Act of 1663 stipulated that foreign goods (with strategic exclusions such as with enslaved people, Madeira wine and salt for the North American fisheries) had to be shipped to colonial markets via England. This provision much favoured the sale of British manufactures in colonial markets by increasing the relative costs of foreign competition.[17]

---

[13] By 1710 the bonded debt of the RAC was reported to be between £300,000 and £400,000: Davies (1958: 316–25, 335–43); Price (1991: 299–305). In 1752 the RAC's assets were transferred to the Africa Company of Merchants, which traded until 1821: Pettigrew (2013).
[14] Donnan (1931: vol. 1, 265, 266; vol. 2, 89–90, 98): https://babel.hathitrust.org/cgi /pt?id=pst.000009721524andview=1upandseq=695.
[15] Davies (1958) quoted in Price (1991: 300); Richardson (2022: 23–44). For a brief survey of the slave trade in Africa and credit practices there see Morgan (2016a: 37–46).
[16] Kelly, Ó Gráda and Solar (2021: 239–76).
[17] Zahedieh (2009: 53–70).

Scotland was included in the Navigation Acts after the Union with England in 1707, enlarging the domestic market for plantation products and providing lucrative opportunities for Scottish merchants and importers. Glasgow came to specialize in the tobacco trade with Virginia. Scottish factors opened stores in the Chesapeake, where they sold imported manufactures and bought tobacco for shipment.[18] Monopoly kept other countries out of Britain's Atlantic trading zone, or greatly increased their costs of engaging. The result for Britain was possession of the largest free trade area in the world for almost two centuries, before the repeal of the Acts in 1849.

The Navigation Acts were a vital support in the rise of London to replace Amsterdam as the leading European entrepôt and international financial centre in the early eighteenth century. Many London merchants, often with origins in the provinces or in Scotland and with mercantile connections around the Atlantic basin, developed interlocking activities in the slave and sugar trades, in banking and finance, in shipping, military contracting, and in government funds.[19] The Navigation Acts, reinforced by the Anglo-Dutch and Franco-Dutch Wars of the later seventeenth century, helped to precipitate the decline of Dutch commercial dominance. It was the French rather than the Dutch who became the main eighteenth-century trading rivals of the British in the staple trades of the Caribbean and in the trade with Spanish America.

Early British sugar planters were hostile to the Navigation Acts because their sugar had first to be transported to England before it could be sold elsewhere. They could not therefore compete effectively in the European sugar market, and the British home market was not yet absorbing enough of their output. Circumstances changed in the early decades of the eighteenth century. Sugar production expanded rapidly throughout the West Indies to meet an explosion in European demand. It grew fastest in the propitious soils of French-owned Saint-Domingue, and French, Dutch and Portuguese sugar all remained cheaper in Europe than British sugar. The planter oligarchy in the British sugar island legislatures, however, was able to use its power to prevent foreign sugars being

---

[18] Devine (1975); Price (1991: 325–6).
[19] Hancock (1995: 115–240).

illicitly shipped to Britain via British colonies. The burgeoning British domestic market thus belonged to British-shipped sugar alone.[20]

Sugar consumption in England increased much faster than on the European mainland due both to rising real incomes and to a shift in consumer preferences for new hot sugared beverages of tea, coffee and chocolate, along with new tastes for distilled liquors relying on sugar: rum, punch and gin. Rapid expansion of the home market and competition from Saint-Domingue sugar virtually ended British sugar re-exports to foreign markets; they declined from 40% in 1713 to only 5% in the mid-1730s.[21] But the West India interest in the British Parliament succeeded in creating increased monopoly power for British sugars in colonial markets. The Molasses Act of 1733 levied prohibitive duties on foreign sugar, molasses and rum imported into the American colonies. Though not always adhered to, the 1733 Act was endorsed by the Sugar Act of 1764: together they substantially increased the market for British sugars in North America. The Molasses Act also barred French sugar, rum and molasses from Ireland and insisted that all sugars imported into Ireland conform with the Navigation Acts. Ireland's trade with the French colonies thereafter declined sharply; instead, Ireland became a vital market for British sugar, taking the greater part of England's sugar re-exports after 1733.[22] West Indian sugar exports to Britain increased in value by 237% between 1714 and 1775, rising to £3.24 million per annum in 1771–5.[23]

By 1770, at a time when recorded British Caribbean sugar exports had expanded to 97,000 tons, 90% was retained in Britain, with much of the rest re-exported to Ireland, leaving the French as the major sugar suppliers to continental Europe until the loss of Saint-Domingue in 1791.[24] The protected market provided by the Navigation Acts and later legislative protections meant that British sugar consumers effectively paid a subsidy to growers and traders because consumers had access only to British sugars, at higher prices than those in continental Europe.

---

[20] Sheridan (1957: 62–83).
[21] Richardson (1987); Zahedieh (2014).
[22] Sheridan (1957).
[23] Richardson (1987: 747, 762).
[24] Richardson (1987); Deerr (1949–50).

Nevertheless, over the eighteenth century, the British consumed around a third of all sugar imported into Europe.[25]

The state supported overseas trading activity with military force throughout the eighteenth century, especially in the Americas. Between 1660 and 1815, Britain was at war for seventy of the 155 years. Most wars were fought entirely at sea and most involved trading rights and colonial possessions in the Atlantic. After 1713 the main adversary was France, and disputes always involved the key Caribbean and Spanish trades. Spending on the navy, from shipbuilding and munitions to the provisioning of voyages, stimulated the economy. The Royal Navy by the mid-eighteenth century maintained a wartime fleet of over 300 vessels, most purpose-built but many captured.[26] War imposed dangers for merchants and increased the cost of insurance and convoys, but it also brought opportunities of greater profits for those merchants who could carry 'Letters of Marque' from the government; 'Letters of Marque' allowed merchants to capture enemy shipping and to retain the proceeds.[27]

Wars in defence of the American colonies and naval action to enforce the Navigation Acts relied on increased government spending and taxation. Tax revenues rose by a factor of fourteen between 1688 and 1815, making the British second only to the Dutch as the most heavily taxed population in Europe.[28] The rise of the excise tax on consumer goods, alongside customs, as a major source of essential revenue created a regressive element in the tax system because it raised the prices of many basic goods. It also created a bureaucracy of inspection of production standards, weights and measures (for consumer goods and essential manufactures) that increased both efficiency and innovation in the manufacturing sector.[29]

The West Africa trade

London was the main slave-trade port in Britain and the main entrepôt in Europe for the African trade in the seventeenth century. Bristol

[25] Davis (1973: 255).
[26] Morgan (2000); Rodger (1998: 169–83; 2004).
[27] Richardson (1976; 79); Inikori (2002: 346); Williams (1966).
[28] O'Brien (1988: 1–32); O'Brien (1998: 53–77, 63–70).
[29] Hudson (1992: 55–6); Ashworth (2003: 261–79; 2017: 117–28).

was Britain's second port, trading in enslaved peoples from the 1680s. However, as early as the 1740s, Liverpool became the leading slave-trading port not just in Britain but in Europe, accounting for 80% of the British trade by the end of the century. Liverpool expanded as a slave port because it had good connections with the sources of both domestic and imported commodities to satisfy African demands, including access to the Isle of Man contraband trade up to 1765. It also developed a group of large, well-established and specialized slave merchants, with close connections to London finance houses.[30]

Merchants traded British, European and Asian manufactured commodities for enslaved people in West Africa. African demand varied by region and shifted over time as English traders moved southwards to avoid competition and to exploit new sources of supply of enslaved peoples at the Bight of Biafra, Old Calabar, Cameroon and Gabon.[31] West Africa's share of direct English exports by the late eighteenth century (excluding re-exports) was around 4%, but added to this were goods made in England that arrived in West Africa via other European ports. Some branches of British manufacturing depended heavily upon African markets. Africa was second only to the American colonies as a destination for wrought iron exports in the eighteenth century. Both the Carron and Coalbrookdale companies had warehouses in Liverpool to supply the trade. Britain supplied brasswares, iron and copper goods, and guns to West African markets, and Africa took nearly a quarter of British cotton exports at the peak of this trade in the 1790s.[32]

Asian and European goods were also much in demand in African markets. They were acquired by London importers, then purchased by slave traders in the outports. Historians rarely consider how significant the re-export trade to Africa was in expanding Britain's Asian and European trade. Between 1699 and 1800 Asian textiles were the largest single item in the trade to Africa, comprising 27% of all goods and

---

[30] For discussion of the shifting pre-eminence of British slave ports see chapter 5.

[31] Richardson (2022: 23–44; 1979; 1976); Drake (1976); Morgan (2016a: 37–46). For a detailed case study of exchanges, 'money' and the role of states in the trade in enslaved people between indigenous African traders and Europeans on the Guinea coast see Polanyi (1966).

[32] Inikori (2002: 405–72); Wadsworth and Mann (1968: 118); Anderson (1977); Evans (2010).

40% of all textiles exported there. Swedish bar iron, German linens and Danish, Dutch and German munitions also featured prominently in the re-export trade to Africa.[33]

The multilateral impact of the slave trade

The export of manufactures to Africa was one side of trade that made the Caribbean plantation system possible. Another was trade from the North American colonies to the British Caribbean; this provided the latter with foodstuffs, livestock, building materials, lumber, in addition to shipping and commercial services. The northern colonies in turn took sugar and sugar products. Supplies from the northern mainland allowed Britain's Caribbean colonies to specialize in cash crops. The gains from this trade also generated the income and profits that enabled a major trade in British manufactures to North America. A huge variety of manufactured goods, from textiles to agricultural implements, was sold to the mainland colonies. British merchants took tobacco, indigo, rice and other North American agricultural products as well as specie and trade bills back to Britain.[34] The absence of a competitive manufacturing base in the colonies, especially for fashionable and better-quality items, including metal tools and many textiles, drove the trade before the 1770s. High disposable incomes of families and firms in the areas of white settlement were also important. Between the mid-century and 1770 North American surpluses from the Caribbean trade appear to have paid for between a quarter and a half of the imports that North Americans bought from Britain.[35]

Caribbean plantations also drew their provisions from Ireland, England, Scotland, Wales, Bermuda and the Atlantic 'wine islands'. The trade stimulated British trade with north European manufacturing regions, as well as with the Caribbean colonies of other nations, the Spanish Main and Brazil.[36] The Scots traded barrelled herring to the Caribbean through Glasgow, and the Irish sent salt beef, salt pork and

[33] Klein (1990: 292); Richardson (1985: 5).
[34] Morgan (2000); Pellizzari (2020: 528–54); Kimball (2016: 181–94); Breen (2004); Maw (2010: 734–68).
[35] Richardson (1987: 766); Harley (2015: 171–2).
[36] Sheridan (1969: 5–25, 13, 16–18); Pearce (2007: 67–8, 230–41).

butter. The value of Irish exports to the Americas nearly tripled between the mid-century and the end of the 1770s, and the West Indies took 85% of this.[37] By the mid-eighteenth century 50,000 to 80,000 cattle were slaughtered and processed yearly in Cork for the trade. Irish receipts from the Caribbean trade paid for English imports to Ireland, especially manufactured goods.[38]

Coarse linens from Lancashire, the west of Scotland and Germany were exported to the Americas in large quantities to satisfy demand for basic slave clothing, as were plain woollens from Wales, the Pennines and Kendal.[39] Britain also supplied machinery and utensils to plantations for processing crops prior to export, including copper boiling vessels and an array of agricultural tools. The wealthy planter classes of the sugar islands actively consumed Britain's manufactured luxuries: fashionable textiles, hats, clothing accessories, fancy goods, domestic decorations and utensils, books, clocks and carriages.[40] Caribbean-generated demands (taking in the African, West Indian and northern colonies trades) between 1748 and 1776 accounted for almost 50% of total British-produced exports, and 95% of these exports were manufactured goods. Home plus European demand still dominated markets for British industry, but these estimates suggest that 'Caribbean-based demand' may have accounted for around 12% of total British industrial output in these years, and much of this was for new and increasingly sophisticated mass-produced goods.[41]

At the beginning of the eighteenth century, Britain's colonies in the Americas accounted for 11% of the value of exports and 20% of retained imports. By the late 1790s North America and the West Indies took 57% of British exports and supplied 32% of retained imports. During the century re-exports, mainly Atlantic colonial crops such as tobacco,

---

[37] Nash (1985: 330–1).
[38] Evans (2010: 45).
[39] Evans (2010: 17–18, 46–54).
[40] Burnard (2001: 506–24); Haggerty (2023: chapter 7).
[41] These are crude estimates by Richardson in the 1980s from official values (taking in the African, West Indies and Northern Colonial trades) but instructive nevertheless: Richardson (1987: 739–69, 76); Eltis and Engerman (2000); Morgan (2000: 18); Berg and Hudson (2021: 259–81).

sugar, coffee and rice, rose five-fold.[42] Such re-exports underpinned imports from Europe, particularly vital supplies of raw materials: 'iron, flax, hemp, masts, deals, pitch and tar – that kept thousands of sailors and tens of thousands of workers busy in Britain'.[43]

The Triangular Trade

The slave and commodity trades between Britain, Africa and the Americas is often referred to simplistically as a triangular trade in which Europe specialized in manufactures, the Americas in the production of intermediate goods and produce, and Africa in enslaved labour.[44] But because many goods that entered into trade with Africa and the Americas were re-exports, especially Indian textiles, the model might better be viewed as a 'diamond-shaped trade' that integrated the Indian and Atlantic Oceans during the eighteenth century.[45]

Before the 1740s, the enslaved were mainly exchanged directly for tropical produce that was shipped home on the same vessels. Such voyages were best suited when the typical unit of cultivation was small and when European merchants supplied both enslaved peoples and other Caribbean imports. But planters needed long credits to purchase slaves to cover their outlays until harvesting. Slave traders by contrast needed speedy remittances to buy their cargoes for their next outward voyage to Africa. This put the old structure of trading under strain. New patterns of larger-scale and more intensive plantation agriculture and growth in the economic and political power of planters led to changes in the way that the slave and plantation trades operated after the 1730s and 1740s. Well-established planters with large businesses shipped staples to Britain on their own account, employing factors and commission agents, largely in London, to sell their produce, to buy plantation supplies, to grant credit and to arrange voyages. Slave merchants in the British outports

---

[42] See tables 2.1 to 2.3, pp. 48–9. Morgan (2000: 18); Zahedieh (2014: 409–13).
[43] Price (1998: 21).
[44] Several historians, Inikori in particular, have claimed, with justification, that this structured an international division of labour and influenced the economic trajectories of the three world regions to the detriment of West Africa: Inikori (2014). Williams (1944) first used the term extensively.
[45] Riello (2021).

gradually came to concentrate upon the 'African trade' or 'Guinea trade' alone: the transportation and sale of enslaved people.[46]

The London commission system was the main beneficiary of the shift in economic and political power in favour of the planters. After 1750 Bristol, Liverpool, Lancaster and Glasgow also had their commission agents, though not on a scale to rival London. Walter Tullideph, a leading Antiguan planter, had agents in all four of these west-coast ports.[47] Bristol merchants, who had spent time learning the trade in the West Indies, returned to Britain and set up merchant brokerage businesses on behalf of planters. Bryan Edwards and John Pinney, both planters from Bristol, returned to establish commission houses.

At the same time that slave-trade merchants withdrew from the staple-carrying trade, they also reduced their involvement in the direct sale of slaves in the West Indies. This was gradually taken over in the later eighteenth century by London commission agents who employed trusted contacts, often family members, resident in the Caribbean.[48] Slave factorage was a valuable adjunct for the London commission agent, who earned interest on credit extension to planters as well as on the sale of West Indian produce in Britain.[49] The British slave trade itself thus became more specialized, bringing greater efficiency and quicker turnaround times. Ships designed almost solely for carrying human cargoes reflected and endorsed the demise of triangular trading and increased the efficiencies of concentrating on the slave trade alone. Because it was uneconomic to keep expensive ships hanging around in the ports of the Caribbean and elsewhere awaiting a return cargo of plantation produce, slave traders instead began to return quickly with bills of exchange and miscellaneous goods such as South American logwood, mahogany, dyes, cacao, African timber, furs and ivory that could be picked up easily en route.

Bills of exchange were negotiable paper credit instruments guaranteed by wealthy finance houses mainly in London. Their growing use from the 1740s and 1750s speeded up and made the trade financially more secure

[46] Sheridan (1958); Radburn (2015a); Morgan (2005; 2016).

[47] He also had agents in Lancaster, Leith, Dundee, Cork and Dublin to whom he consigned plantation produce. Sheridan (1958: 254).

[48] Sheridan (1958: 254–7); Radburn (2015a).

[49] Donnan (1931: vol. 3, 629 n7); Pares (1960: 241); Radburn (2015a).

and predictable.[50] Bills of exchange accounted for the bulk of returns after 1750, and by the 1780s very few slavers returned to England with sugar. William Davenport (1725–94) who was involved in at least 163 slaving voyages from Liverpool between the 1760s and 1786, specialized in quick turnaround times in the Caribbean, his ships returning with 'bills in the bottom'.[51] Specialist bilateral shippers, some connected to the slave trade but many not, carried out the direct trade between Britain and the Americas, taking an increasing share of the westbound trade in supplies and manufactures and the eastbound trade in plantation products.[52]

The plantation trade and the slave trade before 1776

In the first three-quarters of the eighteenth century plantation production expanded, encouraged by improving terms of trade for staples especially between the 1740s and the 1770s. The terms of trade are the relative prices of commodities being exchanged in trade. In this case the prices of plantation products (especially sugar) remained high or increased compared with the combined prices of manufactured goods and enslaved people. Although wartime interruptions of trade caused much fluctuation, the terms of trade in favour of plantation crops increased 4.7-fold between 1701 and 1770, with the steepest increases occurring after 1763. This enabled traders in plantation products to maximize their returns.[53]

The Seven Years War (1756–63) brought significant territorial gains. Acquisition of the Ceded Islands of Grenada, Dominica, St Vincent and Tobago brought increased quantities of sugar to Britain. Later acquisitions of the 1770s to 1810s, principally Saint Lucia, Demerara and Berbice, opened a succession of new British sugar frontiers and investment opportunities. New plantations and the lure of high profits drew in new planters and investors. Enslaved people were in high demand to carve out and cultivate the new frontier, and the slave trade increased.

---

[50] Pearson and Richardson (2008).
[51] Richardson (2022: 81–91); Anderson (1977); Price (1991: 316). For more on Davenport see Radburn (2009). https://core.ac.uk/download/pdf/41336523.pdf.
[52] Minchinton (1979); Hyde et al. (1952–3); Pares (1950: 62, 80–1); Sheridan (1958: 252–7); Richardson (2022: 37–44).
[53] Smith (2002: 457).

Greater demand for capital extended the mortgage market and brought new opportunities for lenders and financial intermediaries to profit from investments in the West Indies. The 'Silver Age of Sugar' (1763–75) was a boom period when demand for sugar was buoyant, the sugar frontier expanded, and the slave trade reached a peak.[54] Metropolitan creditors loaned vast amounts to planters.[55] Land used to cultivate sugar appreciated in value: in Jamaica, for example, the value of estates tripled in the mid-century decades, adding to collateral that could be used to raise loans for further expansion.[56]

In 1763 Britain owned eleven 'sugar islands' in the West Indies plus rice, indigo and tobacco colonies on the North American mainland. Five other European powers owned extensive sugar colonies. Saint-Domingue (French), the 'pearl of the Antilles', then exported 31.7% of West Indian sugar even though the colony also produced cotton, coffee and indigo.[57] Jamaica (British) came next with 18.7%, followed by Antigua (British), Saint Kitts (British), Martinique (French), Saint Croix (Danish), Guadeloupe (French), Barbados (British) and Grenada (French), all of which exported between 8 and 11% of the total. Cuba (Spanish) which was to become the main exporter of sugar after the decline of other parts of the West Indies in the early nineteenth century, ranked tenth at this time with just 2.7% of all sugar exports. The Caribbean on the eve of the American Revolution had an estimated 3,900 sugar plantations, of which 1,830 were British, 1,350 French, 475 Spanish, 195 Danish and 50 Dutch.[58]

Britain did not dominate the sugar or plantation trades of the Caribbean. Indeed, the total value of French long-distance trade (taking trade with Africa, Asia, America and re-exports to the rest of Europe) at the end of the 1780s has been estimated to have been 25% higher than

---

[54] A term coined by Pares (1960: 40, 46, 90).

[55] Checkland (1958a: 461–9); Smith (2002).

[56] Sheridan (1974: 229).

[57] Sheridan (1969: 21–2). The value of sugar arriving in French ports grew at 4% per annum between 1730 and 1790. Between 1750 and 1790 the value rose from 30 million livres to 75 million livres: Stein (1988: 14). On the growth of the French slave trade over the period see Daudin (2004: 144–71).

[58] Sheridan (1969: 21–2); Stein (1988).

Britain's.[59] The main pillar of support for the growth of long-distance trade for each nation was the plantation system, and in the French case this was both a larger and more productive system than the British. Britain was however a pre-eminent force especially in the slave trade itself. Britain reaped an economic stimulus from the slave-plantation nexus that was greater than its rivals overall, especially between 1763 and 1776. British terms of trade helped, but Britain also benefitted from access to provisions from the northern colonies before 1776; enlargement of the protected market area to include Scotland (from 1707) and Ireland (from 1733); by adopting a credit system backed by London finance houses, which increased trade specialization, efficiency and turnaround times; and by maximizing the gains from an aggressive mercantilism. This mercantilism kept British trade in British ships and protected the huge home market for sugar. Above all, Britain benefitted disproportionately because her plantations were not only important in themselves, but were also the foundation for wider British multilateral trading activities in the whole Atlantic basin and beyond (taking in her re-export trade from Asia to Africa). Much of this trading involved the sale of British manufactured goods.

Late century volatility, booms and speculation

The gains from British investment in the slave trade and plantations between the early 1770s and the end of the Napoleonic Wars in 1815 became increasingly volatile. The American War of Independence brought acute provisioning difficulties to the West Indian colonies, particularly for foodstuffs and timber, and cut off a lucrative market for plantation products. Thousands of enslaved people died of malnutrition and attendant diseases. The slave trade declined, plantation returns plummeted, and mortgage foreclosures increased. Hurricanes swept the Caribbean in the 1780s, and older cultivated areas suffered soil exhaustion at the same time as slave prices rose and became more volatile.[60]

[59] Equivalent to £25 million sterling compared with Britain's £20 million: Daudin (2004: 144).
[60] Sheridan (1976: 615–41); Carrington (1987: 823–50); Radburn (2015b).

The period marked a nadir in the fortunes of many planters, who went bankrupt or deeper into debt with their London agents. But the challenges brought opportunities for others to profit from the mid to late 1780s. From this time West Indian finance and lending became the major preoccupation of the London commission agent, whose role evolved into that of a merchant banker. Huge sums of money were extended to planters by their London correspondents. Much was spent clearing and stocking new colonies and extending cultivation in older colonies. In Jamaica alone it is estimated that the number of sugar plantations rose from 400 in 1730 to 648 in 1768 and to 1,061 in 1786. The slave population of Jamaica tripled in the second half of the eighteenth century, to reach over 300,000 by 1801.[61] Very high mortality of enslaved people who were engaged in clearing new land and in cultivating sugar added to the demand for enslaved workers and to the profits of the slave trade. The Free Port Act of 1766 had opened up six British ports (four in Jamaica and two in Dominica), allowing merchants openly to supply the markets of Spanish, Dutch and other non-British colonies with manufactures and enslaved people.[62] This trade increased signifcantly after 1788, when Spain relaxed its trade restrictions, allowing British merchants access to the burgeoning Cuban market for enslaved workers. Indeed, market opportunities for slave traders between 1783 and 1807 were buoyant from South Carolina in the north to Rio do La Plata in the south.[63]

New sources of provisions from Scotland, Ireland and Canada compensated over the medium and longer term for the impact of the loss of the North American colonies. British and Irish exports to the Caribbean islands increased, as did imports of salt fish and building materials from Canada.[64] Intra-island trade also grew, including that between British and non-British colonies in the West Indies and with South American coastal colonies. Planters also drove their enslaved labour harder, producing more subsistence food as well as plantation

[61] Sheridan (1974: 223; 1958: 259).
[62] Before 1766 there had been significant inter-colonial contraband trade and trade with the free ports of other colonies. Zahedieh (2018: 77–102); Keiser (2021: 334–61); Hunt (2013). https://journals.openedition.org/diacronie/672?lang=en.
[63] Richardson (2022: 28–30); Burnard and Garrigus (2016: 164–91).
[64] Sheridan (1976).

crops. High sugar prices in the late 1780s and extension of the sugar frontier into fertile lands rescued plantation profits.[65] And the export of manufactures to the former colonies, now the USA, gradually recovered and expanded, even though they were no longer carried only in British ships.

Earlier in the eighteenth century British planters had been alarmed at the potential competition posed by wartime island conquests. But by the 1790s merchants, speculators and bankers dominated the West India interest and they were much less hostile to retaining new territories. Domestic sugar consumption continued to increase rapidly, prices were generally buoyant and they vied for a share in the anticipated profits. War gains of the later 1790s brought several more sugar colonies into British control, including Demerara, Essequibo, Berbice, St Lucia, Surinam and Trinidad. These immediately became the focus of increases in slave shipments and opened the floodgates for further large flows of investment in new plantations.[66] By 1800 slave imports had doubled to cover the labour-intensive work of clearing and planting new territories.[67] A contemporary source suggested that £18 million had been invested overall in the British West Indies in just five years during the later 1790s, and that cotton as well as sugar was now being grown and exported at 'immense profit'.[68]

The revolution in Saint-Domingue in 1791 boosted profitability for British plantations because it removed the main rival to Britain's sugar trade to Europe and increased sugar prices, which remained high beyond the end of the century. British planters entering the business in the 1790s were mainly speculators able quickly to raise money in London and elsewhere to seize the opportunity for large immediate profits.[69] New planters were under pressure to maximize output and profits in order to repay massive loans and mortgages. They intensified slave work regimes and invested in improved processing technologies. Thus, from the 1790s the older sugar islands had a final flush of prosperity and the newly acquired territories had their first and last boom. The boom

[65] Checkland (1958a: 461–9).
[66] Checkland (1958a: 461–5).
[67] Sheridan (1958: 259).
[68] Checkland (1958a: 462); Lord Brougham quoted by Rose (1929: 35).
[69] Checkland (1958a: 461–5).

seriously faltered with international fallout from speculation in trade, over-extension of credit and the harsh winter that caused a major crisis in 1799. But the last throes of major prosperity and profit-making in the British West Indies did not finally end until the crash of 1806–7.[70] Heavy investment, intensive cultivation and the industrialization of sugar processing continued apace, encouraged by the high sugar prices of the war period. The slave trade also expanded significantly as planters and merchants rushed to stock up and gain profits in advance of the British abolition of the trade in 1807.

The decline of planter power

The economic and political power of planters reached a peak in the mid-eighteenth century. British demand for sugar exceeded supply, and prices rose to double those on the continent. Planter profits and the value of estates were high. Many planters retired to Britain to become leisured landowners. Joseph Massie wrote in 1759 that planters were enjoying 'excessive profits'. They had done so since the 1730s, and this continued until the end of the Seven Years War in 1763. According to Massie, planters had made servants of their London agents and were able to demand that their sugars were sold at excessive prices. They could also threaten to sell their sugar in North America or move to other commission agents if their own did not advance sufficient credit to cover slave purchases. Massie estimated that, as a result of their commercial power and political influence, the 'exorbitant Gain' of the planters in the 1730s, 1740s and 1750s amounted to £8 million, with the loss to the people of Britain from the misdoings of British sugar planters amounting to £20,650,000 over that period.[71] The power that planters exercised over the trade was not, however, to last.

Crises and changes precipitated by the loss of the North American colonies and the expansion of the sugar frontier radically changed the commercial and financial organization of British Caribbean trading. As planter debt rose, it was the London commission agents who became the

---

[70] Rydén (2009); Checkland (1958a: 462).
[71] Sheridan (1957: 73; 1958: 257–80); Massie had an axe to grind, but there is no doubt that the wealth of planters was buoyed up by their economic and political power and influence. Massie (1759: 50–3), quoted by Sheridan (1957: 82).

major creditors and who were thus in a position to dictate most aspects of British Caribbean trade, shipping and finance. Such London houses came to control the trade of the sugar islands, determining which planters could be relied upon to purchase slaves, how many they could buy and the terms of payment. These houses also handled the remittances of the outport slave merchants via the discount of their slave trade bills. In the late century the London commission agent came to act as a broker and banker, reaping lucrative commissions and interest for accommodating the needs of the planters and slave merchants. By the close of the century the vast resources of London were being drawn upon to support the mounting debt burden of Caribbean estate owners and cultivators.[72] The City of London was tied to the slave trade by credits and loans and by the income they generated. It was feared that if the slave trade were to be abolished, the City would be ruined: many financial careers and fortunes were dependent upon it.

Decline of the Caribbean?

A case can be made that the prosperity of the British Caribbean and its value to the British economy began to decline as early as the third quarter of the eighteenth century, exacerbated by the loss of the northern colonies, the declining power of the planter aristocracy and by absenteeism of plantation owners.[73] The period from 1763 to 1776 may have been the peak time of profitability of the plantation and slave trades, but the 1790s was also a boom period across the British Caribbean, even if on the insecure foundation of increasing indebtedness to metropolitan finance. Sugar output and prices continued their rise until 1807. The British Caribbean in general continued to expand until at least the ending of the British slave trade in 1807, and substantial profits continued to be made in the West Indies until well into the nineteenth century. This was particularly the case in the fertile former Dutch colonies of Essquibo, Berbice and Demerara, gained during the Napoleonic Wars and amalgamated to become British Guiana in 1831. The Jamaican economy by contrast experienced increasing difficulties by the 1820s with the collapse

[72] Sheridan (1958: 263); Sissoko and Ishizu (2023).
[73] Williams (1944/1994: 108–34); Ragatz (1931: 7–24); cf. Rosenthal (2018).

of sugar prices and indebtedness, exacerbated by the low reproduction rate of enslaved people. The fortunes of Jamaica are important because it was by far the wealthiest of the British tropical colonies, yielding nearly two-thirds of the total trade of the British West Indies between 1740 and 1813.[74] A recent re-estimation of the national income of Jamaica for benchmark years between 1730 and 1850 shows that it rose to £16 million by 1800, after which it fell to £8 million by 1850, but most of this fall came after the 1830s. Serious decline in Jamaica came only with the ending of slavery and especially with the ending of tariff protection on British sugar in the home market in 1846.[75]

Many planters, factors, merchants, agents, refiners and processors, bankers, mortgagees, traders and retailers continued to gain good profits from the Caribbean throughout the Napoleonic War period, although bankruptcies increased sharply because of speculation and volatile wartime conditions. Caribbean planters fared less well from 1807 to 1818 because coffee and sugar prices began to decline whilst production and trading costs rose. But even then others in the commodity chain and consumers benefitted. The West Indies also became much more important during the Napoleonic Wars for supplying industrial raw materials, especially cotton but also dyestuffs and mahogany, and for importing manufactures when other markets were closed off. The British Caribbean retained its share of world sugar production into the 1820s and continued alone to employ a third of the nation's long-distance shipping. It also supplied one-eighth of Exchequer revenues through customs duties. The tide of prosperity in, and coming from, the Caribbean had turned, but the colonies remained important to the British economy through to the 1840s.[76]

[74] Sheridan (1971: 285–96); Burnard (2015, 2020b: esp. 231); Ward (1978: 201–13).
[75] Graham (2023).
[76] Zahedieh (2014: 404).

CHAPTER 2

Slavery and the British industrial revolution: misleading measures

Contemporary commentators were in no doubt about the central importance of the slave trade and plantations to the economy of Britain in the eighteenth century. In 1712 John Carey, Bristol sugar merchant and creditor of planters, wrote that the Africa trade was key to national prosperity:

> The African Trade is a Trade of the most Advantage to this Kingdom of any we drive, and as it were all Profit, the first cost being little more than small Matters of our own Manufactures, for which we have in return, Gold Teeth,[1] Wax and Negroes, the last whereof are much better than the first, being indeed the best Traffick the Kingdom hath. . . . Hands by which our Plantations are improved . . .[2]

William Wood's *Survey of Trade. . .* (1718) suggested that the African trade was 'the spring and parent whence the others flow'.[3] A decade later Joshua Gee described the trade as 'very profitable to the Nation' because, unlike the Asian trades:

> it carries no money out, and not only supplies our plantations with servants, but brings in a great deal of bullion for those that are sold to the Spanish West-Indies. The supplying our Plantations with negroes is of that extra-ordinary advantage to us, that the planting of sugar and tobacco, and carrying

---

[1] Contemporary expression for ivory.
[2] Carey (1712) quoted by Dresser (2001: 22). Carey was an agent of the Bristol Merchant Venturers in London arguing against reinstatement of the RAC's monopoly and in favour of free trade, so he did have his own ends to pursue.
[3] Wood (1718: part 3, 193). Wood was secretary to the customs at the time of writing this.

on trade could not be supported without them; which Plantations . . . are the great causes of the increase of the riches of the kingdom.[4]

In the mid-1740s Malachy Postlethwayt, compiler of Britain's great commercial encyclopedia *The Universal Dictionary of Trade and Commerce*, argued that the slave trade was 'the first principle and foundation of all the rest, the main-spring of the machine which sets every wheel in motion'. The British Empire was 'a magnificent superstructure of American commerce and Naval Power on an African foundation'.[5]

Many contemporary economic commentators collected data and stressed the contribution of the slave trade and slave plantations to the British economy.[6] They catalogued a range of connections; these included acquiring precious metals and importing slave-produced consumer goods, introducing new commercial institutions, slavery's practical and technical impact on navigation, and the boon to shipping and ancillary trades (carpenters, shipbuilders, provisioners). They wrote of how Britain's textile, sugar and metallurgical industries all benefitted. They also praised the profitability of plantations. Charles Davenant calculated that one person in the Caribbean islands – white or black – was as profitable as seven in England. Sir Dalby Thomas went further in suggesting that every person employed on a sugar plantation was 130 times more valuable than one at home.[7]

Even Adam Smith, who opposed the monopoly aspects of the trade and found slave labour abhorrent as well as economically inefficient, wrote that 'The profits of a sugar plantation in any of our West Indian colonies are generally much greater than those of any other cultivation that is known either in Europe or America.' He also stressed that plantations created vast *private* profits.[8] At the time Smith was writing, in the mid-1770s, George Walker, the agent for Barbados, testified before the

---

[4] Joshua Gee was made a freeman of the Grocers' Company in 1694, and began trading to the colonies from 1700. Gee (1729), cited in Darity (1990: 136).

[5] Postlethwayt (1745: 4, 6); see also Postlethwayt (1757). Postlethwayt was a director of the RAC 1744–5 but was later a critic of slavery. See Pettigrew (2013).

[6] Among these were Josiah Child, William Pitt, Adam Smith, Charles Davenant and Charles Whitworth.

[7] Williams (1944/1994: 52–3).

[8] Smith (1776/1976: vol. 1, 389, 464).

House of Commons on the wider benefits of the sugar islands, including their trade with North America and Ireland, their impact on trade with Asia, and the fact that they repaid the costs of their protection: 'It is not that the profits all centre here; it is that it creates, in the course of attaining those profits, a commerce and navigation in which multitudes of your people, and millions of your money are employed; it is that the support which the sugar colonies receive in one shape, they give in another . . .'[9]

Much of this contemporary political economy, emphasizing the multilateral impact of the slave trade and plantations across the economy and throughout wider trading networks, was soon to be sidelined or forgotten. The nineteenth-century Empire based on 'free trade' and 'free labour' became the dominant story. Contemporary commentary did, however, make its way into the case made by Eric Williams two centuries later in *Capitalism and Slavery* (1944).[10] Williams' book marked a turning point in putting slavery back on the map of historical debate in the twentieth century. It hit a nerve by resurrecting the importance of slavery to the development of the British economy and by suggesting that the slave trade and slavery were abolished only when, and because, their economic importance was on the wane.

Eric Williams

Williams was a young Trinidadian scholar at Oxford in the mid-1930s.[11] *Capitalism and Slavery* was developed from his doctoral dissertation of 1938 on the impact of slavery on the eighteenth-century British economy and the economic background to abolition of the slave trade and slavery.[12] He argued that abolition became a force only when the slave trade, slavery and the mercantilist system on which they depended became a hindrance rather than the 'vital props that spurred the rise of British industry'. This was controversial because the view at the time was that abolition was 'an act of humanitarian national sacrifice'.[13]

[9] House of Commons 1775 cited by Sheridan (1969: 23).
[10] Williams (1944/1994: 51–7).
[11] Williams later became the first prime minister of Trinidad and Tobago.
[12] Williams (1938/2014). For an interpretation of the sharpening of Williams' theoretical position between his thesis and subsequent book see Brandon (2017: 305–27).
[13] Williams (1938/2014: xi, xv, 105).

Williams maintained that the 'Triangular Trade' of the eighteenth century between Britain, the West African coast and the plantation colonies (the West Indies in particular) had stimulated British industry in three ways:

- African slave labour was bought with British manufactures.
- African peoples were transported to the plantations, where they produced sugar, cotton, indigo, molasses and other tropical products. Processing these products created new industries in Britain.
- The maintenance of enslaved peoples and their owners on plantations in the New World provided another market for British industry and for the products of agriculture and fisheries in Britain's northern colonies; these in turn were then better placed to buy British manufactures.

He argued that: 'By 1750 there was hardly a trading or manufacturing town in England which was not in some way connected with the triangular or direct colonial trade. The profits obtained provided one of the main streams of that accumulation of capital in England which financed the industrial revolution.'[14]

Williams never claimed that slavery was the sole cause of the development of industrial capitalism or of the industrial revolution in England.[15] His book did, however, present a mass of evidence and examples connecting slavery closely to Britain's capitalist and industrial transformation. Trenchant criticism of his arguments by the imperial and abolitionist historians of the 1940s soon marginalized Williams' work. For at least two decades it is fair to say that a 'blanket of scholarly silence' covered the study of slavery and its role in the British industrial revolution.[16]

---

[14] Williams (1944/1994: 52).

[15] Williams (1944/1994: 105–6).

[16] Critics included his thesis examiner, Professor Reginald Coupland, who had written *The British Anti-slavery Movement* (Oxford 1933). Williams obtained his doctorate but found it impossible to secure a British publisher for his book until 1964, when it was taken by André Deutsch with a limited print run. *Capitalism and Slavery* was republished in England in January 2022 in the Penguin Modern Classics series. Advance orders broke Penguin's records. The quote is from Darity (1990: 117–49, 143).

Why did Williams' analysis receive such a negative reception in Britain?

Most British historians of the mid-twentieth century subscribed to a heroic interpretation of the history of the British Empire and believed that ideas and social action rather than material forces were the central agents of history.[17] This affected their evaluation of Williams, who emphasized the economic background to the success of the abolitionist cause. He argued further that the origin of chattel slavery was economic: 'it had not to do with the color of the labourer but the cheapness of the labour'. 'Slavery was not born of racism: rather racism was the consequence of slavery.'[18] Williams, however, balanced economic factors with human agency, particularly the agency of the enslaved themselves. He broke new ground in his dissertation in emphasizing the importance of slave rebellions in British Guiana (1808, 1823); Barbados (1816); Demerara (1823); Jamaica (1824 and 1831) and Antigua (1831), and the indirect impact of those in Saint-Domingue (1790–91). He argued that, alongside the rise of East India sugar and ready access to slave-grown produce from countries outside the British Empire (coffee from Brazil, sugar from Cuba, cotton from the US), the growing force of slave rebellions determined the success of the emancipation campaign.[19]

Debate over Williams' work resurfaced with the rise of social and labour history from the 1960s, and his interpretation received some support in both British and US academic circles in the later decades of the twentieth century. Slavery and its role in economic development were, however, much more closely examined in the US academic literature than in Britain.[20] *Capitalism and Slavery* was certainly not at the forefront of studies of the British industrial revolution. This is

[17] Drescher (1977) was central in undermining the materialist interpretation of the ending of British Caribbean slavery.
[18] Williams (1944/1994: 7–29, 19). This is a matter of much debate, especially in the US literature.
[19] Williams (1944/1994: 208, 211). Marx prefigured Williams in treating slavery in the Americas as essential to the rise of British industry: Marx (1867/1976: 915–16). For resistance and rebellion see Morgan (2016a: 87–114). For rebellion in Demerara see Harding (2022) and in Saint-Domingue see Hazareesingh (2021).
[20] Fogel and Engerman (1974) gave rise to global debate on the subject of slavery.

partly because economic history took an increasingly quantitative turn from the 1970s.[21] Aspects of historical development that were difficult to measure were pushed to the periphery of the field, including detailed research on transatlantic trade, the Caribbean economies and the impact of slave-based wealth on the British economy. The data and sources for such work were partial, dispersed and did not start to be systematically collected, digitized or accessible until after the 1990s. In addition, mainstream theories and approaches in economic history focused not on trade but on transnational comparative measurements of economic growth and on sources of growth internal to individual economies. This discouraged analysis of the wider questions that Williams had raised.[22]

Between the 1980s and the 2010s research on the impact of Atlantic trade and of slavery on the home economy finally expanded, with growing emphasis on mercantilism, protectionism and the role of the state. But these contributions had to make their way against the dominant view that free markets, free trade and institutions supporting free enterprise were the key to explaining the rise of the West.[23] Despite the environment of intensified globalization and growing European integration that led growth in the 1990s, many economic historians continued to give more priority in historical work to comparisons of factors internal to individual national economies (endogenous factors) than to international trade and connections. Population expansion, increases in domestic capital formation, labour and capital productivity, agricultural change, the shift to new sources of energy and the rise of the 'knowledge economy' have in recent decades prevailed as explanations for British industrialization. But new studies of global trade in consumer products and raw materials, and of global transfers of technical and design knowledge and material culture, have opened fresh questions on

---

[21] de Vries (2018: 313–34); McCants (2020: 547–66); Boldizzoni and Hudson (2016: esp. 28–9, 38–42).

[22] Institutionalized racism doubtless also played a part in dismissing the role of Africans in Britain's industrial revolution: Palmer (1994: xix).

[23] Compare essays in Solow and Engerman (1987); Brewer (1989); contributions summarized in Bowen (1998); and Inikori (2002); with the following key works, all of which emphasize the central importance of economic liberalism in the rise of the West, including Britain: Landes (1995); McCloskey (2010); Mokyr (2009); Acemoglu and Robinson (2012).

the role of colonial trade and of slavery.[24] Now is the time to re-evaluate Williams' thesis in the light of new evidence and new arguments.

Debates on slave trade profitability and capital supply

Williams emphasized links between slavery and British developments in technology, banking, ancillary trades, textile industries, metallurgy, heavy industry, insurance, infrastructural projects at local and regional levels as well as its part in the growth of Britain's global trade. Williams' critics of the 1960s to the 1980s, however, focused narrowly on only part of his thesis: on the profits of the slave trade, the profitability of plantation agriculture, and the degree to which those profits found their way into the industries that underpinned the industrial revolution. This was encouraged by a preoccupation, at the time, with the level of capital formation necessary to spark the transition to an industrialized economy.[25]

Historians abstracted the slave trade from the Atlantic economy as a whole and attempted to measure the profits accruing to those who literally handled or employed enslaved peoples (traders, shippers and planters). They then claimed that slavery made only a minimal contribution to total domestic investment. This conclusion ignored slave trade and plantation profits that arose from speculation, credit extension, risk capital and other forms of financial intermediation.[26] A key essay of the 1970s concluded that the slave trade itself could have added at best only 1% to total domestic capital formation in the eighteenth century, reaching 1.7% at the peak in 1770. As late as 1998 an influential survey using different assumptions and calculations repeated the 1% figure,

---

[24] Cuenca-Estaban (2004: 35–66); Berg (2005); Findlay and O'Rourke (2007); Hazareesingh and Curry-Machado (2009: 1–5); Rönnbäck (2010: 373–94); van Zanden and Prak (2013); Riello (2013); Zahedieh (2014: 392–420); Berg et al. (2015); Gerritsen and Riello (2016). Key books of the 1990s and 2000s that emphasize the impact of Atlantic colonial trade, including the slave trade, on the British economy of the eighteenth and early nineteenth centuries are: Hancock (1995); Pomeranz (2000); Findlay and O'Rourke (2007); Zahedieh (2010); Ashworth (2017). See also many key essays by P. K. O'Brien and N. Zahedieh cited in the references, and Wright (2020: 353–83, esp. 356–8); Harley (2015: 161–83).
[25] Rostow (1960); Deane and Cole (1962/1967); Mathias (1969).
[26] Robinson (1987: 122–40, esp. 133–4).

although by then it had been pointed out, using the 1970s estimates, that the potential contribution of the slave trade alone to *industrial and commercial* investment rather than to *total investment*, in 1750 and 1770, may have amounted to almost 40%.[27]

Assessments of the contribution of the slave trade to capital formation and to industrial investment have rarely been revised since the 1980s. This is surprising because historians in recent decades have made major revisions to data on the number of slaves carried; the profits per slave; the level of British national income; the ratio of investment to national income and sectoral capital formation; and the capital value of plantations. Estimates of the growth rate of national income in the period 1770 to 1830, and the size of investment ratios, have been revised downwards, by up to 40% since the early 1980s, significantly enlarging the potential contribution of industrial capital from the slave trade, perhaps doubling some earlier estimates.[28]

More slaves were carried than was known in the 1980s, perhaps half as many again,[29] and profits on slave voyages were likely higher, as the widening evidence base for the profitability of the slave trade has shown. Early assumptions of average returns of 6–10% were probably an underestimate; there are examples of voyage profits exceeding 20 or even 30% and a few over 100%, but profits were also volatile and potential losses great, not least from disease.[30] The many years of war in the eighteenth century also yielded large windfall gains to some merchants through state-sanctioned privateering. On the second voyage of the Liverpool slave ship *Hawke* in 1781 the *Jeune Emilia* was seized, netting a profit on the voyage of 147%.[31] In 1793 the Liverpool ship *Christopher* captured

---

[27] Engerman (1972: 430–3, 441); Richardson (1998: 461); Solow (1985: 99–115, esp. 105); Morgan (2000: 46–7); Zahedieh (2014: 403).

[28] GDP estimates of the 1960s by Deane and Cole were revised downwards for the period 1770 to 1830 by Crafts in 1985 and recently adjusted by Broadberry et al. (2015): Deane and Cole (1962/1967); Crafts (1985: 45); Broadberry et al. (2015: 187–244). For capital formation see Feinstein and Pollard (1988).

[29] Compare Curtin (1969) with https://www.slavevoyages.org/ and with Eltis and Richardson (2010).

[30] Profits remained on average well above the returns on investment at home in land or government consuls: Richardson (1976: 79); Morgan (2000: 38–44); Inikori (2002: 116–17, 215–16); Radburn (2009).

[31] Richardson (1976: 79); Williams (1897/1966).

Le Convention en route from West Africa to the West Indies, netting a prize worth £23,800.[32]

The profits and wealth of slave plantations

Calculations of the importance of slave trade profits to the British economy ignore the generation and repatriation of plantation profits. Early estimates of plantation profit rates indicate they were high in Barbados during the later seventeenth century. During the war years 1756–62 profits may have settled down to 11.2% for Barbados and 14.8% for Jamaica. In the 'silver age of sugar' between 1763 and 1775 plantation profits in Jamaica averaged 13.5% per annum but these fell to just over 6% later in the century and elsewhere in the British Caribbean profits may have hovered between 5 and 6% between the 1770s and 1791. Profit rates in the 1790s and beyond on the British sugar frontier were unstable but frequently much higher. Average profits for the whole period from the late seventeenth to the early nineteenth century are generally accepted to have been at least 10%.[33] Adding on the value of repatriated interest on loans and mortgages, it is possible that 8–10% of the national income of Britain came from the West Indies in the late eighteenth century.[34]

Plantation wealth accounted for £104 million or over 64% of British American wealth in 1774. At that date plantation America has been estimated to have been almost three times as economically valuable to the British Empire as Scotland, twice as valuable as Ireland and perhaps equivalent to Lancashire and Yorkshire combined. Total wealth in the British Caribbean in 1774 has been estimated at £51,926,327. With only 16.3% of the total population of British America and 2.4% of the white population, the Caribbean had 32.2% of its wealth. Jamaica in particular was prodigiously rich: it had 10% of the wealth of England and Wales. The wealthiest Jamaicans left estates worth five times those of

---

[32] Inikori (2002: 346).

[33] Ward (1978: 197–213, esp. 204–9); For Jamaica see Burnard (2020b: 220).

[34] Sheridan (1965: 292–311). See also Burnard (2001: 506–24) who estimates the capital stock of Jamaica alone in the 1770s to have been 50% higher than Sheridan's figures.

British North Americans. William Beckford's Jamaican estate was worth £148,401 in 1774; Sir Simon Clarke's was valued at £350,120.[35]

Were the returns from the Caribbean colonies worth the high costs of their defence and administration? Adam Smith thought not, as did a number of economic historians of the 1960s and 1970s.[36] But this misses the point because as long as high net private returns were made, the potential was there for the proceeds to flow into the industrializing economy. The 'cost' of colonial defence was, furthermore, largely offset by the, often innovatory, stimulus it created for the economy, in the demand for munitions, ships, ships' provisions and uniforms. By 1805 a seventy-four-gun ship of the line, fitted rigged and armed, cost £80,000 or the price of sixteen cotton mills. And the navy alone bought a fifth of all products traded on the British agricultural market in the late eighteenth century.[37]

Significantly, there have been few attempts to convey the fuller picture that could be provided by adding together profits from the slave trade, profits from plantations and profits from plantation trade. Conscious of the latitude for error, few historians have attempted these measures in recent years despite the existence of better data than was available in the last century.[38] The equally important question is: were these proceeds invested in productive areas of the economy? There is no doubt that much wealth generated by the West Indies was invested in landownership, in the building of fine country houses and in conspicuous consumption rather than in industry.[39] But this non-industrial spending was not wasted on the economy. New owners brought money to exploit coal and mineral resources on their estates. Landed estates also provided a store of wealth upon which loans could be raised for investment in agricultural improvement, mining, transport or finance. Such spending also impacted upon the building, landscape gardening and fine furnishing industries.

---

[35] Burnard (2019: 102–17, esp. 111); Burnard (2001: 520).
[36] See, for example, Coelho (1973); Thomas (1968) but compare Pares (Pares 1960: 50). For costs in Jamaica see Burnard and Graham (2020); Graham (2023).
[37] Rodger (2010: 1–18, esp. 10, 14); Morriss (2004); See also O'Brien (2021).
[38] Darity (1990: 121, 144); Findlay and O'Rourke (2007: 337–45); Harley (2015: 161–80).
[39] See, for example, Barczewski (2014: 69–89, 164–79); Dresser and Hahn (2013).

Conspicuous consumption created demands for new consumer goods and their industries.[40]

There was also much industrial and commercial investment. Samuel Touchet was a sugar and cotton merchant, speculator, slave trader and plantation owner of the mid-eighteenth century. He engaged heavily in the Liverpool slave trade and had shares in twenty West India ships. With his brothers he ran one of the leading cotton check firms in Manchester, owned another cotton mill in Northampton and bought rights to spindles in the first powered spinning mill developed by Lewis Paul and John Wyatt during the 1740s and early 1750s (an enterprise that failed). His Africa interests extended to an attempt to monopolize the trade from Senegal in slaves and gum Arabic (needed in the cotton calico printing trades). Touchet raised his investment funds for the British cotton industry in the slave trade, on the family Caribbean plantations and in the futures markets of the London sugar trade.[41] Recent research has multiplied the number of examples of these sorts of entrepreneurial and financial overlaps.[42]

Many industries before the 1830s and 1840s needed little fixed capital as manufacturing machinery was not yet complex or expensive. Circulating capital (including credit) was often three or four times greater than fixed asset requirements in the eighteenth century, rising to eight or nine times in the Napoleonic War period, particularly in the consumer goods industries.[43] Assessing the economic impact of slavery needs to include its role in providing credit and in furthering the development of banking and credit instruments as well as its role in supplying fixed capital. Thanks to research of the last decade we can in this volume fully explore how wealth derived from slavery, in many forms, was mobilized for the benefit of the British economy through to the period of slave emancipation and beyond.

---

[40] Mullen (2022: 263–71); Styles (2000: 124–69); Berg (2005: 85–110); Wilson and Mackley (1999: 436–68); Zahedieh (2021: 784–808, esp. 789–90); de Vries (2008; 2015: 7–39); Barczewski (2014: 164–79).

[41] Wadsworth and Mann (1931/1968: 245); Berg (2004: 137–41).

[42] See, for example, Legacies of British Slavery: https://www.ucl.ac.uk/lbs/.

[43] Hudson (1986: 51); Chapman (1979: 52, 66).

The slave trade and overseas trade

In recent decades, historians researching global history and the history of consumption have attributed much more significance to overseas trade in British eighteenth-century economic growth than in the past. They have demonstrated that around 95% of the *addition* to the volume of exports between 1700/1 and 1772/3 was sold on imperial markets, the bulk to North America and the West Indies.[44] Furthermore, exports were increasingly of manufactured goods. The markets of the New World demanded many new types of manufactures that were at the forefront of product and process innovation.[45]

Before the development of a substantial manufacturing base in the North American colonies, these settler and plantation societies were a major source of demand for British manufactured goods. The generally thriving white settler population of the North American mainland colonies numbered 2 million by the 1770s. By 1800 the settler population of the USA had reached 5.3 million, providing the most buoyant Atlantic market for British manufactures, especially textiles.[46] The colonies, and their shipping, lay within Britain's 'free trade'/ mercantilist sphere until 1775. Trade between the mainland American colonies and the Caribbean, which constituted half of the former's total export trade, paid for much of their British manufactured imports.[47] Mass-market plantation demand for coarse plain woollens and linens for slave clothing and for hand tools geared to specific crops and soils brought large-scale British imports of mass-produced items. Sugar cane processing also relied on British-imported copper vessels, windmill parts, hydraulic equipment and steam engines.[48] British manufactured exports for transatlantic markets above all involved significant and fashion-conscious colonial demand for consumer goods – fancy textiles, scientific and musical instruments, clocks, carriages, candlesticks and

---

[44] O'Brien and Engerman (1991: 178, 186).

[45] Inikori (2002); Inikori in Solow and Engerman (1987: 79–101). This case is emphasized fully in Berg and Hudson (2021).

[46] O'Shaughnessy (2000: 9); Riello (2022: 19); Smith (1998: 676–708); DuPlessis (2016); Breen (2004).

[47] Wright (2020: 362); Harley (2015: 171–2).

[48] See chapters 3, 7 and 8.

cruets – sought not just by a wealthy Caribbean and mainland planter class, but also by a rapidly growing northern colonial artisan, commercial and middle class. The British additionally exported these same goods to the slave-plantation colonies of other European powers, especially within the Spanish and Portuguese empires.

Atlantic trade, propelled by the slave trade and by European demands for slave-produced plantation crops, created the main dynamic of Britain's global trade over the period leading to, and including, the industrial revolution.[49] Estimates broadly accepted by economic historians show an increase of the share of Caribbean and North America trade in total British international trade from 11% in 1700 to 56% in 1800.[50] This trade was increasingly integrated with the Indian Ocean trade in Indian textiles, which were in demand as re-exports to Africa and the Americas, and with European trade that also provided re-exports destined to be exchanged for enslaved peoples in Africa or to be traded across the Atlantic.

The West Indies stands out as the major single dynamic source of British imports before the nineteenth century (see table 2.1). The average annual value of imports from the West Indies in 1766–70 was £2,870,000 in comparison with £1,195,000 from North America. The value of imports from the Caribbean remained much higher than from the USA after the 1780s. In 1814–16 they were valued at £16,656,000 in comparison with the £3,976,000 from the USA. British West Indian sugar imports more than doubled in the mid-century decades from around £1.5 million per annum 1746–50 to £3.2 million per annum 1771–5.[51]

British export figures demonstrate the growth, then dominance, of American markets during the classic industrial revolution period, up to the 1830s. The West Indies took a rapidly increasing share of British

---

[49] de Vries (2010: 710–33, esp. 718–19).

[50] See Burnard and Riello (2020: 242); Riello (2022). Trade figures for Britain in the eighteenth century are too unreliable to offer more than an indication of rough proportions and change over time. Official values do not include illicit trade and were distorted by the failure to revalue units of trade goods from one year to the next. The figures do not include Scotland before the 1770s. This must be borne in mind in using the tables in this chapter and with other trade figures quoted throughout the volume.

[51] Richardson (1987: 111). See also Sheridan (1974: 448, 500–1); Davis (1979: 92).

Table 2.1: Geographical distribution of origin of retained imports of England/ Britain 1700–1798 % (total official values in £000s).

	1700–1701 England	1730–31 England	1750–51 England	1772–3 Britain	1797–8 Britain
Europe	62	52	46	34	29
West Indies	14	21	19	24	25
North America	6	9	11	15	7
Africa	1	1	1	1	1
Ireland	5	4	9	11	13
East Indies and other	12	13	14	15	25
Total %	100	100	100	100	100
Total value	£5,819	£7,386	£7,855	£13,395	£23,903

Sources: Deane and Cole (1967: 87), summarized in Morgan (2000: 19) and in Zahedieh (2014: 409). For later figures see Davis (1979: 110–25). (1797–8 was a major war year.)

Table 2.2: Geographical distribution of English/British domestic exports, 1700–1798 % (total official values in £000s).

	England 1700–1701	England 1730–31	England 1750–51	Britain 1772–3	Britain 1797–8
Europe	82	76	69	39	21
West Indies	5	7	5	12	25
North America	6	7	11	26	32
Africa	2	2	1	5	4
Ireland	3	5	8	10	9
East Indies and other	2	3	6	8	9
Total %	100	100	100	100	100
Total value	£4,461	£5,203	£9,125	£10,196	£18,298

Sources: Deane and Cole (1967: 87), summarized in Morgan (2000: 19). For later figures see Davis (1979: 94–101), summarized in Zahedieh (2014: 413). (1797–8 was a major war year.)

exports after the 1770s, accounting for a quarter or more of exports by the late 1790s, but the USA remained the bigger market, taking around a third and far exceeding the value of goods sent to Europe by the end of the century (see table 2.2).

Re-exports were boosted by the slave-based Atlantic trade with Africa taking re-exported goods from Asia (especially textiles and cowrie shells) and from Europe (manufactures) in exchange for enslaved people (table 2.3). North America and the West Indies took even more re-exported goods, mostly manufactures but also iron and timber from the Baltic. But by far the biggest proportion of re-exports by value were plantation products from the Caribbean destined for European mainland markets and for Ireland. These increasingly underpinned Britain's ability to purchase essential supplies from continental Europe, particularly timber, iron, naval supplies and linen; and foodstuffs and linen from Ireland.

Table 2.4 shows the relative magnitude of the different broad market areas for British goods in the Americas (excluding Spanish America) in three decades. This table also considers the value of imports from India as well as exports to Africa and America in the diamond-shaped trade.

The South Asia trade is not our main focus here, but it was doubtless important to the economy aside and apart from its synergy with the slave trade. Profits made by East India Company investors buoyed the domestic economy, and the demands of Asian trade for credit and capital led to financial innovations, not least in joint stock company organiz-ation. But the Asian trade was essentially a London-based import trade; it was a deficit trade dependent upon exports of bullion. Atlantic trade, by contrast, was based on a two-way exchange that included the export of manufactures, and that increasingly drew in enterprise and capital from the north and west of the country was well as London. It therefore

Table 2.3: Geographical distribution of English/British re-exports 1700–1798 % (total official values in £000s).

	England 1700–1701	England 1730–31	England 1750–51	Britain 1772–3	Britain 1797–8
Europe	78	70	62	65	78
West Indies	6	6	4	3	4
North America	5	7	11	9	3
Africa	3	4	3	4	3
Ireland	7	11	18	18	11
East Indies and other	1	2	2	1	1
Total %	100	100	100	100	100
Total value	£2,136	£3,002	£3,428	£6,930	£11,802

Source: Deane and Cole (1967 edn: 87), summarized in Morgan (2000: 20). For later figures see Davis (1979: 102–9). (1797–8 was a major war year.)

Table 2.4: The 'diamond-shaped trade' associated with the British Atlantic system and the Indian Ocean of the eighteenth century in three benchmark decades. Values of trade are by decade, official values, in £millions. Exports include re-exports.

Decade/ World Region	Exports to North America	Exports to West Indies	Exports to Africa	Imports from India	Numbers in slave trade in British ships per decade
1710s	£3.75	£4.1	£0.72 (68% textiles)	£4.52	150,329
1750s	£15.77	£8.3	£2.0 (69% textiles)	£8.1	253,060
1790s	£58.6	£34.3	£10.7 (72% textiles)	£20.3	382,672

Source: Trade figures (by decade): Riello (2022: 134–9), where original sources are listed. Slave trade figures from https://www.slavevoyages.org/voyage/database#tables.

had a greater impact in spreading incomes and wealth more broadly through the economy than did Asian trading. Nabob wealth, derived from the profits of the East India Company, was, moreover, invested more in country houses and estates and less in industry, than was wealth from the West Indies. Planters and Atlantic traders had closer direct links with industries via their two-way trading connections. Absentee planters were also more likely to invest in industry and commerce, alongside or instead of land because they often repatriated wealth earlier in life than nabobs. Where the Asian trade did have a major impact was on consumption. The trade in tea, porcelain and fine cotton textiles shifted consumer preferences. Tea consumption became closely linked to sugar consumption, and Chinese porcelain and Indian cottons drove product and process innovation in British industry.[52]

The wider impact of the slave trade and plantation colonies: shipping, financial services and commodity chains

Alongside the profits directly generated from trading in, or possession of, enslaved peoples and the impact of the Caribbean on manufactured

[52] Berg (2005: 46–110).

goods exports and industries, the economic gains arising from the plantation colonies and trade were distributed over many other sectors of the economy. These included shipping, shipbuilding, refining, insurance, financial intermediation, commodity brokering and retailing.[53] As employment in all of these industries and services expanded, the working lives and wages of hundreds of thousands in manufacturing and processing, shipbuilding, shipping, dock work, clerking, banking and retailing came to rely upon the foundation stone of slavery.

In the 1780s Britain had roughly 50,000 merchant seamen and one million tons of shipping. By 1831 these had risen to 130,000 men and 2.5 million tons deployed worldwide, closely connecting Europe with both the Atlantic and Indian Oceans. The share of the West African and American trades in English tonnage rose from an estimated 30% in the 1680s to 40% by 1770 and 57% in 1836.[54] The demand that shipbuilding and repair in British Atlantic ports created for timber, iron cordage, sailcloth, pitch, tar and hemp provided a major stimulus to the Baltic trades. Linkages extended outwards from shipping to other industries including dock construction and ship provisioning. Copper and iron innovated and expanded in response to the trade, including copper sheathing of ships from the 1770s to protect hulls. From the 1780s regulations stipulating basic conditions for slave transport led to innovations and investment in the remodelling and refitting of ships.[55]

Britain's financial sector was a major beneficiary of the slave and plantation trades. Many of the key financial innovations of the eighteenth century were spawned or intensified by slave trade needs and by plantation investments including payments systems, insurance and mortgaging. Changes in banking promoted by Atlantic credit and payments linked the resources of the London money market with the industrial regions. Prospects of slave trade profits and the influence of the West India lobby helped to secure the national debt and influenced Bank of England policy. All consolidated London's position as the international financial centre for global trading by the end of the eighteenth century.[56]

[53] Inikori (2002); Solow (1987: 72–4); Morgan (2000); Sheridan (1974: 475–8).
[54] Kelly, Ó Gráda and Solar (2021: 239–75).
[55] Inikori (2002: 265–313, 341–2).
[56] See chapter 8.

Opportunities for profit making occurred at every stage in the long and complex transnational production, processing and trading chains that characterized the Atlantic commodity trades. Calculating the value added at each stage in these chains yields much higher and more realistic estimates of the contribution of slave-based economic activity to the British economy than do earlier, more simplistic, calculations. Such measures reflect changing productivity along the product chains; they also highlight the economic rents that have been long neglected in calculations of the proceeds of slavery. Some rents were appropriated through taxation but there were also significant monopoly rents taken by commission agents, slave traders, marine insurers and West India Houses.

One study of the commodity chain of the sugar trade alone has estimated that sugar accounted for 1% of British GDP at the beginning of the eighteenth century, rising to 4% in the 1770s, faster than the growth of GDP in that period. The re-export trade added another 1 to 2% of GDP by the 1770s.[57] This 5 to 6% contribution to GDP in the 1770s, falling to 4–5% at the end of the century, constituted a substantial share of British economic activity associated with just one plantation commodity (sugar).[58] Traders, shippers, wholesalers, processers, retailers, insurers, investors, bankers and other agents and institutions, not in the Caribbean but in Britain, took most of the value added in the sugar chain. If this analysis is extended beyond sugar to include tobacco and cotton, and to include production on plantations as well as the slave trade and industries dependent on the American plantation complex (i.e., all of the trans-national value chains involved), a much fuller picture emerges. The incomes earned were perhaps equivalent to 3% of GDP at the beginning of the eighteenth century, and around 11% of GDP a century later.[59]

Finally, the Atlantic slave economy added significantly to Britain's capacity to feed its growing population and to provide industrial raw

[57] Rönnbäck (2014: 223–45, esp. 236, 232). Eltis and Engerman initially pioneered this approach for sugar, estimating that the value added in British Caribbean sugar production alone in 1805 was £5.4 million (2% of GDP): Eltis and Engerman (2000: table 1).

[58] Rönnbäck (2014).

[59] Rönnbäck (2018: 309–27, esp. 324–6).

materials. Plantation products stimulated new consumer tastes for tropical groceries and their derivatives: sugar, tobacco, coffee, sweetened beverages, rum and other alcoholic drinks, with knock-on effects on domestic processing and manufacturing. At the same time, slave-grown Caribbean cotton was indispensable in Britain's textile revolution.[60]

Britain's gains compared with France and other European rivals

By 1776 the French Caribbean produced 43% more crops by value than did the British Caribbean, and it made significant contributions to French economic prosperity before the Haitian Revolution in 1791.[61] France's foreign trade valued at £25 million at the end of the 1780s was perhaps £5 million more that of Britain, and it had grown at a faster rate in the eighteenth century.[62] Saint-Domingue generated extraordinary wealth: its fertile soils and efficient plantation systems produced sugar more cheaply than did the British colonies. Sugar shipments rose from 15 million livres in 1730 to 75 million livres in 1790, a growth rate of 4% per year, a rate greater than that for the whole French economy. France was also Europe's greatest re-exporter of sugar.[63] Profits on the French slave trade and wider long-distance trade to the West Indies were, as in Britain, higher than those on domestic alternatives. But all this was quickly to change in the wake of the French Revolution, slave revolts, the loss of Saint-Domingue and the decline of French trading power during and after the Napoleonic Wars.[64] Recent reassessments have also highlighted the key role of slavery in the Dutch economy, suggesting a significant contribution in 1770 to the GDP of the Dutch Republic (5.2%) and especially to the province of Holland (10.4%). But this contribution declined thereafter following financial crises in the 1770s and the loss of colonies to Britain in warfare.[65]

---

[60] Pomeranz (2000: 274–5); Cuenca-Estaban (2004: 55; 2014). See also chapters 3, 6, 7 and 10 in this volume.

[61] Eltis and Engerman (2000: 130); Daudin (2004: 144); Burnard and Garrigus (2016: 164–91, 244–68); Hazareesingh (2021).

[62] Daudin (2004: 144–71, esp. 144).

[63] Stein (1980: 3–17); Burnard and Garrigus (2016, 244–8).

[64] Daudin (2004: 164, 167); Potofsky (2011: 89–107, esp. 105).

[65] Fatah-Black and van Rossum (2015: 63–83); Brandon and Bosma (2021: 43–76).

It is often argued that if deep engagement with Africa in slavery was enough on its own to spark an industrial revolution, Spain and Portugal, as well as France and the Low Countries, would have become industrial leaders earlier than they did.[66] However, each European trading empire had a different chronology, different background economic and political conditions, different interactions with different parts of the Americas and thus experienced a different impact. As we shall see in later chapters, Britain's dominance of the slave trade extended the diamond-shaped global trade flows that linked the Indian and Atlantic Oceans, stimulating the demand for manufactures and encouraging commercial and financial innovation. It set up commodity flows not just across the north Atlantic and Eurasia but also with Latin America. The fiscal military state, developed to protect Britain from invasion, also protected and extended Britain's global trade and overseas investments. Britain thus came to dominate international shipping and finance over the course of the eighteenth century. London was already the leading cosmopolitan entrepôt for European trade with the Americas and for the African trade in the early eighteenth century. By 1800 it was the linchpin of international credit and finance in trade and investment in the Atlantic and beyond. Wartime gains greatly enhanced British plantation cultivation, especially after the Seven Years War (from 1763), when gains were mainly at the expense of the Dutch. The financial advantages that Britain drew from plantation commerce and the slave trade were central to her success, particularly after the crises in the 1770s that badly affected Dutch finance. The Napoleonic War period and the revolution in Saint-Domingue together confirmed British dominance of Caribbean trade and investment, largely at the expense of the French.[67]

Conclusion

This volume, like the classic work of Eric Williams, takes a broad and multilateral view of the many connections created by slavery throughout the Atlantic basin, globally and within the home economy. The early critics of Williams between the 1950s and 1990s focused narrowly

---

[66] See, for example, Harley (2015: 161–80); Wright (2020: 358).
[67] For more on finance see chapter 8.

on the profits of the slave trade or on plantation profitability and claimed a minor economic contribution from slavery. Their findings are misleading and no longer acceptable. We now have new data on the scale of the slave trade as well as detailed studies of plantation wealth and investment. More significantly, our historical questions and perspectives have changed. New histories of consumption, global history and capitalism have turned our gaze outwards. To understand the role of slavery in British industrialization and in later capitalist development the net needs to be cast wide and long to include the complex global interconnections of the slave-based British Atlantic system as well as slavery's broad impact on the economic development and wealth of Britain, through to slave emancipation in the 1830s and beyond.

CHAPTER 3

A revolution in consumption: sugar and other plantation products

Sir Dalby Thomas, writing of the growth of the West Indian colonies in 1690, listed the rich variety of their leading staples: sugar, molasses and rum, indigo, logwood, cotton and ginger, 'not to speak of the many *Druggs, Woods, Cocoa, Piemento,* and *Spices,* besides *Raw-Hides,* etc. which comes from those parts'.[1] By the time Thomas was writing, sugar had come to dominate the trade in plantation products. In *A Vindication of Sugars* (1715) Dr Frederick Slare praised the appeal of sugar to the refined palates of women and the activities of the West India merchant 'who loads his Ship with this sweet Treasure . . . By this commodity have Numbers of Persons of inconsiderable Estates, rais'd Plantations, and from thence have gain'd such Wealth as to return to their native Country very Rich, and have purchas'd and do daily purchase, great Estates.'[2] Slare, like many others in the eighteenth century, not only extolled the economic advantages of the sugar trade but became a 'sugar fanatic', adding it to his wine, using it as snuff and even as a toothpaste.[3]

What difference did the new sweet sugar taste and the rapidly expanding importation of other colonial groceries and spices make to the European economy and consumer cultures? There is no doubt that imports of Asian-produced manufactured goods deeply affected material culture and consumer demand, stimulating adaptive and inventive products and technologies that were part of Britain's industrial revolution.[4] But much larger imports of colonial groceries, from the Americas, especially tobacco and sugar joined by coffee, cacao and tea (from Asia), became key goods that shifted European tastes and cultural practices

---

[1] Thomas (1690: 9), cited in Sheridan (1974: 19).
[2] Slare (1715: Dedication).
[3] See British Library introduction to Slare and his pamphlet: https://www.bl.uk/collection-items/a-vindication-of-sugar.
[4] Berg (2004: 85–142).

throughout much of society during the seventeenth and eighteenth centuries. As their supply grew, so did their popularity. They entered social practices, diets, nutrition and drinking habits across a broad social spectrum of the population. These commodities also created demand for ancillary manufactured goods such as kettles and pans, sugar tongs and basins, glassware and other receptacles for rum and punch drinking and for serving desserts, coffee, tea and sugar spoons, crockery of all kinds, tobacco pipes, snuff boxes, tables and many other products. Their consumption provoked widespread debate about social habits and shifted economic thought and policy.[5]

The dramatic growth of Europe's imports from the Atlantic world, produced largely by African enslaved labour, dwarfed the tonnage of its imports from Asia. In the late seventeenth century roughly twice the tonnage of goods was imported from the Americas to Europe compared with return cargoes from Asia. By the 1790s the ratio had risen to more than twenty-fold. Imports from the Atlantic paralleled a rise in the supply of enslaved peoples of more than 2% per annum over the whole period 1525–1790, accelerating after 1650. Atlantic trade (by weight), although very volatile, grew by at least twice the long-term rate of the Indian Ocean trade over the eighteenth century. Chesapeake tobacco exports to Europe grew 5% per annum over the period 1622 to the 1750s, but by the 1770s sugar exports had grown most dramatically to four times the level of total Asian exports to Europe.[6]

Sugar imports

Sugar production in the Western hemisphere was 54,000 tons in 1700; this figure doubled by 1740, tripled by 1776 and had almost quadrupled by 1783.[7] The estimated annual profits on sugar cultivation throughout the British Caribbean reached an estimated £1,700,000 by c.1770.[8] Colonial groceries accounted for 17% of all imports in 1700, rising to

---

[5] See, for example, Edward Misselden's fear of the impact of the sugar and tobacco on England's balance of trade (1622: 12, 108–9), cited in Withington (2020: 384–408, esp. 395). Also see Hirschman (1977); de Vries (2003: 41–56).

[6] de Vries (2010: 718–20).

[7] Solow (1987: 70–2); Morgan (1993a: 184–5).

[8] Ward (1978: 197–213, esp. 209); Morgan (1993a: 184–5).

35% in 1800. The value of British sugar imports from the Caribbean between 1670 and 1820 far surpassed imports of any other commodity in Britain's world trade.[9] Table 3.1 shows the rise of sugar to become the top-ranked import by the early 1770s, and its continued high position into the mid-nineteenth century.

Taxes on sugar contributed significantly to state revenues. Though the percentage rate of tax changed little, valuations of various classes of sugar were doubled, then trebled by the early eighteenth century. Protection given to British over foreign-produced sugars also rose from 2s.5d per cwt in 1787 to £3 6s.2d by 1844.[10] Taxes on addictive goods, like sugar, made for such sure revenue streams that they were among the last to be cut at the end of the nineteenth century.[11] Excise and preferential taxes fell most heavily on consumers raising the price of sugar in Britain above the international level, but domestic demand remained buoyant. The sugar trade continued to boom right through the eighteenth century and into the early nineteenth century, remaining strong and profitable (despite oscillations) until the Sugar Duties Act of 1846, which ended preferential duties on British over foreign sugars. George III, out driving in his carriage with Pitt the Elder one day in the 1780s, noticed a much grander carriage occupied by a West Indian planter. He said to Pitt: 'Sugar, sugar, eh! All that sugar. How are the duties, eh Pitt, how are the duties?'[12]

The history of the sugar trade should not be associated only with a pre-industrial commercial or agrarian capitalism: the industries to which it gave rise and the cultural shifts it created made it fully a part of the industrial revolution. Britain became the key player in the production and consumption of sugar from the later seventeenth century and maintained its place into the nineteenth century. Sugar consumption per head per annum in England and Wales, on current estimates, was already c.7 lbs in 1700; older estimates show an increase from 8.23 lbs in 1710–19 to 24.16 lbs per head in 1790–99.[13] During the 1680s

[9] Shammas (1993: 117–205, esp. 182); Sheridan (1974: 20); Findlay and O'Rourke (2007: table 6.5, 329).

[10] Deerr (1949–50: vol. 2, 427–30).

[11] Ashworth (2003: 47, 52).

[12] Deerr (1949–50: vol. 2, 429n).

[13] Zahedieh (2010: 221); Goodall (2020: 687); Shammas (1993: 117–205, esp. 182).

Table 3.1: Top eight recorded English/British commodity imports (official values) ranked, together accounting for between half and two-thirds of the total official value of imports.

1699–1701	1772–4	1784–6	1824–6	1854–6
Linens	**Sugar**	**Sugar**	Cotton	Cotton
Sugar	Linens	Tea	**Sugar**	Grain
Tea	Cotton	Cotton	Dyestuffs	Silk
Calicoes	Silk, raw/thrown	Asian textiles	Wool	**Sugar**
Silk, raw/thrown	Calicoes	Silk	Tea	Tea
Tobacco	Tobacco	Wine	Timber	Timber
Textile yarns, mostly flax	Iron/steel	Dyestuffs	Silk	Wine
Dyestuffs	Flax/hemp	Timber	Wine	Wool

Source: Based on Davis (1962, 1979: 39) and Zahedieh (2014: 405).

the English Caribbean produced as much sugar as Portuguese Brazil, and much more than the French islands. British West Indies sugar production rose by 80% between 1740 and 1769.[14] It was produced in more and larger plantations; the value (including enslaved peoples) of the median sugar estate in Jamaica rose from £7,956 in 1741–5 to £19,502 in 1771–5. 70,787 enslaved peoples were sold and stayed in Jamaica 1702–25; twenty-five years later a further 122,676 had been retained.[15] The enslaved on William Perrin's five Jamaican estates grew from 135 in 1769 to 950 in 1820. His overseers bought a gang of fifty-four men and women in 1797 for £5,100; two young women field workers in their twenties, Industry and Mary, were valued at £100 each.[16]

Sugar production on the French-owned islands also rose rapidly between the 1740s and 1790, surpassing Britain's plantation production. Saint-Domingue alone exported far more sugar than any of the other sugar islands in the later eighteenth century. Between 1749 and 1790 French imports from her islands rose from 114 to 178 million lbs.[17] British and French consumption patterns were, however, very different. Britain's per capita sugar consumption by 1774 was eight times that of the

---

[14] Pares (1956: 254–70, esp. 257); Zahedieh (2010: 214).
[15] Sheridan (1974: 230–31, 502–3).
[16] Avery (2019: 88–91).
[17] Stein (1980: 3–17, esp. 6); Sheridan (1974: table 6.2, 101); Deer (1949–50: vol 1).

French.[18] Britain accounted for a third of Europe's sugar consumption in the first half of the eighteenth century; her sugar consumption per capita grew by over 250% in the period 1700 to 1775. French per capita sugar consumption grew only 110% over the same period; the French re-exported much of their sugar to supply the rest of Europe.[19] Why did the British consume most of their colonial sugar, while the French re-exported theirs? One of the answers no doubt lies in the different types and levels of refining of the sugar imported and processed by both countries. Another likely lies in different distributions of income between the two countries and different food cultures.

Sugar prices fell relative to wider consumer goods prices in England and Wales from 1660 to 1685, as production and imports rose, thus favouring greater per capita consumption.[20] Simultaneously, slave prices rose and slave mortality did not fall. Rising production was extracted from growing labour forces worked more intensively. Prices for the consumer fell from over 1s. per lb. (the level of a labourer's wages for two days' work) in the sixteenth century to half this level in the seventeenth century. Prices fell by a further third between 1700 and 1750.[21] They fluctuated during the 1760s and 1770s at a level higher than in 1750, but prices rose significantly higher and fluctuated more sharply in the 1780s and 1790s.[22] Sugar prices also depended on the type of sugar. John Dryden in 1719 was charged 7½d for a pound of single refined sugar and 4½d for a pound of brown sugar. The Leighs at Stoneleigh Abbey, Warwickshire, at the end of the century paid 15d for a pound of single refined sugar, 13d for 'Lisbon', 9d for dry sugar and 8d for raw sugar.[23]

Sugar importing, refining and distribution

The supply of sugar coming into the London market doubled in the period between 1740 and 1769, and London intermediaries dictated the

[18] Solow (1987: 70–2).
[19] Stein (1980: 12).
[20] Zahedieh (2010: 221).
[21] Shammas (1990: 81).
[22] Deerr (1949–50: vol. 2, 531).
[23] Stobart (2013: 220).

prices.[24] Specialist sugar commission agents purchased different grades of sugar for different classes of buyer and exchanged knowledge with planter correspondents on improving quality, packing, seasonality and markets.[25] They sold the sugar on commission usually at 2½%.[26] The London commission system came to dominate the trade and finance of the sugar economy. Large planters by the 1730s sent their sugar to London agents. Specialist shipping developed with larger ships than slave vessels, and owned by planters and their agents, prioritizing full loading of sugars and rum for return voyages. This reduced risk, and London agents came to control insurance, finance and banking for their planter clients. These agents were also influential in the sugar markets of the outports of Bristol, Liverpool, Lancaster and Glasgow. In 1749 one pamphleteer commented that merchants in the outports relied on London commission agents 'for negotiating their Bills, receiving and paying their Money, discounting their Tickets and Tallies, purchasing *India* Goods, and many other Commodities for them, at the *London* Market, insuring their Ships, and making a great Variety of Bargains and Contracts for them'.[27]

London, with its concentration of agents and absentee planters, came to exercise control over the sugar economy, its trade, shipping, warehousing and finance. Though most of the sugar imported was consumed domestically, a sophisticated and speculative financial brokerage economy developed balancing harvests, ship arrivals, payments, bill discounting and sales. Refined or semi-refined sugars could be stored longer against a potential price rise, and agents, trading on commission and connected with the great West India merchant houses, speculated on price fluctuations. These agents knew the grades of sugar wanted by their buyers and operated a knowledge exchange on qualities and markets for absentee planters and correspondents. They advised on shipping dates to avoid gluts in the market, but balanced this against access to shipping space and the qualities and spoilage rates of the sugar they contracted to sell.[28]

[24] Pares (1956: 254–70, esp. 254).
[25] Sheridan (1974: 330).
[26] Pares (1956: 255).
[27] Anon (1749: 32–3), cited in Sheridan (1974: 337).
[28] Sheridan (1974: 330–8).

The sugar wholesaling trade was not controlled by monopolistic companies. Cargoes were bought directly from the importers by sugar factors, refiners and specialist wholesale grocers, to be resold to other refiners and all manner of retailing grocers across the country.[29] The sugar factor's art lay in two decisions: when to sell and in what lots. War and the weather raised the risk premium. 'Nothing can be more fluctuating than the Market for Sugar, the Continuance of an easterly wind for a few weeks shall raise it, and a westerly wind with the bare expectation of the arrival of Ships shall lower it again.'[30] Indeed Bernard Mandeville, the early eighteenth-century theorist of luxury, in *The Fable of the Bees* framed his analysis of the role of sociability in the economy in the setting of the price between two sugar merchants as they entertained each other while awaiting news of the arrival of a ship from the West Indies.[31] The London commission house of Lascelles and Maxwell, expecting the arrival of Jamaica sugars in the 1740s, sold its Barbados muscovados. But the Jamaica fleet met a terrible storm, and prices went up. The commission house rushed to sell its sugars after news of declaration of war from France, but prices rose to wartime heights during the rest of the year: a typical story of the risks and bounties inherent in the sugar trade.[32]

Further unpredictability went into the choice of sugar lots, whether single or mixed types and grades. The sugar was judged on colour and grain. On its arrival in London, it was bought by grocers and refiners who took nine-tenths of the trade in the 1730s and 1740s, and by exporters and speculators who took the rest.[33] When the sugar arrived in Britain it was already semi-processed. It was not a colonial agricultural product or raw material; it was a manufactured commodity. Many plantations included large industrial complexes of sugar mills, boiling and curing houses and distilleries. Powered by wind, water and later

---

[29] On the London Grocers see Clifford (2018: 231–7); Austen and Smith (1990: 95–115, esp. 102).

[30] Pares (1956: 262).

[31] Mandeville (1714/1924: Remark B, 60).

[32] Pares (1956: 263–4). On the Lascelles commission house, including Lascelles and Maxwell, see Smith (2006: 73–83).

[33] Pares (1956: 262).

steam engines, they required extensive capital investment.[34] After the cane harvest the sugar moved through a series of powered mechanized processes on the plantations, for the cane had to be crushed and the juice extracted as soon as possible to get sugar into a form that could survive long-distance transport without deterioration. Cane mills powered by wind, water or horse power turned iron rollers for crushing the cane and extracting the juice. The juice then went by pipes or gutters to the boiling house, where it was heated in turn between four and five large copper cauldrons to a very high temperature. Once clarified, the sugar went into copper coolers, then crystallized in a curing house in earthenware pots.[35] Some of the planters took the processing further to produce 'clayed' sugar, a semi-refined type. In this process the white sugar produced at an earlier stage was ground into powder and poured back into the moulds. A layer of clay batter was poured on top of it; this pushed the cruder and treacle-like parts of the sugar to the bottom of the mould, leaving a more refined white sugar.[36] Images of the plantation economy in the seventeenth and eighteenth centuries convey technologically progressive machinery and sophisticated chemical processing. They show little of the enslaved peoples working the mills and sugar-boiling processes: Europeans discounted and rationalized the enslaved labour of the plantations as a necessary part of technological modernization.[37]

The English customs regime ensured that most planters sent semi-processed muscovado sugars to London; indeed they comprised 90% of the volume and 78% of the value of London sugar imports in the 1660s.[38] The proportions of muscovado and further-processed clayed sugars varied thereafter as prices and duties between the two changed.[39] Much of the imported sugar went on to further processing. Sugar houses and sugar bakers in London, other European metropoles and in Britain's outports carried out the more sophisticated refining and processing. Consumers often saw sugar in grocers' shops as conical loaves wrapped at the end in a sugar paper dyed in indigo to keep insects away. Similar

[34] Crowley (2016: 414–16). For more detail see chapter 4.
[35] Sheridan (1974: 112–18); Zahedieh (2013: 805–25, esp. 811).
[36] Sheridan (1974: 117–18).
[37] Crowley (2016: 403–36).
[38] Zahedieh (2010: 217).
[39] Sheridan (1974: 53, 432, 498).

loaves had been poured at the plantation refineries into earthenware moulds imported from the Staffordshire potteries. The loaves were then either further refined in British refineries into many different grades and colour qualities for sale by apothecaries and grocers or broken down into granulated sugar for use in kitchens and at table.

London became the leading centre for British sugar refining: there were fifty sugar bakers in the metropolis by the mid-seventeenth century, and by the mid-eighteenth century 120 refineries in Britain's larger ports and cities, and others in smaller centres in Stockton, Yorkshire, Whitehaven, Preston and Warrington.[40] Amsterdam also had fifty sugar refineries by 1661, and by 1752 the Dutch Republic had 145 refineries, 139 of these in Holland.[41] The furnaces, open pans and utensils of the London and Bristol sugar bakers were notable features of the cities' industrial landscapes, drawing on capital and coal stock, and making their smoke-filled atmosphere.[42] Each of these refineries needed a capital of several thousand pounds and relied on highly skilled labour to produce the many types and grades of sugar demanded. Bristol was especially significant in the mid to later eighteenth century. It had more refineries than any other British outport. The sugar bakers, with large premises on the riverbanks and close to main roads, absorbed up to £200,000 of local capital between 1720 and 1780. These were major industrial enterprises. The refineries and distilleries both on the plantations and in Britain stimulated the British copper and copper-refining industry for inputs to produce the great vessels for sugar boiling and distilling.[43]

Shopping and consuming

The extraordinary growth rate of sugar imports, the levels of consumption of this addictive food additive and its journey through the trading and refining processes are only part of the story. How did sugar make the shift from a luxury to an everyday commodity from the beginning of the

[40] Johnstone (1976: 58–64, esp. 58–9); Berg and Berg (2001: 227, 237, 255, 281, 295, 315).
[41] de Vries and van der Woude (1997: 326–7).
[42] Zahedieh (2010: 218–19); Morgan (1993a: 216–18).
[43] Morgan (1993a: 215–17); Zahedieh (2013: 805–25); Zahedieh (2021: 784–808); Zahedieh (2022: 149–66).

seventeenth to the end of the eighteenth century, and especially during the mid to later eighteenth century?

Large numbers of sugar varieties and qualities were soon available across the country. As early as 1686 Whiston's price current listed eighteen grades of sugar priced from 45s per hundredweight for the finest to 8.25s for molasses.[44] Place names indicated quality and cost. Jamaica sugar was cheaper but considered poorer quality than those of some rivals; Barbados was associated with muscovado sugar, while St Kitts was known for its fine sugars. Labels often identified specific plantations as well as refining centres in Britain and Europe.[45] The Leigh family of Stoneleigh Abbey, Warwickshire, bought five different types of sugar between 1630 and 1701, six different types between 1710 and 1738, and between 1768 and 1792 eight different types were purchased. A specialist grocer, Alexander Chorley of Manchester, stocked ten types of sugar in the mid-eighteenth century.[46]

By the mid-eighteenth century, grocers and tea dealers, 62,000 of them, comprised a quarter of all shops, and sugar, tea and coffee were defining elements of their stock.[47] The sweetness described and demanded in English recipe books came from dried fruits and honey but, above all, from sugar. Arresting visual images of the period illustrate the luxury sugar desserts and products consumed in elite households and displayed in the windows of confectioners' shops. The widespread presence of sugar in small quantities in gentry and upper-middle-class households from the sixteenth century was to become, by the early eighteenth century, embedded among all social classes. If not regularly consumed, it was desired, craved and even expected.[48]

Production, supply and distribution provide one side of the story behind sugar's meteoric rise in the British economy. Markets, taste and consumer practices make up the other. They explain the rapid percolation of a taste for sweetness throughout society in the eighteenth century. Sugar in the sixteenth and early seventeenth centuries had been

[44] Zahedieh (2010: 220).
[45] Pares (1956: 260); Stobart (2013: 220, 55, 60–3).
[46] Stobart (2013: 55, 193).
[47] Bickham (2008: 71–109, esp. 76).
[48] Thirsk (2014: 27–58, 157–67). For the consumption of sugar in the Anglo-American world see Goodall (2022).

used as a medium of exchange, with fees in Oxford colleges and colonial America's Yale University paid on occasion in sugar cones. In the eighteenth century casual labourers in the customs houses were still often paid in tobacco and sugar.[49] But it was as a foodstuff, a component of drinks and medicines and as a preservative that sugar began to impact upon the wider society. Recent work on bread, potatoes, tea and coffee has highlighted the importance of finely grained consumer preferences, medical and social policy prescription and social and cultural context, in the spread of tastes and choices.[50] For sugar this was even more the case.

Sidney Mintz in his classic book of the 1980s, *Sweetness and Power*, set out how an exotic commodity which first entered the social life of the powerful became a type of 'kingly' luxury for commoners, then later a necessity with sugar calories in a hot drink or with porridge or bread often substituting for a more expensive meal.[51] Appearing early on in the medical pharmacopeia, it was used as a medicine and as a spice. Sugar became a key part of the gum paste of the confectioner's art in the making of sweet condiments and sugar sculptures to decorate the dessert tables of the rich.[52] Used more widely as a preservative of fruits and vegetables, it added valuable calories and vitamins in the winter months, and was vital to a new commercial production of jams and chutneys.[53]

As early as 1700 sugar was a common additive to hot beverages. Rituals of social connection embedded sweetened tea and pastries consumed in the material culture of the tea equipage, not only porcelain cups and saucers imported from China, but mahogany sugar boxes and silver bowls, sugar nippers and tongs and silver teapots. The material culture of sugar consumption was a major stimulus behind the rapidly growing ceramics industry. The number of potteries in England grew by 47% between 1680 and 1710, and by another 25% between 1745 and 1780. Employment by 1780 was ten times its level in 1745.[54] Equally

---

[49] Smith (1776), cited in Sheridan (1974: 347); Goodall (2020; 2022); Ashworth (2003: 157).

[50] See de Vries (2019); Earle (2020); McCants (2007: 433–62).

[51] Avery and Calaresu (2019: 82–7); Mintz (1985: 95, 115, 173); Zahedieh (2010: 225–6).

[52] Brown and Schwarz (1996: 83); Day (2002; 2019: 95, 115, 173).

[53] Weatherill (1990: xxiv).

[54] Berg (2005: 130).

affected were the silver and silver-plate industries, where the silver tea equipage with its sugar bowls, sugar shakers and tea and sugar spoons became symbols of refinement. England's Sheffield silver plate became a new internationally desirable commodity made with new technologies and design skills.[55]

There was a clear link between the rapid growth of sugar imports and East India Company tea imports in the first half of the eighteenth century. The East India Company fostered a tea taste associated with sugar; sugar consumed in this way became 'virtuous' as opposed to the extravagance of sugar decorations.[56] Frederick Slare in his *Vindication of Sugars* made this point in 1715: 'I have frequently commended the Ladies well-chosen Morning Repasts, call'ed Break-fasts, as consisting of good Materials; namely Bread, Butter, Milk, Water and Sugar; Chocolate and Tea are also endow'd with uncommon Vertues ... Nor do I decry and condemn Coffee ...'[57]

Tea dealers and grocers sold tea and sugar together, often provided in small quantities to suit the pockets of a range of consumers. Sugar was commonly advertised on grocers' trade cards alongside tea, chocolate and coffee.[58] Colonial hot drinks became the occasion for new eating and drinking customs among the middle classes at breakfast and tea-time, with sugar not only consumed in hot liquids but also in sweet breads, pastries and preserves.[59]

From luxury consumption to the industrial revolution

Exactly how far down the social scale the dramatic increases in sugar consumption extended and at what point is difficult to establish. Certainly the wealthy consumed large quantities from an early date, as the data of *average* consumption suggests. The political arithmetician and pamphleteer Joseph Massie (1760) estimated sugar consumption by social group. Massie had interests as a sugar merchant or factor and his pamphlets conveyed an extensive knowledge of the sugar trade and

[55] Clifford (1999: 241–56; 2005: 147–68); Berg (2005: 162–7).
[56] Austen and Smith (1990: 95–115, esp. 102–4, 106).
[57] Slare (1715: Dedication).
[58] Austen and Smith (1990: 102–7).
[59] Berg (2005: 228–30).

sugar estates. He divided the English population into four categories, according to the frequency with which they consumed coffee, tea or chocolate, and with these, sugar. He counted 400,000 middling-sort households drinking tea or coffee occasionally, and consuming half as much sugar as those 236,000 households consuming it once a day.[60]

Historians of diet and nutrition do not tell us a great deal about working-class sugar consumption: they confine most discussion to wheat, oats, barley and meat.[61] It has, however, been estimated that the gains in wellbeing from sugar consumption for the lower classes in 1800 was around 13%. By 1800 the 'average Englishman' would have been 'willing to forego 10% or more of his income to maintain access to sugar and tea alone'.[62] 'Far from a side-show in the history of living standards, the introduction of caffeinated hot beverages and sugar contributed substantially to the welfare of the first industrialized country.'[63] The much-cited budgets of Frederick Eden and David Davies, at the end of the eighteenth century, strengthen this conclusion, though their writing was suffused with moral judgement. They give estimates of over 10% of food budgets spent on sugar, treacle and tea: 'instead of two meals a day of hasty-pudding [oatmeal-based], beer and milk . . . the labouring people, in general have substituted the less substantial food of tea, sugar, wheaten bread and butter; which cost double the sum'.[64]

One study drawing on these reports found that over 11% of money spent on food went on sugar, treacle and tea across a sample of 193 labouring families with little difference between the north and south.[65] Certainly sugar consumption was widespread across the country. Samuel Finney considered treacle, brown sugar and tobacco among the 'small necessities' he recorded being bought in the rural districts south of Manchester in the 1750s; by the 1770s he added tea, coffee and loaf

---

[60] Massie (1760); Hersh and Voth (2011: 13); Mathias (1979: 171–89, esp. 175–7); Lindert and Williamson (1982: 385–402, esp. 394–99).

[61] There is little discussion of sugar in analyses of calorific intake and nutrition: Muldrew (2011: 135–40); Meredith and Oxley (2014: 163–214); Allen (2009: 28–36; 2019: 109); Zylberberg (2015: 91–122); Griffin (2018: 71–111).

[62] Hersh and Voth (2011: 1).

[63] Hersh and Voth (2011: 30, 35; 2009).

[64] Eden (1984: 254–69, esp. 257).

[65] Shammas (1984: 257).

Table 3.2: Wages and spending on new drinks by class, 1760.

Families which drink coffee, tea or chocolate	Number of households	Average expenditure £	Average sugar consumption lbs per annum	Average spending on sugar £
Morning and afternoon	70,000	250	369	12
Tea or coffee in the morning	236,000	49	92	3
Tea or coffee occasionally	400,000	44	45	1
Labouring families	750,000	18	14	<1

Source: Adapted from Hersh and Voth (2011: 45), drawn from Massie (1760).

sugar.[66] William Ellis, a Hertfordshire farmer, in 1750 fed his farm servants at harvest five times a day, and included sweet pastries or puddings made with added sugar.[67] Richard Latham, a Lancashire smallholder and labourer who kept a diary of his expenditure between 1724 and 1767, spent between £7 and £11 a year on food and other consumables for his family up to the 1750s. He bought ('on average') 50 lbs of sugar (about a pound a week for a large family) and 20 lbs of treacle each year in the 1740s.[68]

Sugar appears in the records of hospitals and workhouses in the late seventeenth century, and was widely reported by the 1720s. The St Albans workhouse in 1725 spent 3.7% of its budget on sugar and molasses; the Clerkenwell workhouse in 1732, 4.5%. The Norwich new workhouse spent 2.7% of its expenditure on sugar in 1787.[69] St John's workhouse in Chester bought 6 lbs of treacle in 1731 and 1732 and small amounts of sugar by 1738.[70]

Colonial groceries, particularly sugar, played a pivotal role in shifting the composition of diets across society, including those of the labouring poor. When forced to choose, the labouring poor took sugar, tea, butter and wheat bread, rather than larger quantities of oats and milk. This shift in the diet was rarely a choice of luxury over necessity, but a greater

[66] Stobart (2013: 221).
[67] Thirsk (2014: 157).
[68] Weatherill (1990: xxiv).
[69] Mintz (1985: 170); Shammas (1990: 143).
[70] Stobart (2013: 221).

reliance on appetite appeasers coupled with the addictive pull of tea and sugar.[71]

Sugar and intoxicants

A European sweet tooth was also a taste for intoxicants. The key by-products of sugar refining, molasses and sugar syrup, were widely used in rum, brandy, gin and whiskey. The eighteenth century saw a shift in the consumption of alcohol from beer and wine to brandy, gin and rum. Distilled molasses yielded rum, consumed among the rich and the middle classes in the newly popular rum punch, served up from large porcelain punch bowls, first obtained in a trade with China, drummed up by the East India Company, and later provided by local porcelain and earthenware manufacturers. Among the poor, a taste was fostered in rum rations for the navy, which rose from half a pint in 1731 to a pint a day in the late eighteenth century, and watered-down grog took over from the gin craze. England and Wales by 1769 absorbed 1.12 million gallons of West India rum; even more was re-exported to Ireland, which in the same year consumed over 2 million gallons.[72] To the domestic material culture of tea and coffee drinking was added another around clubs, punch houses and taverns serving the new spirits in the vessels that helped to underpin Britain's innovative and rapidly advancing glass and ceramics industries.[73] English manufacturers of newly invented flint glass produced the full range, from cheap dram and gin glasses to the jelly and sweetmeat glasses of the dessert table to fine wine and cordial glasses, decanters, salvers and punch bowls, which came to dominate world glass markets in the eighteenth century.[74]

Rum was also consumed in the West Indies itself on the plantations and in the towns, estimated at nearly 32% of Jamaica's production in the 1770s. The enslaved on the island consumed over a quarter of this.[75] Rum was, in addition, a major player in the trade between the

---

[71] Shammas (1990: 146–8).

[72] Sheridan (1974: 348–51).

[73] Berg (2005: 117–54); Brown and Schwartz (1996: 45–54).

[74] Berg (2005: 121–4).

[75] As the enslaved comprised over 90% of the population, their per capita consumption was limited compared with elite consumption. Sheridan (1974: 342–3).

West Indies and British North America. By the 1770s British North Americans of European ancestry consumed over four gallons of rum per person, per year, a level double that of modern US consumption of all distilled spirits. There were more than 25 sugar refineries and 140 rum distilleries in the British North American colonies by 1770.[76] Rum was also traded by the North American colonies to the coast of Africa in exchange for slaves. The Royal African Company between 1700 and 1727 shipped 182,347 gallons of rum from Barbados, Antigua and Jamaica to its forts on the African coast.[77] Sugar syrup derived from British and European sugar refineries also formed a base, as an alternative to grain mash, for the greatly increased gin production of the 'Gin Age'. Dutch distillers had discovered the mixing of juniper berries with the sugar syrup base to produce their gin; the English used the same base for English gin and English brandy. The Irish added sugar syrup to local grains to create Irish whiskey.[78]

Tobacco, coffee and other plantation consumer goods

Tobacco and coffee were the other key colonial consumer imports, alongside sugar. The plantations produced other groceries, such as rice – 82 million lbs was imported from South Carolina and Georgia in 1790–95, and various spices, especially ginger, cultivated in Jamaica and imported for medicines and cooking.[79] Tobacco was the pioneer, and the most rapidly diffused of any colonial grocery. Tobacco plantations in the Chesapeake as well as in the West Indies, developed on indentured, then enslaved labour, provided a mass consumer market in Britain for smoking, chewing and snuff-taking as early as the 1630s and 1640s. Much tobacco was re-exported to Europe in the eighteenth century. Glasgow merchants and the wider Glasgow economy captured most of the economic gains. Tobacco gave rise to changing gendered social practices in new rituals of sociable smoking and snuff-taking, among the better-off, often wearing particular dress and using fancy pipes and

[76] McCusker (2000: 186–224, esp. 211); Stobart (2013: 221, 217).
[77] Sheridan (1974: 344).
[78] McCusker (2000: 209–10).
[79] Duisenberre (1996: table 22, 89); Shammas (1990: 144). Shammas (2000: 63–185); Avery and Calaresu (2019: 66–8); Higman (1984/1995: 16, 212–14).

snuff boxes. For those lower down the social scale it spawned a large, widely dispersed mass manufacture of basic clay pipes for everyday use. Before the later seventeenth century clay pipe bowls were small because tobacco was relatively expensive. In the eighteenth century larger novelty bowls were produced with moulded designs showing popular celebrities and politicians, commemorative events and advertising wording.[80] Consumption averaged 2 lbs per capita per annum from the 1690s into the late eighteenth century. It was smoked or chewed by many lower down the social scale as an appetite suppressant.[81]

Tobacco cultivation first motivated Caribbean colonization on St Kitts and Barbados, but it was the Chesapeake region of Virginia which was to provide most of Europe's tobacco by the end of the seventeenth century. English and Scottish ports in the next century re-exported 85% of their tobacco imports. From the 1720s most of the field labourers in the Chesapeake tobacco plantations were African enslaved people; by the 1750s they comprised 37% of the Chesapeake population, rising to 39% by 1782.[82] When British consumption of tobacco levelled off in the mid-eighteenth century, that of the other great plantation crop, sugar, stepped up.[83]

Samuel Pepys and Robert Hooke, visiting their London coffee houses in the 1660s and 1670s, drank sugared coffee, but there were a number of other beverages on offer including ales, wine, distilled liquors and another plantation crop: chocolate.[84] Coffee consumption was slower to grow than were the coffee houses, which often became centres of commerce, information flow and male sociability. Retained imports of coffee rose from 360,192 lbs (1701–10) to 627,648 lbs (1711–19), a rise to 0.12lbs per capita per year over the period, small amounts in comparison with sugar. Coffee remained a rare and exotic beverage. Initially it was brought from the Levant and Mocha but it became a colonial plantation crop harvested by enslaved labour from the late seventeenth century, cultivated especially by the Dutch and the French. Coffee cultivation did not

---

[80] http://www.pipearchive.co.uk/; https://www.museumofcambridge.org.uk/2021/03/cambridges-archaeological-pipe-finds-tracking-a-history/.
[81] Shammas (1993: 177–205, esp. 179–81).
[82] Price (1995: chapters 1–4).
[83] Sheridan (1974: 394–5); Watts (1987: 224–5, 290).
[84] Withington (2020b: 40–75).

start in the British West Indies until 1728 on Montserrat, then Jamaica. It was always sugar's 'poor relation' in the British plantation system, and never contributed more than 5% of British coffee imports before the 1750s. Arabian coffee was still preferred by British coffee drinkers and tea much preferred to coffee.[85] By mid-century Saint-Domingue had become the world's leading coffee producer, supplying France and much of the rest of Europe.[86] After the Haitian Revolution of 1791, however, Jamaica took the lead in world coffee production for a few decades, adding to the continued profitability of the British Caribbean into the early nineteenth century. It was cultivated on 700 estates but by the mid-1830s this had declined to just over 350 as planters came to face an increasingly competitive international marketplace.[87]

Plantation groceries and the wider economy

The production of colonial groceries, especially sugar, by enslaved labour stimulated both supply-induced and demand-induced shifts in popular consumption in new ways that were to affect waged work in manufacturing. The supply-effect of higher production and lower prices together with the demand created by new tastes and cultures of consumption of colonial groceries had a wide social impact in Britain and other parts of northern Europe. Colonial groceries and the products made and distilled from them likely encouraged what has been termed an 'industrious revolution' that preceded and paved the way for the industrial revolution. The concept of an 'industrious revolution' epitomizes how the desire for a variety of commodities provoked gradual changes in the household behaviour of ordinary people in western Europe. Families and households shifted from subsistence activities to wage labour, and they worked harder and longer in order to purchase new wider-world commodities.[88] One outcome was a more intensive pace of waged work; another was a growing separation between home and workplace.[89] This capitalist

---

[85] Smith (1996: 183–214); Cowan (2005: 72–7); Watts (1987: 503).
[86] Greggus (1993: 73–98).
[87] Monteith (2019); Graham (2021: 570–1); Smith (2008: 68–89).
[88] de Vries (2008).
[89] Mintz (1985: 151–86); Pomeranz (2000: 281).

transformation of the household increased the economy's labour supply; a labour supply further increased by the enslaved labour in the colonies.

Migrants and travellers moving in and out of London and between other urban and rural areas spread new consumer tastes across the country. Britain's rapidly urbanizing economy further reinforced this shift in consumer tastes towards colonial groceries.[90] In the 1770s Adam Smith in *The Wealth of Nations* wrote that rum, sugar and tobacco had become objects 'of almost universal consumption'.[91] Malthus followed by emphasizing that the attractions of addictive colonial groceries may have propelled the shift to wage labour more readily than the attractions of new clothing: 'The peasant, who might be induced to labour an additional number of hours for tea and tobacco, might prefer indolence to a new coat . . .'[92]

Plantation groceries were part of the achievements of a British agricultural revolution, though they are rarely so considered by historians. By contrast, contemporary merchants and economic policy-makers had a unified imperialist vision that incorporated the plantations within a wider Britain. As Malachy Postlethwayt put it in 1766, 'Our colony trade is our own trade, under our own conduct and control'.[93] Historians debate the capacity of domestic agricultural output to provide sufficient calories for Britain's growing population during the crucial decades of the industrial revolution.[94] Certainly, grain was being imported in substantial quantities during the Napoleonic War period, especially from eastern Europe and Ireland. Foodstuffs in total accounted for between 42 and 48% of imports by value between 1784 and 1815.[95] To what extent did colonial groceries contribute to ecological relief at a time of rapid population growth? Most current historical debate on meeting Britain's food needs in the period is confined to grain and meat products. It ignores colonial groceries (still considered rare luxuries by many historians), yet these, including tea, accounted for over 60% of

[90] Wrigley (2018: 9–42, 19).
[91] Smith (1776), cited in Sheridan (1974: 347).
[92] Malthus (1820), in Sraffa and Dobb (1966: 355–6).
[93] See Price (1998: 80); Postlethwayt (1766: I, xxxi).
[94] For a survey of these debates see Schneider (2013: 340–63, esp. 341–3). Also see Wrigley (2018: 21); Meredith and Oxley (2014: 163–214, esp. 171–2).
[95] Davis (1979: 36, 40–2).

imported foodstuffs by value in the 1790s and 67% by 1814–16.[96] Sugar contributed energy and calories; tea and coffee were stimulants, and tobacco an appetite suppressant. All were addictive. The addition of sugar promoted the consumption of inferior grains such as oats and rice to supplement wheat. Consuming sugar in hot drinks depressed beer drinking such that per capita beer consumption fell by almost 50% over the eighteenth century, relieving pressure on grain supplies.[97]

Plantation groceries should be seen as part of Britain's agricultural output, an output taken from colonial plantations within the zone of the Navigation Acts. Britain's plantation colonies added to what are now widely referred to as 'ghost acres' that contributed to Britain's advantageous lead in the 'great divergence'.[98] Slave-produced foodstuffs from the Caribbean, the Carolinas and Georgia provided 'ecological relief' as Britain's population growth pressed against the limits of her domestic food production.[99] Estimates of the 'ghost land' of sugar production added to Britain's own arable land (using the excessively modest assumption that sugar contributed 4% to caloric intake by 1800) suggest that 1.3 million acres was added to Britain's 17 million domestic acres, not a trivial component.[100] These plantation ghost acres played a significant part in providing the food resources that boosted Britain into industrialization.

Conclusion

Slave-produced plantation groceries, especially sugar, transformed consumer culture, created new refining and processing industries and stimulated a wide range of new manufactures associated with their use. Demand for these goods helped to cause a shift to waged working, and an

---

[96] Davis (1979: 37); Mintz (1985; 1993: 261–73, esp. 266); Shammas (1983: 89–100, esp. 97–100; 1990).

[97] Mathias (1959: 375).

[98] Term referring to the divergence in development and economic growth between western Europe and Asia initiated at some point between the seventeenth century and 1800: Pomeranz (2000) identified the turning point around 1800.

[99] There is some debate about this but see Allen (2005); Broadberry et al. (2015: 80–129, 288–95); Meredith and Oxley (2014); Floud et al. (2014).

[100] Pomeranz (2000: 274–5, 281–2); Zahedieh (2014: 392–420, esp. 410).

'industrious revolution' that provided the labour force for the industrial revolution. The trade in plantation produce greatly expanded long-distance commercial exchanges, wholesaling, retailing and commodity broking and introduced institutional innovations that formed a basis for later economic expansion. Specialized plantation systems producing colonial groceries and using enslaved labour also formed a little-acknowledged part of the broader agricultural transformation that fed the British people during the industrial revolution.

CHAPTER 4

Plantation innovation and Atlantic science

Britain's prominent role in the slave trade, plantation agriculture and in wider Atlantic exchanges placed the country in a favourable position to benefit from new forms of science and technology. Europe's trade brought encounters with distant cultures, flora, fauna and indigenous systems of knowledge, which added to biological and scientific advances. The home economy benefitted, as did plantation agriculture and the processing of its produce. Britain's mainland American and Caribbean colonies became sites of agricultural, technological and organizational innovation that were fully a part of Britain's agricultural revolution and industrial transition.[1]

The sugar revolution

The 'sugar revolution' of the 1640s to 1670s in the Caribbean was associated with a rapid shift to specialized plantation cultivation of sugar by enslaved labour. It comprised six elements of change: from diversified agriculture to sugar monoculture, from production on small farms to large plantations, from free to slave labour, from sparse to dense settlement, from white to black populations, and from low to high value per capita output. 'The sugar revolution constitutes the defining moment of the region's economic and social history, a history characterized by the synergy of sugar and slavery.'[2]

This rapid and extensive agrarian and social transition in Britain's sugar islands, and predating the longer process of Britain's eighteenth-century agricultural revolution, has been easy for British historians to

---

[1] See Overton (1996). Also see Wrigley (2018: 9–42), and the debate on Wrigley's exclusion of non-domestic land-intensive food and raw materials. Kumar (2020: 297–9) and Wrigley (2020: 301–2).

[2] Higman (2000: 213–36, esp. 231). Also see Sheridan (1969: 5–25); Sheridan (1974: 128–34); Curtin (1998: 81–5).

forget. Histories of English agricultural change have generally overlooked innovation in plantation agriculture.[3] Yet a near monoculture in sugar emerged in Barbados, and sugar came to account for around three-quarters of plantation output in Jamaica and some of the other British Caribbean possessions.[4] The sugar plantations on Barbados by the late seventeenth century, where sugar was grown on every piece of cultivable soil, were 'laboratories' of agricultural experimentation, as planters responded to soil erosion, fuel shortages and the depletion of soil fertility. A detailed plantation manual, laying out some of these challenges and possible solutions, was written by a Barbadian, William Belgrove: *A Treatise upon Husbandry or Planting* (Boston, 1755).[5]

Both Barbados and Jamaica initially experimented with other cash crops, especially cotton in Barbados and coffee in Jamaica; they produced clayed sugar and rum, they kept livestock, primarily for the fertilizer it provided, and they became relatively self-sufficient, producing their own provisions. Cotton was introduced from South America into Barbados, where it was developed as a commercial crop in the 1630s by James Drax, owner of several sugar plantations. Also cultivated early in St Kitts, it was well adapted to the drier coastlands and grown alongside other commercial crops, such as indigo, tobacco and ginger, by small-scale planters.[6] But the significance of all of these developments was cast into the shadow by the sugar revolution.[7]

Despite a growing market in Europe for West Indian cotton, and its new significance on several of the islands, sugar dominated. Planters wrote about their experiences of crop specialization and sent notes on plantation management to Arthur Young's *Annals of Agriculture*. One Jamaican planter wrote in 1776 that 'husbandry ought to be more generally understood as a science'.[8] Many small changes in plant types and practices accumulated over the eighteenth century. Planters adopted Guinea or Scotch grass in the last half of the century and introduced

---

[3] They have similarly overlooked Scottish and Irish agricultural changes that were also important in the eighteenth century.
[4] Sheridan (1969: 5–25, 22); Ward (1978: 207).
[5] Roberts (2013: 9–10).
[6] Smith (1998: 68–89); Stephens (1976: 391–9, esp. 394–5).
[7] Watts (1987: 158–60).
[8] See Blake (1798: 360–70), cited in Roberts (2013: 33).

thick-stemmed cane varieties from Tahiti, the Malabar coast and Batavia in the 1790s, such as Otaheite and Bourbon cane, acquired from the French. They improved their livestock care and their manuring of crops with dung. They rotated the cultivation of provisions with cash crops. Henry Drax was known for his early cotton cultivation and for a plantation manual that was later appended by William Belgrove to his famed instructions on sugar planting. This went through many editions, becoming an evolving document as community knowledge on sugar planting grew and was added.[9] Careful attention attuned to the distinct environmental conditions of the West Indian islands went into preparing the fields, digging the cane holes and harvesting the cane. Digging cane holes replaced trenching in early eighteenth-century Barbados. It was extremely labour-intensive, but with careful attention it minimized soil erosion, preserved moisture, created more even soil fertilization and allowed intercropping of food crops.[10]

Careful attention to crop development and environment was only one side of plantation innovation. It also required specific tools that were made by English ironmasters and hardwaremen. The plantation hoe was developed to high specification to meet varied Caribbean and American mainland conditions. British hardware manufacturers strengthened the blades to cope with cane holing. The Crowleys in County Durham, England, made a specific style for Barbados, Nevis and Jamaica, and others for Virginia and Carolina. British producers made the heads; the handles were fitted by local Caribbean users, who shaped the tool's final form. Attempts were also made to invent a suitable plough. A Barbadian planter appealed to Matthew Boulton to invent a mechanism that would cut through the hard-baked Caribbean soil. Edward Long, the powerful plantation owner and author of *The History of Jamaica* (1774), wrote of efforts to substitute the plough: 'a spirit of experiment has of late appeared which, by quitting the old beaten track, promises to strike out continual improvements'.[11]

[9] Belgrove and Drax (1755). See discussion of Drax's 'Instructions' in Thompson (2009: 575–604).
[10] Watts (1987: 402–5, 432–4); Roberts (2013: 43); Thompson (2009); Roberts (2013: 107).
[11] Evans (2012: 71–100, esp. 81–90). See Martin (1765: 38n) and Long (1774: vol. 1, 435), both cited in Evans (2012: 98).

The sugar plantations required livestock, less for the meat and dairy products consumed in some amount by the small planter class, than for fertilizers, transportation and energy production. Jamaica, especially, developed a system of specialized cattle pens by the 1740s, to provide the much-needed manure for fertilizing the cane fields. The enclosed livestock pens also provided the mules, oxen and cattle used for carting and for animal-powered mills. Newly arrived enslaved Africans were often employed in the pens for a period of 'seasoning' (harsh and violent training and acclimatization to enslavement).[12] In Jamaica alone, 82,810 cattle serviced 340 sugar works in 1740, and 142,216 cattle provided the energy for 612 sugar works in 1768. There were 656 cattle-powered sugar mills out of a total of 1,077 in the Cornwall, Middlesex and Surrey counties of Jamaica in 1804. Water mills were more efficient, but water sources were unreliable, and wind power was locationally constrained and capricious.[13]

Innovation on British and other plantations was not confined to agriculture. Planters, their managers and overseers developed improved processing techniques of curing, drying, hulling, fermenting, distilling, ginning and refining to make staples less perishable and less bulky for long-distance transport. They also improved the quality of their semi-refined cash crops and extended the variety of their products. With sugar this involved an increased ratio of semi-refined clayed sugar to muscovado sugar and of rum to molasses.[14]

Invention and innovation

Invention, innovation and investment occurred in both the cane fields and in mechanical and chemical processing for refining and claying sugar, distilling rum, curing coffee, processing indigo and cleaning cotton. Greater capitalization of processing plants and inventiveness were the main strategies allowing planters to respond to the rapidly growing British demand for sugar and other products. Great efforts were made to adapt water and wind power, and soon afterwards steam power, to sugar milling. The profits to be gained from sugar stimulated planters to build massive

[12] Radburn (2021).
[13] Shepherd (1991: 627–43, esp. 635, 638).
[14] Sheridan (1969: 19); Pares (1956: 250–70). For clayed sugar see chapter 3.

wind-tower mill structures and extensive water courses. The widespread use of sophisticated windmill technology came earliest in Barbados, where 356 windmills were operating by 1750 at a density unknown in Britain.

Improved waterwheels and steam engines were also developed. John Smeaton, the celebrated English millwright and engineer, designed a specialist overshot waterwheel for a Mr Gray of Jamaica, and Newcomen engines were used at an early stage to pump water over the waterwheels. Plantation owners adopted steam engines for industrial purposes, including for rotary force, in the British West Indies from the third quarter of the eighteenth century, at a time when they were rare in Britain outside of pumping engines in mining. John Steward, a millwright, petitioned the Jamaican House Assembly for a patent for a fire engine to power sugar mills in 1768, arguing that enslaved labour could be trained to operate the machinery.[15] In the five years to 1785 Boulton and Watt supplied twenty-one engines to overseas customers, with the West Indies a significant market, as the engines were sent to power sugar mills and other machinery. There were steam engines on Lord Penrhyn's Jamaica estates from 1796, and James Mitchell on the Moreland estate had a steam engine by 1800. Boulton and Watt sent 132 steam engines to the sugar plantations between 1803 and 1830.[16] This plantation innovation did not just happen. Planters, plantation managers and black overseers sought it out and made it workable, often with the assistance of highly skilled enslaved labour. Enslaved Africans and indigenous peoples provided knowledge of crops and uses of local resources; they were also the ones who 'worked' the new technologies.

Caribbean invention was facilitated by 'a tiered and flexible system of Imperial patenting . . . which inventors used strategically to promote technological innovation and a two-way flow of inventive, adaptive activity between the colonies and the metropole'.[17] The British colonial patent system had no counterpart in the French or Spanish colonies before the 1820s. John Greenhill Yonge obtained a Jamaican patent for his new sugar mill in 1762, an Imperial patent for his 'Hydraulic machine' in 1766 and seven years later a further Jamaican patent for

[15] Satchell (2010: 114–15, 223, 123–6).
[16] Andrew (2009: 63–70); Satchell (2010: 130–1).
[17] Graham (2020a: 940–63, esp. 940).

the same machine to give him additional protection. Patents issued by the colonial authorities frequently included a range of legal rights that amounted to an 'industrial subsidy'. At least ninety-four patents were passed by colonies in the British Atlantic before 1780, two-thirds in the West Indies (Barbados and especially Jamaica) and the rest in North America, most notably Carolina – in the major exporting regions that had the most to gain from rising productivity. In addition to the patents themselves, island assemblies also offered grants, bounties, prizes and subsidies, sometimes worth several hundred pounds each, for invention, research and innovation particularly where there was potential public utility. Francis Coke petitioned the Jamaican Assembly in December 1768 that his new sugar mill would be 'of infinite service to the country', whilst John Ashley argued that his pumping engine would have general utility.[18] This civil society of patents, prizes and protections underpinned a 'spirit of improvement' in much the same way as they functioned during Britain's 'industrial enlightenment' on home soil.[19]

Plantation 'improvement'

Promoting technologically advanced sugar mills was part of a wider programme of economic improvement on the plantations and in the colonial assemblies. This spirit of innovation also extended to improved crops and botanical experimentation. British historians have long written about the improving agricultural societies of eighteenth-century Britain and their interest in economic botany, but few mention the role of such bodies in the improvement of crops and practices carried out in the plantations. The Society for the Encouragement of Arts, Manufactures and Commerce (now the Royal Society of Arts), founded in London in 1754, made colonial as well as domestic agriculture central to its mission. Its first colonial premium in 1755 was for the cultivation of silk in the American colonies. It also announced premiums for introducing a whole range of Asian and African plant varieties into the New World, including indigo and cotton, breadfruit and mangoes, coffee and a range of spices from nutmeg, mace and pepper to cinnamon and cloves. The many

[18] Graham (2020a: 943–4, 950).
[19] Mokyr (2009: 63–99).

British agricultural improvement societies also included the Society for the Encouragement of Natural History and Useful Arts of Barbados (1784) and the Physico-Medical Society of Grenada (1791). A botanic ground was established on St Vincent in 1765 to test Asian and American plants in the West Indian environment, and the planters of Jamaica voted in 1775 to establish two botanic gardens and to fund a full-time botanist.[20]

The transfer of crops from Asia and Africa to the West Indies was part of the programme of economic improvement of the French and British enlightenments as well as of state mercantile policy. The French deployed colonial priests then secular full-time botanists and physicians to establish botanical stations in Guadeloupe, Martinique and Cayenne. They also set up government gardens in Saint-Domingue. They attempted to transfer cochineal production to Saint-Domingue from the Spanish possessions in Oaxaca, Mexico, and they brought large shipments of Indian Ocean plants to the colony in 1773 and 1788. They also exchanged plants with the British in Jamaica.[21]

The Society for the Encouragement of Arts, Manufactures and Commerce engaged from its early days in many projects of improvement in the West Indies, offering premiums as an inducement to experiment or innovate, and also corresponding about sugar production, mills and refining.[22] John Pownall, one of the early very active chairmen of the

---

[20] Drayton (2000: 64–6, 80). See Guilding (1825); Ellis (1770).

[21] McClellan III (2010: 114, 149, 154–62).

[22] Royal Society of Arts (RSA) Archives. See 'Letter from William Homer on growing various spices in East and West Indies', RSA/PR/GE/110/3/35, 21/7/1760; 'Letter from Edmund Augustus Turner about material for drying cotton', RSA/PR/GE/110/8/104, 20/2/1760; 'Letter from John Carlier about refining sugar', RSA/PR/MC/102/10/99, 18/8/1794; 'Letter from Joshua Steele about an engine for sugar mills', RSA/PR/GE/110/28/34, 18/5/1768; 'Letter from John Stewart about a machine for compressing sugar cane', RSA/PR/GE/110/28/31, April 1768; 'Letter from Sir Robert Clement about a sugar boiler', RSA/PR/MC/105/10/315, 17/10/1774; 'Letter from Sir Joseph Senhouse about improvement of windmill vanes', RSA/PR/MC/104/10/192, 7/11/1780; 'Letter from John Carlier about refining sugar', RSA/PR/MC/102/10/99, [1794]; 'Letter and printed notice from William Archdeacon about his 48 discoveries and improvements including methods for refining sugar', RSA/PR/MC/105/10/457, [1794]; 'Observations and advices for the improvement of the manufacture of Muscovado Sugar and Rum', RSA/SC/EL/1/72, [1797]. For a recent history of the Society, now the Royal Society of Arts (RSA), see Howes (2020).

Society, was also secretary of His Majesty's Commission for Trade and Plantations. Indeed, the Society had a Standing Committee for Colonies and Trade, which recommended a peak number of awards to the Society, 123, in 1764.[23]

Joshua Steele, a prominent member of the Society of Arts and owner of a 1,068-acre estate in Barbados, founded the Barbados Society of Arts in Bridgetown in 1781 to promote innovation, and allied it closely to the London and Dublin Societies of Arts. This Society offered premiums, bounties and medals for schemes of economic diversification, including the cultivation of dyestuffs, coffee and cocoa. Corresponding closely with the celebrated British natural historian and President of the Royal Society, Joseph Banks, Steele transplanted Egyptian wheat, mangoes, 'silk grass' (of the *Bromeliaceae* or pineapple family) and camphor trees.[24] Jamaica attracted as much attention from the Society of Arts as Barbados with correspondence and awards over the introduction of new plants from dyestuffs and breadfruit to cinnamon trees. The Society's projects in Jamaica garnered greater local support than in Barbados, aided by the active role of Dr Thomas Dancer, another correspondent of Banks, and curator of the Jamaica botanic garden from 1787 to 1804.[25]

These individual examples were part of a wider process of active planter engagement with innovation. Ideas were spread by word of mouth and demonstration. Home-country sugar lobbies also sent information about new methods. By the mid-eighteenth century there were 'schools of plantership' on several of the islands providing informal residential

---

[23] Allan and Abbott (1992: 215–16).

[24] Steele left Britain for Barbados in 1780, dying there in 1796. Joseph Banks (1743–1820) was the foremost botanist of his day and President of the Royal Society for forty-one years. He had been on James Cook's first voyage 1768–71 and was the leading force behind the development of the Royal Botanical Gardens at Kew. Steele's early correspondence with the Society of Arts about sugar refining can be found in: 'Letter from Joshua Steele about an engine for sugar mills', RSA/PR/ GE/110/28/34, 31/3/1768. See 'Joshua Steele', Legacies of British Slavery: https:// www.ucl.ac.uk/lbs/personview/2146643119; Lambert (2005: 41–72, esp. 55–60).

[25] RSA Archives, 'Copy of a letter from Charles White of Jamaica about experiments with the plaintain', RSA/PR/GE/110/25/40, 20/9/1768; 'Letter from William Kinsbury about cultivation of annatto and cochineal', RSA/PR/MC/104/10/198, 10/9/1785; 'Letter from Samuel Long about medal to Thomas Dancer about cinnamon trees', RSA/ PR/MC/104/10/16, 18/5/1790.

courses such as that organized by Samuel Martin in Antigua. Manuals on planter practice multiplied alongside agricultural societies. Although many of the schools and societies were short-lived, their existence was a testament to the politics of innovation.[26]

Planter innovation also extended into cotton cultivation as demand for cotton in Britain grew. Early planters on the islands experimented with small-scale cotton crops in efforts to develop a species of strong long-stapled cotton, *Gossypium Barbadense*. This species of cotton (named after Barbados) originated in South America before spreading to the Caribbean. It was introduced from Barbados to the coast of the Carolinas and Georgia and their offshore islands, where it was developed into a high-quality strain called 'Sea Island cotton', but it proved unsuited to the inland climate and soil conditions of the North American mainland.[27] In the later eighteenth century Barbadian planters had four different strains of *Barbadense* cotton, which spread to St Kitts, Dominica and Jamaica, where they were cultivated alongside sugar. The Ceded Islands, acquired after the Seven Years War, produced a variety of tropical produce including cotton, as did the Bahamas. The French also expanded their cotton production in Saint-Domingue and later Trinidad. One of the Ceded Islands, Carriacou, only 8,000 acres, produced cotton as its main crop on large plantations as well as a number of smaller farms. Cotton boomed on the island between the 1770s and the 1790s; good soils and a gang system of cultivation and harvesting produced the highest-priced, high-quality British Caribbean cotton. A type of 'cotton gin' machine, not entirely effective, complemented hand-picking of seeds and trash from the harvested cotton. By 1790, with two-thirds of households in cotton cultivation, the island was among the most densely populated, with 270 enslaved people per square mile.[28] By the 1780s Lancashire drew 82% of its raw cotton from the Caribbean and Brazil compared with only 18% from the Levant. This cotton was higher-priced than old-world varieties, but its soft, strong, long staple made it ideal for the wefts of high-quality Lancashire cotton/linen mixes and later for the machine-spun warps of all-cotton cloths:

---

[26] Watts (1987: 391–2).

[27] Russell (2011: 103–31); Stephens (1976: 391–9).

[28] Riello (2013: 200); Stephens (1976: 391–9); Rydén (2013: 547–51, 557).

it encouraged and enabled both product and process innovation in the British industry.[29]

Slavery and scientific collecting

Caribbean cotton growing and its recognized significance to Lancashire's manufacturers prompted state-endorsed expeditions and experiments to transfer other cotton-plant varieties to the Caribbean. In the late 1790s, Joseph Banks organized a Board of Trade-funded expedition aiming to transfer varieties of Gujarati cotton from India to the Caribbean. He sent the young botanist Anton Hove to Bombay, then on to Ahmadabad and further into rural Gujarat, although the venture was difficult and yielded little of value.[30]

The plantations were thus part of the wider scientific and technological change of the agricultural revolution. The economic botany developed in the botanic laboratories and gardens of the West Indies, in their improvement societies, and in transfers of plant varieties from other parts of the world to New World plantations, was a vital part of the wider knowledge revolution of the Enlightenment. The indigenous peoples of Africa and the Americas, and the enslaved working on plantations, assisted explorers and collectors, adding their own knowledge and insights to the projects.[31] Slave traders, slave ships and ships' captains also played a role in collecting and transporting specimens. European scientists, indigenous peoples and traders together provided the infrastructure that helped to build the great natural history collections that underpinned medical developments and Europe's knowledge of the natural world. The material culture of the period of state-funded expeditions and private initiatives between the seventeenth and early nineteenth centuries is now held in many botanic gardens: in Kew (London), Oxford, Edinburgh and around the former British Empire. It also forms the core of Britain's

---

[29] Wadsworth and Mann (1931/1968: 520–1); Styles (2020: 1–42, 5); Russell (2011: 103–31). See chapter 7.
[30] Berg (2013: 117–41).
[31] See Poskett (2022: 135–46); Delbourgo et al. (2009); Ogborn (2013: 251–82, esp. 271, 274–5); Schiebinger (2017).

great museums, especially the British Museum, the Natural History Museum and the Ashmolean.[32]

Hans Sloane (1660–1753) collected plant and soil specimens on slave plantations in Jamaica and married into a slaving family whose money enabled further collecting. In 1727 he succeeded Newton as President of the Royal Society. When Sloane died in 1753 he willed his collection to the British government, and it became the foundation of the British Museum. The museum collections were later divided, and Sloane's specimens formed a vital part of the Natural History Museum. His bequest incorporated the specimen collections of others, especially James Petiver (1665–1718), a London apothecary who had amassed the largest natural history collection in the world in the late seventeenth and early eighteenth centuries through employing a network of ships' surgeons and captains. Between a quarter and a third of these worked in the slave trade; only they had regular access to botanical and entomological specimens from West Africa, the Caribbean and Latin America.[33] One later collector, Henry Smeathman (1742–86), an entomologist, sailed for Sierra Leone in 1771, and collected for Joseph Banks and others. He was an avowed opponent of slavery, but in Sierra Leone he became dependent on slave traders for food, protection, transport and even company to alleviate his loneliness. By 1774 he was working for a slaving company in Liverpool and started himself to trade in enslaved people to finance his expeditions. He planned and created a garden on Bunce Island to provision slave ships and sent a total of 600 specimens of plants and 710 insects back to England from West Africa.[34] Among his most valued specimens was cinchona bark containing quinine. Cinchona bark had long been used in the region to treat malaria. Smeathman's specimens also included varieties of indigo and cochineal, used in blue and red textile dyestuffs.

The impact of Atlantic science on the industrial revolution is still largely unexplored partly because economic historians and historians of science tend to work in isolation from one another. They differ in their approaches and ask different questions. As a result, too little connection has been made between those studying adaptive manufactures such

[32] For a general discussion see Kean (2019: 16–20). For greater details see Delbourgo et al. (2009), Delbourgo and Dew (2007); Roberts (2017).

[33] Delbourgo (2017); Delbourgo (2010: 113–18); Murphy (2013: 637–70).

[34] Coleman (2018: 80–3, 162–71, 238–40).

as windmills or ploughs and those studying characters such as Henry Smeathman. The English ironmaster Ambrose Crowley illustrates this point. He is much celebrated as an industrial pioneer. His great ironworks in the northeast of England, the largest industrial works in Europe in the later seventeenth and early eighteenth century, produced all manner of iron and steel goods for industrial and domestic uses. Among those goods were tools such as the plantation hoe and machine parts made specifically for plantations. Crowley's connection with the West Indies needs to be integrated with those histories of knowledge and experimentation that bound Joseph Banks and his army of collectors to the slave traders of Sierra Leone.

Knowledge in the Caribbean

The history of crop development and plant varieties transferred into plantation agriculture is often written as one of scientific endeavour led by enlightened planters or entrepreneurs. All of this depended, however, on the tacit knowledge and skills of indigenous and enslaved inhabitants. Not only did they broker the knowledge of explorers and collectors but they also provided the skills that made new technologies work. Jamaica and Saint-Domingue, by the later eighteenth century, had significant concentrations of enslaved workers with highly skilled scientific and tacit knowledge. It was these people, mostly the enslaved, who created a favourable environment for the introduction and adaptation of new plant strains and new technologies.

Planters relied on enslaved artisans; a number came from parts of West Africa with highly developed metallurgical industries. Their blacksmithing skills were deployed in manufacturing and repairing plantation equipment, and they acted as mill engineers. The foundry master John Reeder stated that 'Africans were perfect in every branch of iron manufacturing.' William James' foundry in Kingston in 1817 employed thirty-seven apprentices (it is likely many were black), twenty-one enslaved people, one black journeyman and two whites. With these workers he claimed he could 'manufacture and repair all manner of machinery, steam engines etc.'.[35] Enslaved artisans took charge of milling

---

[35] Satchell (2010: 67); Graham (2018b: 323–9).

and grinding sugar cane, seeing to the repair and operation of the mill; they also acted as sugar boilers, bearing responsibility for the successful processing of a crop. Evidence of their place can be found in the writings of those who thought more codified scientific practices should be deployed. The Jamaican writer I. P. Baker wrote in his *Essay on the Art of Making Muscovado Sugar* in 1775 that planters should employ scientific principles in the boiling house rather than trusting enslaved sugar boilers.[36] The Barbadian Society for the Improvement of Plantership, at the beginning of the nineteenth century, agreed that its members needed to study European 'chemistry, agriculture and mechanics' to devise the best systems of plantation management.[37] But on the ground it was generally enslaved workers who adapted European techniques and technologies and made them operate efficiently.

Enslaved people could not own property; their inventions either went unpatented or were patented by their owners. The many local patents granted on the islands were, however, taken out by a large cross-section of their populations, especially by millwrights and artisans, including free people of colour. One such, Dugald Clarke, who owned the Arcadia estate in St Thomas-in-the East, Jamaica, is said to have invented twelve new machines and pieces of equipment. Clarke was born in Jamaica, but went to Britain in the 1760s to train as a millwright. He focused on raising the efficiency of the sugar business, but in 1787 he also invented a 'method of freeing ships at sea of water'.[38]

Plantation management and accounting

Plantations were 'unlike anything known in mainland Europe at the time'. They were an 'agri-business', 'a synthesis of field and factory' employing extraordinarily large workforces and amounts of fixed capital.[39] New organizational forms and new techniques of accounting in addition to technological innovations to improve efficiency and hence profitability were essential to repay the credit extensions, loans and mortgages that were integral to Caribbean business. The plant varieties, tools and

---

[36] Satchell (2010: 67). See Baker (1775), cited in Roberts (2013: 37).

[37] Roberts (2013: 33).

[38] Satchell (2010: 66).

[39] Mintz (1985: 47).

technologies, heavy fixed capital structures and mechanization of the sugar plantation economies relied upon management and accountancy techniques that were little used in British industrial production until a century later. This arose from the size and technological complexity of plantation agri-business, from the harsh labour discipline imposed on the enslaved by the small white minority, and because of the amount of record keeping required in reporting to many absentee owners back in Britain.

Planters of the British Caribbean were responsible for some of the earliest large-scale integrated businesses in the Western world. A typical sugar plantation in the late seventeenth and early eighteenth centuries required 80 acres put to cane in rotation and at least 100 workers, predominantly enslaved people, to produce 80 tons of sugar per annum.[40] And because the sugar cane had to be milled, boiled and crystallized immediately after harvesting the enterprise also needed one or two mills, a boiling house to clean and reduce the juice, a curing house for drying the sugar heads and draining off molasses, a distillery to make rum, as a by-product, plus warehousing to hold products awaiting export.

The median sugar plantation in Jamaica by 1774 had 600 acres and more than 200 slaves, 174 head of livestock and sugar works with associated utensils: a total equity of £19,502. Nathaniel Philips, who arrived in Jamaica in 1759, returning to England in 1789, owned more than 500 enslaved people across four estates. His estates were valued at £110,000 in 1789. He returned to England with £20,000 in liquid assets, which gave him a life of luxury and allowed rich bequests when he died. Most of the enslaved worked on plantations of much greater size than those held by Philips, with between 500 and 1,500 workers.[41] In 1779 Henry Dawkins owned 1,797 slaves in Vere and Clarendon parishes in Jamaica and a further 449 elsewhere, while two of the richest Jamaican planters, Simon Taylor and John Tharp, owned 2,990 and 2,228 slaves respectively by the beginning of the nineteenth century.[42] With very few exceptions, the industrial employers of Europe did not

[40] Mintz (1985: 48–9).
[41] Sheridan (1965: 296–306); Koth and Serieux (2019: 59–91, 84); Burnard (2015: 159, 15).
[42] Rosenthal (2018: 14, 19).

approach this size of workforce until half a century later.[43] The amount of fixed capital investment in large plantations which included capital in enslaved people as well as land, processing plant and equipment was also unusual in European enterprise and precocious for the time.[44]

Accounting was a major innovative tool of management in these large concerns.[45] Written records became increasingly important as absentee ownership in the British plantations increased in the later eighteenth century. As early as 1774 Edward Long estimated that there were as many as 2,000 'annuitants and proprietors non-resident' in Jamaica alone. In order to prevent fraud or breaches of trust by attorneys or agents of absentee proprietors, the Jamaican Assembly passed the 'Account Produce' law in 1740, which required attorneys and overseers to submit annual accounts of all rents, profits, produce and proceeds'[46] It thus became essential for plantation managers to be able to account for their activities and the sources of success or failure to a much greater extent than was common at the time in British domestic, generally family-owned and managed, businesses. Managers and attorneys had to send accounts back to Britain yearly or even quarterly, and they needed detailed recording systems at every stage of plantation activity. This presentation of accounts, balanced at regular intervals, assessed the return on fixed assets and depreciation, as well as trading, something that was not common in British mainland industries until into the nineteenth century.[47] Enslaved people, along with draught animals, tools, equipment and even slave clothing, were regularly evaluated to calculate the depreciation of capital.[48]

Plantation managers also developed assessments of productivity and profit generation ahead of other merchants and manufacturers on both sides of the Atlantic. Double entry bookkeeping systems became common, in advance of their general use in capital- and labour-intensive

[43] As late as 1881 438 firms in Britain employed over 1,000 workers, 149 of which had over 2,000: Hannah and Bennett (2022).
[44] See, for example, Chapman (1979); Hudson (1986: 14–15, 46).
[45] Rosenthal (2018).
[46] Sheridan (1974: 385); Carrington (1999: 28).
[47] For innovation in accounting in domestic firms during the industrial revolution see Fleischman and Parker (1997).
[48] Rosenthal (2018: 85–120).

manufacturing in Europe.[49] Numbers of bookkeepers and appraisers on the islands increased rapidly, as did the volume of paperwork. Best practice spread partly through attorneys such as John Shickle and William Miller, who managed several plantations. By the early nineteenth century Miller was supervising twenty-six estates, eight cattle pens, two plantations and 7,000 slaves, for several owners.[50]

Separate accounting books were kept for boiling and still houses, with accounts of any increase or decrease in enslaved workers kept in detailed work logs. Clement Caines in his *Letters on the Cultivation of the Otaheite Cane* (London, 1801) wrote that the work log exhibited 'at one view every application and misapplication of labour on a West Indian estate'.[51] Slavery became a laboratory for accounting because theoretical control was easier to match with the reality of the plantation, much more so than in regimes of waged labour at the time. Plantation manuals included record keeping and accounting advice. Standardized accounting practices made possible the separation of ownership from management, a separation once again that was rare in British or European businesses until a century later.[52] Such accounting was practised alongside of, and encouraged, complex hierarchical forms of management and control of labour. Plantation hierarchies in the British West Indies were often organized in a multi-divisional or 'M-form', which became a feature of American capitalism a century later. The 'M-form' characterized the fourteen properties owned by Henry Dawkins in 1779 and managed for him by John Shickle. On Dawkins' Parnassus plantation alone there were thirteen hierarchical levels, ten exclusively drawn from the enslaved.[53]

Labour intensification

Many of the cane-cropping techniques introduced from the later seventeenth century required great labour intensity, as did the livestock pens. The cane-holing system, which replaced trenching, needed much more labour and took up more days from slaves than any other single task

---

[49] Rosenthal (2018: 17); Parker and Yamey (1994); Hudson (1994).
[50] Rosenthal (2018: 17–23); Hudson (1994); Higman (2008: chapters 5, 9).
[51] Roberts (2013: 58–67); Hudson (1994).
[52] Rosenthal (2018: 4); Chandler (1969: 19–21); see also Pollard (1965).
[53] Williamson (1985); Rosenthal (2018: 16–17, 24–5).

in the sugar cycle. Livestock pens were an innovation, and dung, marl, lime, sand and seaweed improved the fertility of the cane fields, but the work of 'throwing out dung' onto the fields was very labour-intensive. Enslaved field workers on the Newton and Seawell estates in Barbados and at Prospect in Jamaica in 1790 worked an average of 279 to 297 days a year. The Barbadian Society for the Improvement of Plantership met in 1805 with the purpose of calculating the number of days slave gangs could work, and how labour should be distributed across those days. Harvesting the cane usually took place between January and July before the hurricane season. Gangs of over fifty enslaved people spent thirty-seven work days harvesting each hogshead of sugar; and the pace and hours of work were strictly enforced. Jobbing gangs of enslaved workers were also often hired out between plantations.[54] Work regimes worsened over time with improved management and technologies. Both brought opportunities to intensify rather than to save labour. On Berbice managers gained commissions of 2–10% of an estate's production, a great incentive to speed up production and drive the enslaved workforce harder. A task-work system, rather than set hours, measured tasks by distance, area or volume. Five women on the plantation La Penitence in 1829 complained that their task of taking the megass or sugar cane waste from the logie demanded they work all the time without a break to eat, and they refused to carry out their task.[55]

The life cycle of the enslaved woman Sarah Affir (known as Affey) depicts the regimes. After serving five years as a house girl on the Mesopotamia estate in Jamaica she went to field work at the age of twelve. She was among 159 field workers on Mesopotamia in 1779 and progressed from 'grass gang', the children's gang, to second, then to the great, gang of prime field workers. All were supervised by black 'drivers', vigorous in imposing labour discipline, and worked in regimented lock step. Sarah Affir transferred to the great gang in 1780 when she was twenty and worked there for the next ten years six days a week in hard, labour-intensive work. The months of planting and crop time were most onerous; crop time work weeks were ninety hours including three nights a week in the boiling house. 140 men and women fled the estate at least

[54] Roberts (2013: 83, 84, 107, 114–15, 123); Radburn (2019); Morgan (2016a: 71–5).
[55] Burnard (2020a); see also Burnard and Garrigus (2016: 5–9, 25–49).

once between 1762 and 1831. Sarah Affir moved into the second gang during her pregnancies and in older age into the laundry.[56]

Behind this life cycle of labour lay the value of the enslaved person as an asset. By the end of the eighteenth century the price for an enslaved person of average skills was £55.[57] Unlike the white servant, who was contract labour, an enslaved person was a capital investment that could be used as collateral to raise further funds. The subsistence costs of slave labour were much lower than the wages that would have been needed for contract labour. It was access to rising supplies of enslaved people, and growing exploitation, that enabled sugar producers to move their product from luxury to mass markets in Europe.[58] But slave prices relative to sugar prices (in real terms) rose in the later eighteenth century (table 4.1). From the 1760s the relative price differential increased, and the increase accelerated between the 1780s and the 1810s.[59] In response, planters pursued labour intensification and cruelly harsh work regimes.

Accounting provided the measures. Beatings, whipping and hanging enforced control. The violence witnessed through the 'shrieks of some poor wretch' and 'the most dreadful cries' in the torture of the runaway woman 'Old Quasheba', hung by her hands from a beam in a washhouse until she died, became routinized. Planter society became inured to it, and public spectacles of violence and technologies of torture developed alongside the bookkeeping.[60]

Conclusion

Plantations were novel in European terms because of the size of the workforces; their hierarchical organization across agrarian, provisioning and industrial activities; the level of work discipline and human exploitation; and the capital as well as labour intensity of their operations. They presaged later developments in the industrializing economies of

[56] Sarah Affir was invalided with scrofula at the age of fifty-seven: Dunn (2014: 75–88).
[57] Zahedieh (2014: 402–3); Ward (1978: 197–213).
[58] Harley (2015: 25).
[59] Prices rose most rapidly for male enslaved workers, suggesting that planters were training men as artisans while leaving women as field hands: Burnard (2015).
[60] Fuentes (2016: 139, 142, 101). See a history of the counter-arguments on plantation improvement developed from the eighteenth century in Herschtal (2021).

Table 4.1: Real slave and sugar prices in the western Caribbean in pounds sterling, 1674–1804.

Date	Real slave price index (1674 = 100)	Real sugar price index (1674 = 100)
1674	100	100
1700–4	127	194
1720–4	134	133
1740–4	166	151
1760–4	196	174
1780–4	219	173
1800–4	247	129

Source: Derived from Eltis, Lewis and Richardson (2005: 673–700, table 2). Prices and indices are five-year averages.

nineteenth-century metropoles in their record keeping, as well as their constant search for higher profitability through technological as well as organizational innovation. The pressure to maintain high returns on high levels of fixed capital investment drove technological innovation and slave exploitation.[61]

West Indian plantations were a focus of innovative activity in cultivation, in commodity processing, in the use of animate and inanimate sources of power, in business accounting and in the management of large hierarchical labour forces, their discipline and punishment. The history of plantation innovation is, however, rarely included or even mentioned in accounts of changes in British agriculture, technologies or business management. This history does not figure in accounts of the industrial revolution, even though it was an integral part of the economic growth and economic gains accruing to the British economy. The slave-based Atlantic trading world was also a fulcrum of the advance of enlightenment scientific knowledge: a neglected part of the history of the knowledge economy that historians regard as integral to the industrial revolution.

---

[61] For the association between the drive for profit and slave regimes in capitalism see O'Sullivan (2018: 751–802).

CHAPTER 5

British 'slave ports' and their hinterlands: structural and regional transformation[1]

The composition of British trade shifted during the eighteenth century: non-industrial exports declined, and exports became predominantly manufactured goods. There was also a change in favour of Atlantic markets. By the 1770s exports to the Americas and Africa exceeded those to Europe, and by the 1790s continental Europe received only a fifth of total British domestic exports. Atlantic markets demanded new and more varied products, such as lighter, more colourful textiles, a wide range of metal tools for cultivation, guns, pottery, pans and other vessels, that were at the forefront of innovation and mass production. Many of these industries became concentrated in specialized regions and localities, within the hinterlands of Atlantic ports.[2] Atlantic ports also had easier access to some key raw material imports: indigo and other dyestuffs, Senegalese gum, tobacco, Iberian wool, tropical timbers and, above all, both sugar and New World cotton. Atlantic ports and their hinterlands pioneered new manufactures and techniques using these imported raw materials. Regional industrial clusters developed advantages of industrial agglomeration, including transport, trading and financial infrastructures as well as dense networks of knowledge and information flows. Such agglomeration was central to the dynamics of the industrial revolution.[3]

[1] The term 'slave ports' is most often used for ports that exported or imported large numbers of enslaved people. Used here, we refer to port cities that benefitted significantly from the British slave-based Atlantic trading system. Very few enslaved people were brought to any of the British ports. 'Hinterland' refers not simply to a confined geographical area but to one in which shape and distance were determined by the strength of economic, trading and financial connections.

[2] See pp. 48–9, table 2.2. Riello (2022: 116). A close connection between slavery, Atlantic trade and the regional nature of British industrialization was first strongly emphasized by Inikori (2015: 224–65).

[3] For a survey of the advantages of agglomeration and examples of such dynamics see Hudson (1989). For a case study see Stobart (2004).

Most British ports felt the pulse of Atlantic commerce, but west-coast ports had the advantage of facing the direction of trade. Those to the northwest could use the route around the north of Ireland in wartime, avoiding enemy shipping, and could access cheaper European goods for the African trade via contraband dealings in the Isle of Man. Whitehaven, for example, became an important importer and re-exporter of tobacco in the 1730s and 1740s. It did not grow into a major international port, however, because, cut off by the topography of the Lake District, it could not develop a manufacturing or trading hinterland. Liverpool, Bristol and Glasgow were better placed in this respect. But London remained 'the Metropolis of the slave trade'[4] through the whole period from the sixteenth to the nineteenth centuries.[5]

London

Slave trading from London grew out of long-standing bilateral trade with Africa and the Americas, accelerating after the Restoration with the extension of sugar cultivation in the Caribbean. The bilateral trades depended upon gathering together the range of manufactured commodities and other goods demanded by Atlantic markets. London had a great advantage here because, before the mid-eighteenth century, practically all long-distance internal and external trade in manufactures passed through London. Most of the domestic wool textile trade, for example, passed through Blackwell Hall factors, who organized dying, finishing and final sale.[6] London was also the centre of British trade with Asia via the East India Company. This supplied much-desired Indian textiles, cowrie shells and other manufactures that were re-exported to the West African coast to exchange for enslaved peoples.[7] London merchants were further aided by the proximity of Rotterdam, where consumer goods suitable for the African market, and ships' supplies, could be bought more cheaply than in England.[8]

[4] The epithet comes from Rawley (2003).
[5] Morgan (2000: 84–98).
[6] Hancock (1995: 115–42); Hudson (1989: 156–7, 262).
[7] The East India Company also ran a small slave trade between Madagascar and the Caribbean in the 1730s: Platt (1969: 548–71).
[8] Rawley (2003: 40–56).

Bristol eclipsed London as a slave-trading port in the 1720s, before Liverpool surged into a lead position from the 1740s, a lead it maintained until the end of the slave trade. London, however, remained vital, responsible for twice the slave traffic of Bristol over the eighteenth century as a whole.[9] London was the home port of the RAC and of the South Sea Company, which was granted the *Asiento* in 1713. But private traders rapidly became the most important figures in the slave trade.[10] Between 1698 and 1809 at least 2,461 slave ships were cleared from London, delivering 597,812 enslaved Africans to the Americas.[11]

More important than its direct role in shipments of enslaved people, London provided key investment, financial and trading services for the plantation and staple trades and for the slave trade of other ports. London earned much from the extension of trade credit, freight handling and consignment, insurance, ship broking and warehousing, much of which concerned the Atlantic trades. London's trade and finance expanded the roles of her commercial institutions, including private banks, the Bank of England, Lloyds Coffee House (opened 1686 initially as a centre for information and transactions relating to maritime insurance, trading and ship broking) and the Royal Exchange (where stocks and shares in the trading companies came to be routinely traded). The city's European and global connections made it the premier European hub of commercial information and intelligence.[12]

London was a giant city, by far the largest in Europe, almost doubling in size during the eighteenth century to approach a million in population by 1801. It was the largest consumer of necessities and luxuries and the main focal point for the distribution of food and manufactured goods throughout the country. This, coupled with its colonial import, export and re-export trades, assured its key position as a booming national and international processing, refining, manufacturing and finishing centre. As early as 1686 London imported over £1 million worth of goods from the colonies, and 25% of the workforce was employed in occupations connected with the port. London's imperial trade in general and her

[9] In the later eighteenth century it became the second British slave port again behind Liverpool: Rawley (2003: xii, 18, 39); https://www.slavevoyages.org/.

[10] Donnan (1931: vol. 2, xxxv–xxxvii); Pettigrew (2013).

[11] https://www.slavevoyages.org/; Eltis and Richardson (2010: 39).

[12] Morgan (2000: 91–3); Zahedieh (2010).

transatlantic trade in particular, even before 1700, 'raised England to technological leadership in Europe'.[13] By the early eighteenth century a relatively small group of powerful mercantile firms, among them Robert Heysham, Humphrey Morice, Richard Harris, Frances Chamberlayne and Isaac Milner, controlled the African and American trades. The slave trade was often only a small part of their business as they focused upon bilateral trades which were greater from London than from any other port in Europe. Forty-nine London slave-traders owned over 25% of London's slave-carrying capacity, but partnership arrangements for individual voyages spread the risks and the rewards of the African trade widely through the mercantile community. Wealthy London merchants, especially those dealing with the Caribbean, moved into sugar importing and refining and became commission agents, bankers and brokers for both planters in the West Indies and for traders in the outports.[14]

Humphrey Morice (c.1671–1731) was England's foremost slave merchant in the 1720s. His seven ships undertook fifty-two voyages to Africa from London and delivered 11,443 enslaved Africans to the Americas, mainly to the Caribbean. Morice became a director of the Bank of England and served as its governor 1727–8.[15] Forty years later John Fletcher, a slave trader active between 1771 and 1782, directed his ships' captains using the wealth of commercial information available to him in London. Increasingly, captains like Peleg Clarke were told to deal only with factors who had reliable financial backing in London; the guarantee of London finance was key to the mechanics of the trade by the third quarter of the eighteenth century.[16]

London's overseas trade grew on a grand scale through the eighteenth century: London imported around seven times more sugar in the late century than did either Bristol or Liverpool.[17] Yet *relatively*, within Britain, its commercial dominance declined in favour of other ports. In 1700 London handled 80% of the exports of England and Wales, 65% of imports and 85% of re-exports. By 1772–4 72% of exports 62% of

---

[13] Morgan (2000: 91–3); Zahedieh (2010: esp. 285).

[14] Rawley (2003: 13, 40–81); for the London mercantile elite and their operations in the late seventeenth century see Zahedieh (1999: 143–58).

[15] Rawley (2003: chapter 3, 42–4).

[16] Donnan (1931: vol. 3, 251, 296, 298–9), discussed by Sheridan (1958: 261).

[17] Morgan (1993: 190).

imports and 72% of re-exports passed through London. Between 1700 and 1776, imports into the other major ports grew more than twice as rapidly as into London and re-exports grew three times as rapidly.[18] The outports were now drawing on their industrial hinterlands, exporting mass-produced manufactures and importing and re-exporting Atlantic staples. The outports also rapidly developed efficiencies and advantages in handling the Atlantic trades, including the slave trade. London remained the focal point of British international trade and finance, but the shift over the course of the eighteenth century of a share of the dynamism to the outports was pivotal to the economic growth and industrialization of the British economy.

Bristol

Bristol's role in the slave trade also grew out of its longer history of African and transatlantic trade. From the 1620s and 1630s Bristolians traded with Barbados and the Leeward Islands and several had contracts to carry convicts to the West Indies in the 1650s. By the time Jamaica was captured from Spain in 1655 the West India trade was already a major sector in Bristol commerce.[19] As with London, Bristol's interest in Africa initially centred around gold, ivory and other goods rather than slaves. The conversion of England's Caribbean islands to sugar culti-vation from the 1640s changed this. Bristol became a major centre for the import of sugar, tobacco and other staples and a key player in the slave trade.[20]

Over 2,000 slave-trade voyages from Bristol between 1698 and 1807 delivered almost half a million slaves.[21] A small number of merchants dominated the trade. John Duckinfield was typical in the early century. He owned seven ships and became Master of the Merchant Venturers of Bristol in 1736, trading direct to the Americas as well as via Africa. He died wealthy, leaving £30,000, which enabled his son to become a planter in Jamaica, owning 5,000 acres by 1750.[22]

---

[18] French (1992: 27–35).
[19] Dresser (2001: 12).
[20] Dresser (2001: 7–52); Morgan (1993: 7–32).
[21] Eltis and Richardson (2010: 39); https://www.slavevoyages.org/.
[22] Dresser (2001: 34–7).

As in London, many Bristol merchants of the early eighteenth century, who did not specialize in the slave trade themselves, invested in such voyages as partners. Others, such as Mary Baker, invested via the London slave-trading companies; she had £300 worth of shares in the South Sea Company when she died in 1739.[23] Profits from the slave trade were thus widely dispersed and found their way into sugar and tobacco processing and into other industrial sectors such as brasswares and copper manufacturing in the city. As with London, it is difficult in Bristol to separate the profits made in the slave trade from other businesses in which individual merchants and slave-trade investors were involved. Philip Harris's slave trading, for example, was aided by his dealings in East India goods and his investments in sugar refining.[24] The slave trade and those trades based upon it, such as sugar and tobacco importing and processing, employed a large number and a huge range of tradespeople in the city, including ships' captains, shipbuilders and repairers, sailmakers, coopers, retailers of ships' supplies, carters and port labourers.[25]

Some of Bristol's export goods for Africa and the Americas came from industries based in the city and its locality, such as copper, brass and glasswares, but most came from further afield, especially from the midlands via the River Severn and from south Wales and London by sea.[26] Bristol did not develop an industrializing hinterland in the same way as Liverpool and Glasgow. This, together with silting and congestion in the port, contributed in the later eighteenth century to its decline as a slave-trading centre. Bristol's share in the British slave trade fell from 42% in 1738–42 to 10% in 1783–7 and to just 1% in 1803–7.[27] Bristol's customs receipts, however, remained on a par with Liverpool's until the 1780s, and it continued to grow rich from importing, processing and selling sugar, tobacco and other high-value plantation staples.[28]

Bristol's sugar trade made it 'Brittania's second mart and eye' (after London) before being overtaken by Liverpool around 1800.[29] There

[23] Dresser (2001: 29); Carlos et al. (2008: 33–45).

[24] Dresser (2001: 13, 29–34).

[25] Morgan (1993: 7–32); Dresser (2001: 29–34); Richardson (2005).

[26] Morgan (1993a: 89–127).

[27] Morgan (2000: 90).

[28] Morgan (2000: 90; 1993a: 189–90).

[29] Grainger (1764) quoted by Dresser (2001: 1); Morgan (1993a: 190).

were four large refining partnerships involving wealthy merchants such as Edward Colston from as early as the 1680s. By the 1790s the city had dozens of sugar refineries, together with tobacco processing, rum distilling, cocoa processing and brewing businesses. Many sugar merchants became fabulously wealthy and, as in London, this wealth enabled them and their descendants to invest further in plantations abroad and in urban and rural property, finance, banking and industry at home.[30] William Miles used his wealth to make more money by acting as guarantor to slave traders in Liverpool.[31]

Bristol's concentration on the narrow base of staple imports, especially sugar, weakened its potential as an export port. Instead, it developed as a consumption and distribution centre. This did not create the level of structural change and industrialization that occurred in other Atlantic port hinterlands. Nevertheless, Bristol played a part in transforming the rural, urban and financial economy of the southwest of England, industrial south Wales and other areas that were in the catchment of her trade or that benefitted from the investment of Bristol's slaving and plantation wealth.[32]

Liverpool

Hanging in the Walker Art Gallery in Liverpool is a 1768 portrait, of Richard Gildhart at the age of ninety-six, painted by Joseph Wright of Derby. Gildhart was a leading Liverpool merchant of the first half of the eighteenth century, making his wealth from salt and slaves. Like many slave merchants, he became politically powerful, serving three times as mayor and representing the city as MP for twenty years (1734–54). Similarly, John Tarleton, a prominent West India merchant and slave trader of Liverpool, with much invested in plantations, built his personal fortune from £5,874 in 1748 to £53,900 in 1763; this included interest in a sugar house, the rum trade and a tea house in the city.[33]

Between 1750 and 1807 Liverpool slave merchants transported well over a million enslaved Africans across the Atlantic, a much

---

[30] Morgan (1993a: 97–8, 102–3, 184–218; 1993b).
[31] Morgan (2016b: 334–52).
[32] Morgan (2000: 88–91); Morgan (1993a: 89–218).
[33] Tarleton papers LVRO 2/1–2/11, quoted by Longmore (2006: 113–70, 139).

larger number than from any other European port and more than all French slave shipments combined.[34] Liverpool had many factors in its favour which enabled it not only to become the premier European slaving port, but also to figure importantly in tobacco, sugar and, later, cotton importing, processing and broking. Its coal exports, largely to London, forged important links between Liverpool and the capital. Salt exports, principally exchanged for Baltic timber, underpinned Liverpool's key position in the Baltic timber trade, crucial for expanding its shipbuilding and for timber re-exports.[35] Coastal trade brought in vital raw materials such as linen from Ireland and foodstuffs. Shipping from Liverpool to the West Indies equalled that going to Europe even in the early eighteenth century. The Caribbean trade was by far the most rapidly growing: the number of ships coming to Liverpool from the West Indies rose from 21 in 1687 to 188 in 1764. A contemporary source documented fifteen slave traders in Liverpool in 1730 and over 100 by 1753. Between 1700 and 1807 Liverpool launched over 4,600 slaving voyages.[36]

Liverpool's involvement with the slave trade took off in the 1740s, aided by the collapse of the trade monopoly of the RAC, and by the African Trade Act of 1750, which enabled all slavers to use the RAC forts on the West African coast. But these factors were less important than others. Liverpool benefitted from pioneering new areas of slave supply further south along the West African coast. Trading at the Bight of Biafra, inland from Bonny and Calabar, and dealing through indigenous Aro traders gave Liverpool merchants an advantage. They obtained enslaved people for lower prices, experienced fewer attacks from shore, incorporated indigenous credit practices, such as pawning the kin of borrowers, raised loading rates and speeded up turnaround times.[37]

Liverpool traders also excelled at assembling the mix of exports that appealed in various African markets.[38] They benefitted from proximity to the linen-, cotton- and woollen-producing areas of south Lancashire, Cheshire, Derbyshire and west Yorkshire, important because textiles were

---

[34] Richardson (2022: 36); Eltis and Richardson (2010: 39).
[35] Longmore (2006: 127–8).
[36] Williams (1753); Longmore (2006: 132); https://www.slavevoyages.org/.
[37] Richardson (2022: 46–66).
[38] Richardson (2022: 56–66); Lovejoy and Richardson (2007: 43–65); Drake (1976).

major commodities in both African and transatlantic trades. Liverpool merchants also developed close links with metal-manufacturing centres and pottery suppliers in the west midlands and used their London connections to buy imported goods and manufactures from further afield for re-export in the Atlantic.[39]

Liverpool merchants appear to have benefitted more than their rivals from credit extended by suppliers of trade goods in Birmingham, London, Manchester and elsewhere, and from their suppliers of ships' provisions. The ratio of credit to cash payments in overall voyage outset costs was commonly more than 60%.[40] Liverpool slave traders were also the first extensively to prefer bills of exchange in payment for slaves in the Caribbean; this brought quick and predictable returns. Such bills were issued with the backing of London finance houses and could be used as a means of payment before they reached their maturity date. They thereby enabled reputable slave traders in the city to buy their Africa trade goods on credit and to tap the resources of both the south Lancashire and London money markets.[41] One effect of this was to concentrate the slave trade into the hands of fewer merchants. Liverpool slave traders declined in number from forty-two in 1783 to twenty-five in 1793, with the ten largest firms each transporting more than 1,000 enslaved people a year and accounting for 60% of the ships employed.[42]

Five new wet docks were constructed in Liverpool in the 1730s, allowing speedy and efficient loading and unloading compared with the congested ports of Bristol and London. Two new dry docks facilitated ship repairs. Between 1756 and 1836 the dock area grew ninefold with the merchant-led Corporation taking financial and technical risks of a kind not contemplated for this purpose in either Bristol or London until the end of the century. The total cost of Liverpool's dock works (around £4 million) was largely financed by loans on security of the Corporation's landed property and in expectation of rising dock duties. A further £1 million was spent during the eighteenth century on private warehousing.

---

[39] Morgan (2007); Longmore (2006); Richardson (2022: 87–93).

[40] Richardson (2022: 41–2).

[41] Morgan (2007: 43–65); Richardson (1976, 2022: 86–93); Anderson (1977); Hudson (2014).

[42] Donnan (1931: vol. 2, 628); https://babel.hathitrust.org/cgi/pt?id=pst.000009721 524andview=1upandseq=695.

These investments allowed the annual tonnage of Liverpool shipping to rise from 14,600 in 1709 to 450,000 in 1800, outstripping Bristol by the end of the century.[43]

An effective transport infrastructure of improved roads, river passage, coastal traffic and canals developed inland from Liverpool in the middle decades of the eighteenth century with much investment coming from Liverpool merchants and the Corporation of the city.[44] The Mersey and Irwell navigation connected Liverpool more easily to Manchester from 1721, a connection further improved by the Bridgewater Canal in the 1770s. The Leeds and Liverpool Canal, opened in 1816, completed a dense transport infrastructure of roads, waterways and coastal trade that turned the entire hinterland of the port (including south Lancashire, west Yorkshire, Staffordshire, the west midlands and parts of north and mid Wales) into an increasingly well-integrated industrial region dealing in coal, salt, textiles, pottery, metalwares, watches and many other manufactures.[45]

As with London and Bristol, what Liverpool and its hinterland gained from the slave trade went far beyond the estimates indicated by narrow quantification of the profits of slave traders or plantation owners. Each slave trade voyage had multiplier effects throughout the local economy because investment was spread across many individuals (including 'attorneys, drapers, ropers, grocers, tallow chandlers, barbers and tailors') who had a financial interest, shared the risks and reaped the rewards.[46] By 1790 around £1 million a year was invested in Liverpool slaving voyages.[47] Slave vessels were built and repaired in Liverpool shipyards, and provisions for the trade came from merchants and shopkeepers of the city. Demand for trade goods had a transformative effect on manufacturing throughout Liverpool's extensive hinterland. Finally, Liverpool became the site of trades and traders dealing with the import, sale and

---

[43] Longmore (2006: 129–33, 137); Morgan (2000: 88–9).

[44] Longmore (2006: 127–30); Weatherill (1971).

[45] Longmore (2006: 113–69); Clemens (1976: 211–23); Bogart (2022).

[46] Donnan (1931: vol. 2, 627); Longmore (2006: 60–1). Investments in voyages, and in other commercial and industrial enterprises in Liverpool, involved many women perhaps because so much male capital was already tied up in trade: Ascott et al. (2006: 54).

[47] Richardson (2022: 37).

processing of various plantation commodities – sugar, cotton, tobacco, indigo. It has been suggested that Liverpool may have directly and indirectly derived more than 40% of its wealth from the slave trade at its height, the same figure associated with Bristol in the early century.[48]

Thanks in no small part to slavery, Liverpool also became a major centre of shipping, marine insurance, commercial finance, commodity broking and the mass export of cotton piece goods in the early nineteenth century. Liverpool's population grew to 83,000 by 1801. It had become second among English provincial towns behind Manchester/Salford (with 89,000 population), which had grown in tandem with it.[49] By the 1760s Liverpool's occupational structure indicates that almost 60% of the employed population was in the industrial sector. By 1810, however, a remarkable transformation had taken place: the industrial share of the population had declined to under 30%, reflecting Liverpool's growing specialization as a port rather than as a manufacturing centre. The number of labourers rose from 10 to 30% in the same period, with most engaged in retailing, trade and transport, especially in seafaring and port activities.[50] In 1801 6,000 sailors were recorded resident in the town.[51] Thus, by 1801 Liverpool was a specialized port with its population focused on port-related activities and tertiary-sector occupations. Commercial manufacturing for the home market and for export to the Americas now took place almost entirely in Liverpool's huge hinterland, which was being transformed largely as a result of the existence of the port. And, as the slave trade ended, merchants trading manufactured goods to North America came to dominate.[52]

Glasgow

Glasgow played only a minor part in the slave trade itself, but the economic history of the port and of Scotland as a whole can be understood only with reference to slavery. The slave-based Atlantic directed

---

[48] Richardson (2005: 35–54, esp. 49); Longmore (2006: 134).

[49] Morgan (2000: 88–91); Wrigley (1985: 683–728, table 1).

[50] Langton and Laxton (1978: 78, 81–2).

[51] Longmore (2006: 160).

[52] Checkland (1958b: 141–60 esp. 142).

Scotland's economy (with Glasgow as its main trading city) to a greater degree than any other part of Great Britain.

Scots played a disproportionately large role in Caribbean plantation settlement and development even before the Act of Union in 1707, but especially after. The Highland clearances, agricultural change, primogeniture, population growth from the 1730s, and the prospect of making money on a scale impossible at home drove a high rate of emigration of Scots of all social classes. Throughout the Caribbean they became prominent in trading, slave factoring, planting, as agents and attorneys and in medicine and politics. Scottish literacy rates were high – around 98% – and universities in Scotland were renowned for scientific training. Scots were therefore in demand as surgeons, bookkeepers and factors. Nearly a quarter of the 71,000 Britons who emigrated to the Caribbean in the period 1655 to 1780 were Scots, and between 1750 and 1834 between 37,000 and 46,000 Scots travelled to the West Indies.[53] A third or more of the white populations of Jamaica, Grenada, St Vincent and Antigua were Scots by the 1770s and they became equally prominent in Tobago, Demerara, Essequibo and Berbice by the 1790s.[54] The Grants of Monymusk had interests in Antigua, Jamaica and the Windwards after 1763, for example, while James and Alexander Baillie purchased the Hermitage plantation in Grenada in 1765. Scots in the Caribbean were aided by dense 'clannish' networks of information flow and credit.[55] Slave ownership compensation claims after 1834 show that Scottish ownership of enslaved peoples was, relative to population size, much greater than in England, Wales or Ireland.[56]

The close relation between the economy of Scotland and the Atlantic started with the growth of the tobacco trade from the Chesapeake in the early eighteenth century. Glaswegians came to dominate British tobacco importation: they developed new purchasing arrangements with smaller lower-cost planters of the Piedmont area, they increased productivity in tobacco shipment and they introduced new marketing strategies.

[53] Hamilton (2005: 2–6, 12–19); Nesbit (2015: 62–81); Mullen (2022: 119–46, 296)
[54] Burnard (1996: 769–96); Mullen (2022: esp. 183–210); Alston (2021); https://www.spanglefish.com/slavesandhighlanders/.
[55] Hamilton (2005: 5, 55–83, esp. 70–1).
[56] Devine (2015b: 4). See also Draper (2015a: 166–86); https://www.ucl.ac.uk/lbs/maps/britain.

Glasgow merchants sent factors to run stores in the Chesapeake. These factors supplied a large range of consumer goods to American customers and purchased tobacco directly from planters. By the 1770s there were many independent Scottish merchant houses in Virginia and Maryland, and Glasgow overtook London as the leading British tobacco port. Scots also pioneered direct re-export of the tobacco crop from the Clyde to France, the Netherlands and Germany. Tobacco was the most valuable of the West Indian staple crops by weight even with the darker and cheaper Oronoco tobacco, which had mass appeal and in which the Scots specialized.[57] Growth of the tobacco trade and the wealth of Glasgow's tobacco lords underpinned growth in other trading activity on the Clyde and elsewhere in Scotland. There are many examples, particularly after the 1780s, of wealth from the tobacco trade flowing into industry, shipping and banking. Importing such large quantities of tobacco depended on increasing Scottish production and trade in colonial supplies. Many businesses grew to straddle both manufacturing and trade, aided by Scottish law that allowed merchant firms to form large interlocking partnerships. This gave better access to capital and credit.[58]

The role of Scots in the Caribbean increased with expansion of the sugar frontier after 1763. And when the American War of Independence seriously disrupted the tobacco trade with the mainland colonies, Scottish merchants and investors further expanded their activities in the West Indies. They played a dominant role in the growth of sugar cultivation, investment and speculation in the 1790s.[59] Houston and Co., the greatest of the Glasgow West India houses, expanded its trade rapidly after 1763. By the 1790s it served over 220 clients in eighteen territories.[60] By the 1790s Glasgow was the fourth-largest sugar importer after London, Bristol and Liverpool.[61]

Many Scots merchants, like the Houstons, became heavily involved in sugar and later cotton importing and invested in both sugar refining and cotton manufacturing. Of seventy-six Caribbean merchants identified as based in Glasgow at the end of the century twenty-one were partners in

[57] Devine (1975); Price (1995); Morgan (2000: 86–7).
[58] Devine and Jackson (1995: 77, 139–83); Price (1995).
[59] Hamilton (2005: 2–6, 55–83); Checkland (1957); Mullen (2022: 147–252).
[60] Hamilton (2005: 87–8).
[61] Morgan (2000: 87); Morgan (1993a: 190).

cotton manufacturing and fourteen in sugar refining.[62] The Campbells of Possil epitomize Glasgow's elite sugar aristocracy. After abolition, in 1835 partners of the firm received £73,000; they were the eighth-largest mercantile beneficiary of compensation money and the largest in Scotland. Partners of the firm held enslaved people across at least twelve estates throughout the Caribbean. John Campbell Snr (*c.*1735–1807) made money through shares in one of the largest tobacco firms, John Glassford and Co. Campbell and Co. imported sugar from several islands but also cotton from Carriacou on consignment. In return they exported herring to feed slaves, linen and other manufactures. After 1791 the firm, like other Scots speculators, financed and bought plantations on the South American mainland, particularly in Demerara, and many highlanders went to Berbice in the 1790s.[63]

Glasgow's trade to the West Indies 'was fundamental to industrial expansion after the 1770s' and had a major impact on industrialization in the lowlands and beyond. From 1815 to 1820 between a quarter and two-thirds of all goods exported from Scotland, mainly textiles, were destined for the West Indies.[64] Between 1765 and 1795 there was a ten-fold increase in Scottish linen exports to Jamaica, mostly coarse 'Osnaburgs' used for slave clothing.[65] The Scottish cotton industry took off from the 1790s based on imported Caribbean cotton and Atlantic, as well as domestic, demand for cotton manufactures. By the 1820s, 86% of the cotton workforce in Scotland produced goods for export, most going to the Americas. Investment entered the industry from Scotland's tobacco lords and sugar aristocracy. By 1819 in Glasgow and its hinterland there were 52 cotton mills, 16 weaving mills, 18 calico printing works and 32,000 handloom weavers employed by manufacturers in the city. At least 15% of the entire Scottish population of 1.5 million was employed in textiles, mostly in cotton manufacture, at this time. Glasgow and its region also developed iron, shipbuilding and coal-mining enterprises which drew on West Indian finance and benefitted especially, as did cotton, from West Indian mercantile and banking

---

[62] Devine (1978: 40–67, esp. 43).
[63] Mullen (2015: 124–44); Alston (2015: 99–123).
[64] Mullen (2022: 294, 253–302); Devine (2015b: 11).
[65] Hamilton (2005: 15).

connections.[66] Unlike Liverpool, which became a specialized port city by the early nineteenth century, Glasgow was the one British port city where 'innovative industrial development and international trade took place in the same urban space'.[67] But this did not prevent the broad hinterland of Glasgow from also becoming a fulcrum of change. In 1700 Glasgow's population was on a par with Bristol's, but it grew to 77,000 by 1801 and was coming to rival Liverpool (with 77,653) in size.[68] Glasgow's population and that of its industrial hinterland grew rapidly in the last two decades of the eighteenth century, reflecting Scotland's unusually rapid economic transformation, especially in its lowland belt.

National and regional perspectives

For many decades historians of the British industrial revolution underplayed the significance of relations between the dynamic Atlantic trading ports and their industrial hinterlands. Working at the national level of aggregated statistics, they identified only moderate growth in national income and industrial output before 1830 and thus confined their explanations of change to the slow evolution of economic and social stimuli internal to Britain. Recent recalculations of output (GDP) and of shifts in the labour force have, however, partly restored the traditional picture of significant change during (and also before) the classic industrial revolution period.[69] New occupational data show a gradual decline of the agricultural labour force from around 50% to around 32% between 1710 and 1831, a *modest* rise in the already uniquely high industrial total to around 45% over the same period, and a large increase in the service sector share to 23% by 1831.[70] Industry accounted for 42%

---

[66] Devine (1976: 1–13); Durie (1979: 152); Mullen (2022: 274–9, 300).

[67] Devine and Jackson (1995: 14, 235).

[68] Morgan (2000: 86).

[69] Revisions to GDP are by Broadberry et al. (2015); revisions to sectoral labour force shares are by scholars at the Cambridge Group: Shaw-Taylor and Wrigley (2014: 53–88). The implications of the new work are debated by Crafts (2021: esp. 320). The new occupational data produced by the Cambridge Group can be seen at https://www.campop.geog.cam.ac.uk/research/occupations/.

[70] Derived from the Cambridge Group figures referenced above and discussed in Shaw-Taylor and Wrigley (2014: 53–88). See also Keibek (2017).

of employment by 1800 rather than the 25% previously estimated.[71] We also know that the service sector share grew by 53% *c.*1710–1817, suggesting that increased activity in trade, transport and finance deserves a greater weight in accounting for growth and change than has formerly been the case. A new consensus is emerging among historians that Britain was less agricultural and much more industrial at the *start* of the eighteenth century than was thought in the 1980s. And labour productivity growth in industry was thus significantly higher from 1759 to 1801 than estimates of the 1980s suggested.[72] These recent findings at national level provide a new context for re-appraising the causes of growth and innovation in industry and of the part played by the colonial trades, including the slave trade.

Slave ports and the industrialization of Britain

The British industrial revolution was first and foremost a regional phenomenon.[73] Rapid growth and transformation of production and trade, largely in Atlantic port city hinterlands, was accompanied by deindustrialization and decline in many older centres of industry and commerce. The fastest-growing sectors of overseas trade, concentrated in London, Liverpool, Bristol and Glasgow, grew in symbiosis with the home market in their regions. Commercial manufacturing increased the amount of waged work available and encouraged in-migration. The number of households and individuals who were wage dependent and who therefore bought more of their food, drink and manufactured goods in the market increased in these regions, and there was a marked decline in the number of subsistence households. This shift in the allocation of household labour, prompted by the growing availability of waged work, and by increased availability of consumer goods, gave rise to

[71] Shaw-Taylor and Wrigley (2014: 56, 59, 61); cf. Crafts (1985); Crafts and Harley (1992).

[72] Shaw-Taylor and Wrigley (2014: 62–5, 84); Broadberry et al. (2015: 364–9); Crafts (2021: esp 318–19). For sectoral distributions of male and female labour and their spatial character see: https://www.campop.geog.cam.ac.uk/research/occupations/; https://www.economiespast.org/.

[73] For early surveys of the evidence and arguments for this see Hudson (1989); Pollard (1981). For a case study see Stobart (2004).

increasing consumerism and increasing industriousness: both associated with industrialization.[74]

Nowhere was this more obvious than in the textile regions of south Lancashire, west Yorkshire and the Scottish lowlands, where the stimulus of both overseas and domestic markets went hand in hand in promoting industrialization.[75] Similar concentrations of activity occurred in metals and hardware manufacturing (in the west midlands and south Yorkshire), in heavy industries (in south Wales, the west midlands and Northumberland) and in specialized processing and finishing centres for manufactured consumer goods and colonial groceries, notably sugar and tobacco.

Demographic indicators of port-hinterland industrialization

New population figures at local and regional levels demonstrate the structural transformation of the Atlantic port hinterlands. In-migration and high birth rates in the industrializing regions together created rapid population growth. Between 1700 and 1750 population in the industrial counties in the hinterland of Liverpool (Lancashire, Cheshire, Staffordshire, the West Riding of Yorkshire and Warwickshire) grew by 36.5%; in agricultural counties it grew by only 5.2%. Between 1750 and 1801 the population of the industrial group rose by 87.4% compared with that of the agricultural group at only around 29%.[76] The national population of England and Wales grew, between 1750 and 1801, by around 46%. In west Yorkshire it grew by 82%, and in Lancashire by 122%. That such unprecedented rates of population growth occurred without creating local mortality crises is testament to the achievement of 'modern economic growth' in these regional economies.[77]

Trade routes from the west midlands, Lancashire and west Yorkshire, for both internal and external trade, focused less upon London from the mid-eighteenth century and, in many cases, bypassed the capital

---

[74] See chapter 3, p. 73; de Vries (2008: 1–121).
[75] See, for example, Stobart (2004).
[76] Shaw-Taylor and Wrigley (2014: 79). East Anglia's growth, for example, was only 27% in the half century: Wrigley (2009: 21).
[77] Modern economic growth alludes to growth that is self-sustaining because innovation creates positive feedback loops: Wrigley (2018: 9–42).

altogether. London thus saw a *relative* decline in its position as a centre of population. The percentage of total population of England and Wales resident in London in the eighteenth century stabilized at around 11%, whereas it grew in other towns and cities from 5% in 1700 (in total) to over 18% in 1800 (and took off further to around 30% by 1851), with growth particularly strong in northwest port and trading cities.[78]

London remained of vital importance in trade and in the generation of national wealth and incomes. It remained larger and had a higher proportion of national population than any other capital city in Europe. It continued to play a central role in the colonial trades both directly and via financial services. But Britain's most significant population growth and urbanization in the eighteenth century took place in the provinces and in manufacturing towns geared to both export and inland trades. Older centres such as Norwich and Exeter gave way in size order to Manchester, Liverpool, Birmingham, Bristol and Leeds, the five urban centres of England and Wales that grew rapidly to rank in size order, respectively, immediately below London by 1801.[79] It has been suggested that over half of urban growth (occurring largely in the Atlantic port hinterlands) in the seventeenth and eighteenth centuries was attributable to empire.[80]

Structural change

Occupations shifted towards industry in the northern industrializing areas of England and Wales in the century or so *before* 1750, just as the Atlantic trading system was taking off. In the most intensively developed manufacturing hinterlands of Liverpool (in industrial Lancashire and Yorkshire) already by 1755, stimulated by both domestic and overseas demand, two-thirds of employed adult males worked in industry.[81] The proportion of Britain's industrial workers living in these heartlands increased continuously between 1701 and 1817, accelerating between

---

[78] The urban share is here defined as all towns and cities over 5,000 population. Shaw-Taylor and Wrigley (2014: 76–7).

[79] Wrigley (1985: 683–728, table 1).

[80] Allen (2003: 403–43).

[81] It is likely that including female workers would not materially alter this measurement: Shaw-Taylor and Wrigley (2014: 53–88, esp. 66–70); Keibek (2017: 185).

1700 and the 1760s, and decreasing after 1817.[82] Absolute numbers employed in industry in the industrial areas continued to rise as population and in-migration increased. But further structural change in favour of industrial employments tended to stabilize in the classic industrial revolution period.[83] Reasons behind this likely lie in increasing labour productivity and a substitution of capital for labour in manufacturing. Both were markers of industrialization and both occurred particularly in the economic catchment areas of the Atlantic ports.[84] Decline in the geographical concentration of industrial employment after 1817 suggests the spread of new technologies to wider areas of Britain during the nineteenth century, serving broader internal and global markets.[85]

High rates of population growth and structural change in the economy overall, and especially in the hinterlands of Atlantic ports, were rooted in changes in the century before the 1780s. Overseas trade in general and slave-based colonial expansion in particular played an important part in stimulating mass manufacturing at a time of sluggish domestic population growth. The copper industry rose from its Elizabethan doldrums on the basis of the colonial export trade; overseas demand also stimulated the sailcloth, linen, woollens, cottons and metalwares industries in the early eighteenth century. Change precipitated by domestic and overseas demands in tandem altered the types of goods favoured, as well as the volume, and the regional location of their manufacture.

Mapping clearly indicates the geographically concentrated structural transformation of the economy of England and Wales in the eighteenth century and its relationship to the Atlantic port hinterlands. Maps 5.1 and 5.2 demonstrate the changing levels and regional divergence of employment in the industrial sector between 1710 and 1817.

The same information about population and structural change in Scotland is not yet available, but we know that Scotland had a significantly lower proportion of occupations in the industrial and service

---

[82] Shaw-Taylor and Wrigley (2014: 64).

[83] Keibek (2017: 197).

[84] At the same time, some counties including Hertfordshire, Northamptonshire and Bedforshire saw a rise in the proportion of the population employed in agriculture because of the collapse of rural industries. Shaw-Taylor and Wrigley (2014: 53–88); https://www.campop.geog.cam.ac.uk/research/occupations/; https://www.economiespast.org.

[85] Keibek (2017: 210).

Map 5.1: The regional concentration of secondary-sector employment (adult males, excluding mining), 1710.

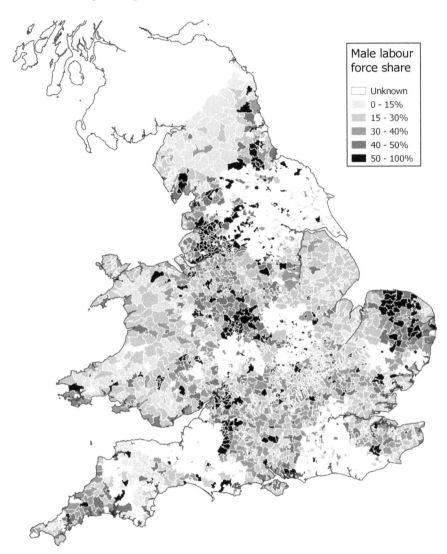

Source: based on probate data and parish register information collected as part of the CAMPOP project on Occupational Change in England and Wales. Map drawn and supplied by Sebastian Keibek and Leigh Shaw-Taylor. For full details of sources and more detailed maps see www.economiespast.org.

Map 5.2: The regional concentration of secondary-sector employment (adult males, excluding mining), 1817.

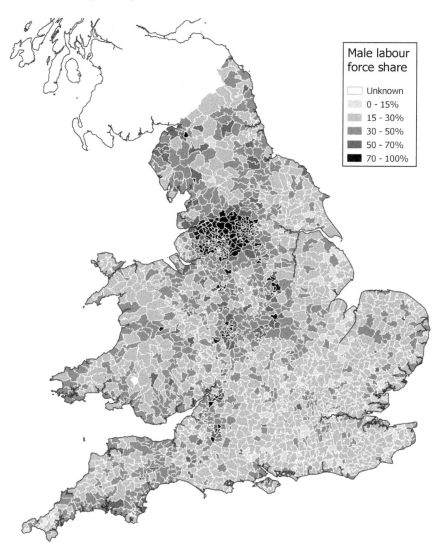

Source: based on probate data and parish register information collected as part of the CAMPOP project on Occupational Change in England and Wales. Maps drawn and supplied by Sebastian Keibek and Leigh Shaw-Taylor. For full details of sources and more detailed maps see www.economiespast.org.

sectors than did England before the later eighteenth century. By 1851, by contrast, the proportion of male occupations in industry was higher in Scotland than in England (47.1% compared with 42.6%). Scotland also had a higher proportion of employment in textiles (15% compared with 8.8%), and a service-sector share that was rapidly catching up with England's.[86] Scotland's industrialization in the late eighteenth and early nineteenth centuries was strikingly rapid and driven by change in the hinterlands of Glasgow, much influenced by slave-based Atlantic trade.[87]

Coal and markets

The parish level and probate data used in maps 5.1 and 5.2 show that concentration of industry occurred *within* counties as well as between them. Industries favoured easy access to markets: these connections were significant in Cheshire, for example, where the textile industry was concentrated in the north and east of the county, nearest to Manchester with its huge pull as an Atlantic marketing centre.[88] Locations also favoured proximity to rivers for power and to coal for heating. Access to cheap coal was important in the geographical concentration of industry long before the widespread use of steam power. Heat was needed for many industrial processes from smelting and metal processing to dyeing cloth, boiling sugar and brewing. Heating domestic and workshop premises was also important to the productivity and nutrition of dispersed labour forces in rural and workshop manufacturing. As Adam Smith emphasized in 1776, cheap coal kept down the cost of labour.[89] It also enabled more work to continue through the winter months. Easy access to coal reinforced the advantages of particular industrial clusters within the Atlantic port hinterlands.

Coalfields were, of course, also locationally indispensable for the manufacture of some key producer goods. The south Wales coalfield

---

[86] Shaw-Taylor and Wrigley (2014: 70–2). Male tertiary-sector employment was 22.9% compared with 29.7% in England.

[87] Mullen (2022: 20–7, 293–302).

[88] Keibek (2017: 193), who also emphasizes the agricultural potential of west Cheshire driving textile manufacturing to the north and east.

[89] Smith (1776: book IV, 338–9); Zylberberg (2015: 91–122).

enabled innovative copper and iron smelting from the beginning of the eighteenth century. However, the coal trade should be seen as a 'social artifact as well as a natural fact' activated by the growth of the international economy.[90] The coal-using heavy industries of south Wales depended on their financial and trading connections with the ports of Bristol and London bringing investment and extended markets for their products.[91] Similarly, the main stimulus to expansion of the northeast coalfield was the demand for domestic coal in London, the nodal city of international trade, including colonial trade, its defence, finance and administration. These brought population, wealth and a huge demand for coal to the capital.[92] This in turn promoted change in mining technologies, including the use of steam engines in mine drainage, and further secured the later foundation of the northeast as a leading centre of heavy industry and shipbuilding.

The pattern of regionally based manufacturing transformation, established long before steam power and coal use in industry became widespread, was dictated not by coal *per se* but by access to markets, particularly markets stimulated by the demand for new sorts of mass-manufactured and specialized commodities.

Conclusion

Growing Atlantic demand for innovative products and new supplies of slave-grown industrial raw materials favoured those industrial regions with access to the main Atlantic port cities. Access to Atlantic trading, to the capital and credit generated by it, and to the buoyant incomes created in its wake, brought wider economic change that rippled out from Britain's 'slave ports'. Most causal analyses of industrialization in Britain fixate on the national level and look to internal factors for their explanations. They point to coal as the determining locational factor. They thus underestimate the causal connections between Britain's industrial revolution, her Atlantic ports and slavery.

[90] Allen (2009: 80–105, esp. 84, 90).
[91] Evans (2010).
[92] Zahedieh (2010); French (1992).

CHAPTER 6

Iron and copper revolutions: metals, hardware and mining

British industry responded quickly to expanding colonial markets. Metals and mining, so often identified with domestic priorities and incentives, led the way. Plantation demands, both in the Caribbean and in the northern colonies, for metals, engineering products, agricultural implements and other metalwares, initiated technological, organizational and regionally concentrated changes in Britain. A study of overseas trade in the early 1960s argued that: 'the process of industrialization in England from the second quarter of the eighteenth century [was] to an important extent a response to colonial demands for nails, axes, firearms, buckets, coaches, clocks, saddles, handkerchiefs, buttons, cordage and a thousand other things'.[1] Metals made up the highest value by far of London exports to Jamaica in 1771–3, at £121,834 in 1772 and £154,958 in 1773. The West Indies took between 54% and 67% of Britain's wrought copper exports between 1740 and 1760 and continued to take over 50% up to 1774. Over the whole eighteenth century the Americas, together with West Africa, took well over half of British metal exports.[2]

A major part of Britain's industrial revolution was based, even from an early stage, on heavy, capital-intensive, industry. Metals manufacture and engineering technologies and skills associated with the sector were fundamental to wider processes of industrialization.[3] Substantial innovatory investment went into mining, iron and copper smelting by tobacco and sugar merchants and banks based in London, Bristol and Glasgow. They financed investment in the south Wales coalfield, in Cornish copper mines, in copper refining in the Swansea Valley, in iron refining in south Wales and the west midlands, in coal mining in the northeast for the

---

[1] Davis (1962–3: 285–303).
[2] Zahedieh (2021: 784–808, esp. 789–90); Inikori (2002: 456).
[3] Mokyr (2009: 99–144); Cookson (2018: 11–58).

London market and in mining and iron manufactures on the Scottish coalfield. The Swansea Valley and other parts of the south Wales coalfield became some of the earliest sites of industrialization, with centralized wage-dependent workforces. This transformation was intimately linked with plantation and slave trade profits and with the demands of Atlantic trade and shipping. The industrializing Birmingham metals region and the west midlands coalfield were also very closely connected with Atlantic markets.

Metals, mining and regional industrialization

The regional shifts in the occupational distribution of the British labour force, explored in chapter 5, are reflected in mapping the distribution of males occupied in the metals and mining industries in England and Wales in 1817 (map 6.1). By 1817 the concentration of metal working alone indicates the prominent place of the west midlands and south Yorkshire, both with significant Atlantic markets and Atlantic port links. There is concentration also in south Wales with its links to Bristol, London and Atlantic demands. The regional concentrations of manufacturing and the commodities explored in this chapter illustrate the importance of industrial clustering. Specific localities specialized in particular carefully targeted types of ironmongery and other light metal goods, copper vessels, wires or plates and heavy iron goods. Geographical concentration combined commercial knowledge with skill development and created synergies among investors, manufacturers, bankers, engineers and traders that brought positive externalities to whole regions.[4]

Combining the share of the male labour force in mining as well as metals manufacture (map 6.2) shows the much stronger place of south and north Wales as well as the northeast coalfield, the growth of the latter connected closely to the growth of the London market for domestic coal. The concentration of copper and tin mining in Cornwall, the former so important to the development of copper smelting in south Wales in response to Atlantic and, later, Asian demands, really stands out. What is striking is the relatively low concentration of male occupations in mining in the south Lancashire coalfield, which may reflect the dominance of

[4] Allen (1966); Hudson (1989).

Map 6.1: The regional concentration of adult males employed in the metals industries, 1817.

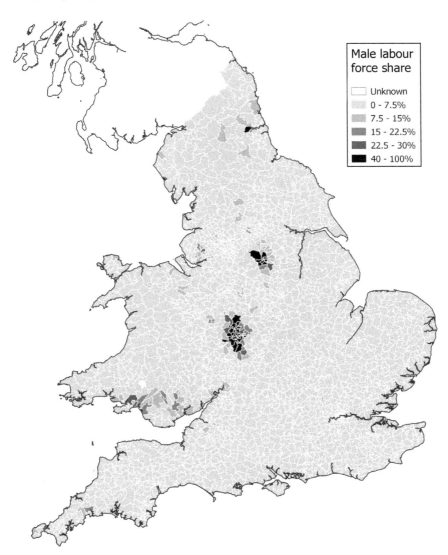

Source: based on probate data and parish register information collected as part of the CAMPOP project on Occupational Change in England and Wales. Map drawn and supplied by Sebastian Keibek and Leigh Shaw-Taylor. For full details of sources and more detailed maps see www.economiespast.org.

Map 6.2: The regional concentration of adult males employed in the metal trades and mining combined, 1817.

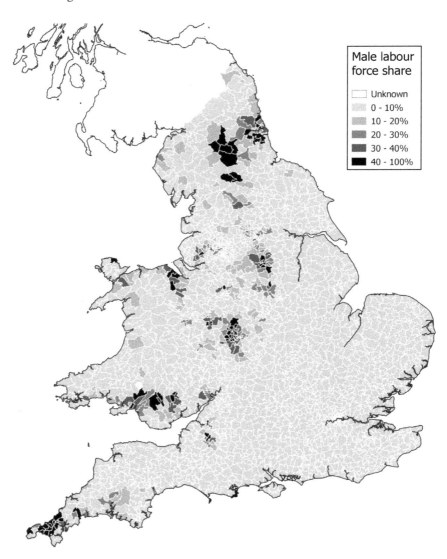

Source: based on probate data and parish register information collected as part of the CAMPOP project on Occupational Change in England and Wales. Maps drawn and supplied by Sebastian Keibek and Leigh Shaw-Taylor. For full details of sources and more detailed maps see www.economiespast.org.

textile occupations and/or the relatively low industrial reliance upon coal in the region until after 1817.

These regional occupational concentrations not only reflect growing domestic demands but also show just how deeply into the country the Atlantic port hinterlands cut. The Swansea Valley with its more obvious links to Bristol had clear Atlantic connections, but what of the west midlands in the centre of the country? Birmingham was no port city, but it looked west, joining the hinterlands of Bristol and Liverpool in networks of navigable rivers and canals that its manufacturers and entrepreneurs developed at an early stage. The River Severn was important in connecting the midlands with Bristol via Shropshire and elsewhere, but it was canals that made the difference. The first canal boom of 1768–76 was followed by another in the 1790s. The trunk canals joined river systems, making for interior lines of communication into the country. The Mersey was linked to the Severn at Stourport in 1772; the Trent to the Mersey in 1777. The Severn was joined to the Thames in 1789; the Mersey was joined to the Trent and the Thames in 1790. By 1790 London, Bristol, Birmingham, Liverpool and Hull were all joined. Birmingham's easy connections with London were finally achieved with the opening of the Grand Junction Canal in 1805. The central pivot of the national canal system was between Birmingham, Coventry and Stafford; there were 160 miles of canals within easy reach of Birmingham.[5]

The Birmingham industrial region and the midlands coalfield, by early in the nineteenth century, connected with the major ports on all sides of England. In the first instance the canals carried coal, but their local economic impact on midlands metals was enormous. Birmingham made a transition from its eighteenth-century place as a supplier of light metalwares, muskets and some ironworks to the major nineteenth-century world supplier of domestic and industrial hardware; the waterways made this possible.[6] Arthur Young wrote on his visit in the early 1790s:

> The port, as it may be called, or double canal head in the town, crowded with coal barges, is a noble spectacle, with that prodigious animation, which the immense trade of this place could alone give. I looked around me with

[5] Mathias (1969: 112).
[6] Turnbull (1987: 537–60, esp. 544).

amazement at the change effected in twenty years; so great that this place may now probably be reckoned, with justice, the first manufacturing town in the world.[7]

Cheap, canal-borne coal attracted industry. The midlands and the north, with their networks of canals, became industrial heartlands; the port hinterlands moved inland. As John Phillips put it in 1805, 'the internal parts of our island [had been converted] into coasts'.[8]

Copper

The three sectors of the heavy and light metal industries that had significant connections to Atlantic world markets – copper, iron and guns – were all embedded in connections with the coalfields. Copper is little considered in many histories of British industrialization, yet it was the fastest-growing industry to the 1770s, and the first to adopt innovations that were later applied in other metals manufactures, and beyond. Recent research has uncovered the deep dependence of the early transformation of the industry on colonial demand.[9] In the early seventeenth century the English copper industry was almost non-existent. Some brass and copper objects were made from imported copper from Sweden, and many English slavers continued to rely to a great extent on this source. But from the late seventeenth century African (slave trade) demand for copper and brass items (thin rods, manillas, pans and kettles) and West Indian plantation needs, especially for copper vessels used in boiling and crystallizing sugar and distilling rum, underpinned a great surge in the industry and much technological change. Copper and brass goods made up an important part of slave trade cargoes, the second most valuable after textiles. John Atkins, a British naval surgeon, in his *Voyage to Guinea, Brasil and the West Indies* (1737), wrote that the men of the Windward Coast (between Liberia and the Ivory Coast in West Africa) wore 'manilla's about their Wrists and Ancles, of Brass, Copper, Pewter, or Ivory'.[10]

[7] Young, *Annals* (532), cited in Turnbull (1987: 544).
[8] Phillips (1805/1970: viii).
[9] Evans (2010); Zahedieh (2013). Also see earlier research of Harris (1992).
[10] Atkins (1737: 61), cited in Evans (2010: 30).

The Africa trade drew in copper works in several parts of the country. Reinhold Angerstein, the Swedish traveller and industrial spy, visiting Mr Pattens' works in Warrington, which supplied 40 tons of copperwork a year to West Africa, found the workers 'busy drawing down copper to rods for the Guinea trade':

> The production would take much less time if the rods were drawn through holes in an iron plate, as is done with heavy brass wire, but I was told that this way of processing would not give the copper the same degree of ductility that it gets from the forging which is required for this part of the operation. The Negroes in Guinea use the rods as ornaments and wind them around arms and legs.[11]

Another brass works near Bristol, part of the Bristol Brass Wire Company, manufactured copper and brass dishes in a variety of sizes in large quantities for the West Africa trade, with the racialized perceptions of the trade embedded in commodity design: 'It was said that of this article alone, Guinea uses 80–90 tons per year. The negroes are supposed to use the large dishes when they wash or when they coat themselves with ointments to become even blacker.'[12]

British copper and brass exports rose from 140 tons in the 1650s to 220 in 1700, with the plantations and Africa taking 90%. Colonial demand transformed the market for invention. It stimulated the substitution of coal for charcoal in metal smelting. Pioneered in lead manufacture, charcoal smelting succeeded much more spectacularly in copper, then spread to other non-ferrous metals. Expansion of copper mining in Cornwall, for most of the eighteenth century the main domestic source of raw copper, depended upon mine drainage and provided one of the key markets for the steam engines of Savary, Newcomen and, later, Watt.[13]

Exports of ornamental copper and brass, vessels and other objects to Africa, while significant, were nowhere near as important as those going to the West Indies. Exports of copper from Britain quadrupled in the last three decades of the seventeenth century; by 1730 there had been a further threefold increase to 247 tons, with the West Indian market the

[11] Berg and Berg (2001: 324).
[12] Berg and Berg (2001: 145).
[13] Zahedieh (2013: 817–23). Also see Evans and Miskell (2020).

Table 6.1: Exports of metal goods from London to Africa and the colonies, 1701 (% of total exports of each good by weight).

	Africa	North America	West Indies	All three Atlantic regions
Wrought brass	26	28	19	73
Wrought copper	36	2	50	88
Nails	0.2	44	31	75.2
Wrought iron	16	23	31	70

Source: The National Archives (TNA) CUST. 2/9, adapted from Zahedieh (2010: table 6.9, 272).

mainstay and with Africa and plantation demand together accounting for some 90% of copper exports.[14] In 1771 the West Indies took over half the export of wrought and unwrought copper, much of it used for the vats for sugar refining; these copper imports were not far off twice those going to the northern American colonies.[15] Estimated exports of wrought copper from London to the West Indies rose from 12,760 cwt in 1740–4 to 57,041 cwt in 1770–4. Estimated stocks of copper utensils on British sugar plantations rose from 146 tons in 1650 to 4,243 tons in 1770, not including the amount of copper used in renewals, repairs and replacements.[16]

The great plantation sugar works and distilleries described in chapter 3, and their European counterparts, required huge copper cauldrons and coolers as essential equipment. Some of these vessels reached a capacity of 1,000 gallons. A suite of three of these on large plantations could boil off 30 hogsheads of sugar a week during the harvest. In the case of rum distilleries, the largest stills might hold between 1,000 and 3,000 gallons of liquor. A great expansion of copper manufacturing first in the Bristol area and in London, and later in the west midlands, supplied much of plantation demand. The manufacture depended in turn on developing the copper mining industry in Cornwall, and the new copper smelting and manufacture region in the Swansea Valley.[17]

[14] Zahedieh (2013: 812).
[15] Harris (1964: 10–12).
[16] Zahedieh (2021: table 2, 790); Zahedieh (2022: 149–66); Zahedieh (2013: 811).
[17] Evans (2010: 40–1); Evans (2014: 61–75, esp. 66; 2010: 35–9). For greater detail on the Welsh copper industry see Evans and Miskell (2020, esp. chapter 4); Royal Commission on the Ancient and Historical Monuments of Wales (2000, esp 1–71).

Late seventeenth-century innovations that brought coal into copper smelting occurred first north of Bristol, in the Wye Valley and the Forest of Dean, and were driven in turn by colonial demand. These innovations reduced fuel costs without markedly increasing the impurities imparted from ore or fuel, or reducing the quality of the finished product. Improvements based on expensive programmes of research and development relied for their finance on wealthy investment partnerships, vertical integration and mergers.[18] The number of stages required in smelting increased from the early eighteenth century, and the industry relied heavily on coal fuel. The smelting sector migrated to the Swansea Valley on the edge of the south Wales coalfield. Here the 'Welsh Method' was pioneered, technologically well ahead of its time, by a small number of leading business concerns, many with close links to Bristol and to slave trade or plantation profits. Welsh copper smelting and the Bristol slave trade developed in tandem between 1710 and 1740. Swansea became the centre of Europe's copper industry as the Bristol slave trade intensified. Those with interests in the slave trade financed huge capital-intensive ventures; their driving incentive was the rapidly expanding markets of the Atlantic world, especially the West Indies.

The copper master Thomas Coster financed slaving expeditions at the same time as developing the great White Rock smelting works in the Swansea Valley. Thomas Williams, who became known as the 'Copper King', developed an enormous copper-mining venture on the island of Anglesey, the Parys Mine company, in the 1770s, then several smelting furnaces to the west of Swansea. These became 'one of the most commanding industrial complexes of the age'. Thomas Williams wrote to the House of Lords in 1788 during moves to regulate the slave trade that it was the demand for copper in Africa that had stimulated him and his associates to invest £70,000 in fixed capital at smelting works at Holywell and Penclawdd, and that they manufactured 'entirely for the African market'.[19] By this stage both domestic and East India Company demand for copper was also significant, but African and West Indian demand dominated the industry for the first two-thirds of the century. By 1800 the global output of smelted copper was around 17,200 tons, of which

---

[18] See Evans and Miskell (2020: chapter 3).
[19] Evans (2010: 37; 2014: 67, 68); Harris (1993/2003).

41% came from Wales. Coal production in south Wales expanded to fuel this great copper-refining region; the output of the western coalfields of Britain grew from 70,000 tons in 1700 to 250,000 tons in 1775, with south Wales doubling its contribution to national coal output.[20]

Although the Caribbean islands took nearly half of the copper exported, with the slave trade also taking a significant quantity, even the copper consumed internally was significantly stimulated by the expansion of Atlantic trade. Demand for copper vessels used in sugar refining and distilling both on the plantations and at home drove an industry in copper rolling and copper smithing in works along the Thames, powered by the river. William Forbes, one of the specialist London coppersmiths producing for sugar refiners, drew on investment from merchants and manufacturers in the wider copper trade, and in turn invested in shares in other firms such as Lockwood, Morris and Co.[21]

The copper-boiling vessels and distilling stills were an enormous capital expense both for plantation works and for British sugar factories. William Belgrove in his *Treatise on Husbandry and Plantations* (1755) estimated capital expenses on copper furniture for a boiling house and curing house at £2,380 out of an estimated capital on a 500-acre plantation of £31,405, which included £12,000 for 300 enslaved peoples. William Forbes, who started his London copper smithing firm in 1771, had, by 1775, supplied vessels to eleven London sugar refiners as well as many plantations across the West Indies. In that year he took an order for a large sugar boiler for the Mesopotamia plantation in Jamaica. It required 8.25 cwt of refined copper ore to manufacture.[22]

The copper sheathing of ships to protect timber hulls from the *teredo navalis* worm in tropical waters created further innovation in the industry. The Royal Navy made its first serious efforts with copper sheathing in 1761 on the *Alarm*, a frigate for the West India station. Over a two-year period the whole of the navy was coppered, but problems ensued over galvanic action on the iron bolts holding the copper plates in place.[23] The research and development to solve this problem brought together

---

[20] Zahedieh (2021: 797); O'Sullivan (2023).
[21] Zahedieh (2021: 792, 798–9).
[22] Zahedieh (2021: 793–4).
[23] Rees (1972: 85–94); Inikori (2002: 470–1); Harris (1998: 263–5); Solar and Rönnbäck (2015: 810–11).

key capitalist entrepreneurs and technologists of the day and the state. James Keir, leading chemist, inventor and member of the Lunar Society, worked with Matthew Boulton and with William Forbes, who was now also acting as copper contractor to the navy, to develop a copper alloy for bolts; Forbes later patented one of these. The main beneficiaries were slave ships and other vessels sailing to Africa and to and from the West Indies, together with the British naval vessels that protected them. The coppering of ships speeded the voyages by preventing seaweed and barnacles gathering on the ship base and greatly reduced the costs of refitting between voyages. One coppered slave vessel in 1785 made sixteen voyages compared with the eleven voyages possible on comparable ships with no sheathing. Copper firms multiplied in Liverpool as it became a centre for copper bottoming, as well as for slave voyages.[24] This new demand for copper stimulated industrial growth particularly in Wales. Two large specialist firms were devoted to sheet copper in the Neath Valley, and a manufacturing plant owned by Thomas Williams in north Wales (at Holywell) manufactured 40,000 copper bolts weekly at its peak for fixing the copper plating to the ships.[25]

Copper ore, supplied initially from West Country deposits, was soon drawn from Cornwall's deep mining sources, from where it was easily transported by sea to Swansea. The number of mines grew from about thirty to ninety between the 1740s and the 1770s, with a workforce that grew more than sevenfold. Mine adventurers, cartels and monopoly dictated prices and drew in metropolitan and midlands finance. It is no accident that the first experimental steam pumping engines in Britain were used in Cornwall in copper and tin mines in the 1700s, and that the region became a centre for steam-engine development in mining after 1712. In 1733 Cornwall had at least five engines working in copper mines at a time when output was about 8,000 tons compared with the entire coal industry which had fewer than thirty and an output of 2.6 million tons. Boulton and Watt by 1780 had made and sold forty pumping engines for Cornish mines. By 1785 Boulton had shares in several of the Cornish copper mines; he was a lead player in the Cornish Metal Company and, with his close associates, had a controlling interest

---

[24] Harris (1992: 176–94, esp. 183, 192).
[25] Evans (2010: 38–9).

in the monopoly supply of this crucial metal of eighteenth-century manufacture. Boulton was not the only figure connecting investment in mining with innovatory manufacturing: entrepreneurs, and mining engineers such as the Trevithicks moved between Cornwall and south Wales.[26]

Atlantic markets for copper expanded rapidly into the 1770s, but were badly hit by the disruption of the American Revolution. Compensation came from growing East India Company demand for wrought copper, copper utensils and copper coinage. The part played by Boulton's Cornish enterprises at this stage of the development of steam power cannot be underestimated. James Watt came to Cornwall to supervise the erection of the first Boulton and Watt pumping engine in the region in September 1777. By the early 1780s Boulton was spending many months of the year in Cornwall, supervising the erection of the mine engines.[27] Boulton was also well aware of the wider potential of the steam engine, and by 1781 was pushing Watt into working on the rotative engine: 'the people in London, Manchester, and Birmingham are Steam Mill Mad . . . I think in the course of a Month or two we should determine to take out a patent for certain methods of procuring Rotative Motion from the . . . reciprocating Motion of the Fire Engine.'[28]

Boulton and Watt as well as other British steam engine manufacturers and engineers acquired new markets in the plantations providing parts and engineering for wind and water mills, and eventually for steam engines to power cane-crushing mills and refineries. Boulton and Watt sent 132 steam engines to the sugar plantations between 1803 and 1830. Lord Penrhyn (Richard Pennant) made contact with James Watt on one of his trips to England in 1786, writing: 'I wish much to have the pleasure of conversing with you on the subject of steam engines for Jamaica'.[29] James Mitchell of the Moreland estate in Vere had a steam engine by 1800 to power his sugar cane mill. Boulton and

[26] Hamilton (1926: 167, 171, 195). Also see Zahedieh, who cites forty Cornish orders for Boulton and Watt engines as well as thirty 'pirate' engines supplied, with fifty-two constructed by 1802. See Zahedieh (2021: 796–7); O'Sullivan (2023: 1–45, esp. 6–8).
[27] O'Sullivan (2023: 26, 31–6); Jones (2009: 80, 149).
[28] Schofield (1963: 333).
[29] Satchell (2010: 130–1).

Watt engines spread rapidly across the islands in the early nineteenth century.[30]

Iron

The growth and technological transformation of the British iron industry, often seen as central to the industrialization process, had its own close links to the slave trade and plantation business. Both contributed investment funds, while Atlantic trading was a major source of demand for iron goods. Atlantic markets took 63% of wrought iron exports in 1750 and 73% in 1770; the West Indies took around 28% and North America around 34% of British wrought iron and nails exported during each decade of the eighteenth century.[31] Cheap coal and suitable home-produced iron encouraged Britain's notable trade in nails and wrought iron. The official values of iron exports from England and Wales rose from £85,000 in 1700 to £400,000 in 1748, to more than double again by the early 1770s, reaching £1 million in 1791, and a level of £1.5 million in 1792, with more output from Scotland and Ireland added.[32]

Innovation in the industry did not significantly increase Atlantic trade in British bar iron until the second half of the eighteenth century, and especially at the end of the century, when iron puddling became a major success in increasing the malleability of the product. Prior to this, much of the iron used in British manufacturing and trading came from Sweden and Russia. The extent of Baltic-sourced 'voyage iron', bar iron traded on by British slave traders as currency to Africa, troubled British policymakers, who planned to outsource production of the required iron to their North American colonies. Iron produced in the Chesapeake by enslaved tree fellers, charcoal makers and ironworkers was, however, already mostly taken up by markets in the Thirteen Colonies and the Caribbean. The American Revolution ended any further possibilities.[33]

Britain's own iron production had many Atlantic world connections. A number of the great ironmasters came from mercantile backgrounds in

[30] Satchell (2010: 132–64).

[31] Zahedieh (2021: 786); Inikori (2002: 457, table 9.11).

[32] Harris (1988: 51–3); Evans (2005: 15–28).

[33] For discussion of the integration of the Baltic into Britain's Atlantic iron trade see Evans and Rydén (2018: 41–70; 2007: 157–73).

Table 6.2: Share of Atlantic markets in total quantity of British wrought iron and nails exported, 1700–1800.

	Total exports of wrought iron and nails (tons)	West Indies %	North America %	Southern Europe %
1700–20	1,639	28	34	14
1725–45	3,666	23	34	15
1750–70	9,594	29	34	9
1775–1800	15,201	27	24	12

Source: Derived from Inikori (2002: table 9.11, 457).

Bristol and London, their capital investment drawn from these sources. One-third of a sample of 16 iron entrepreneurs in 1788 and half of a sample of 35 in 1796 came from mercantile backgrounds. Six out of 25 iron entrepreneurs in south Wales in 1788 and 10 out of 25 in 1796 came from Bristol and London.[34] Even early on, Abraham Darby, well known for developing the coke smelting of iron, spent his earlier career connected first with the Bristol Brassworks, then in the copper-smelting works at Crew's Hole near Bristol. He moved on to Coalbrookdale in 1703, setting up his famous iron works and developing coke smelting; he found ready markets for his cast goods and pipe work among the Cornish engine makers. Darby's major investor was the Bristol merchant Thomas Goldney, who had made his fortune in shares in merchant and slaving vessels to the West Indies, and acquired a controlling interest in the works by 1718. Goldney was best known as a shareholder in Woodes Rogers' ships, the *Duke* and the *Duchess*, said to have rescued Alexander Selkirk (the model for Robinson Crusoe) from San Fernandez Island. Darby's works also produced manillas and brass objects sold in the slave trade.[35] Goldney's son, also Thomas, became Bristol agent for Coalbrookdale and held major shares in at least four other iron works, in brass and lead works and in several mines. He became a partner in one of Bristol's first banks, Goldney, Smith and Co., the origin of the National Westminster Bank.[36]

Anthony Bacon's story even more vividly illustrates these connections. Bacon was born in Whitehaven and was early involved in that port's

[34] Birch (1967: 282–3).
[35] Birch (1967: 61); Zahedieh (2021: 798).
[36] Morgan (2004b).

tobacco trade with the Chesapeake. Following the Seven Years War he won a contract for victualling garrisons in forts on the Senegalese coast that were ceded by France. Between 1768 and 1776 he and his partners won government contracts worth £67,000 to supply slaves to the West Indies to work on fortifications and harbours. About the same time he started taking out mineral leases in Merthyr Tydfil and followed the spread of coke smelting of iron to the south Wales coalfield in the 1750s. His giant works at Cyfarthfa, begun in the 1760s, were not the first in the region but they were the most technologically sophisticated. Bacon's wealth from his African/Caribbean contracts enabled him to invest lavish amounts of capital in transforming the technology of the iron industry in south Wales. He bought further smelting capacity and connected coal-fired refining with John Wilkinson's cannon founding technique to become the largest supplier of cannon to the Admiralty. When Bacon died in 1786 the Cyfarthfa Works were taken over by his former partner in the gun trade, Richard Crawshay. Crawshay developed and exploited another famed iron technology, Cort's puddling process. A later partner, William Brownrigg, devised a method of refining pig iron into malleable bars using mineral coal rather than charcoal. They thus pioneered the integration in a single enterprise of smelting and refining, both using mineral fuel. Crawshay's son, William, the 'uncrowned iron king', also had a merchant house in London, Crawshay, Routh and Moser, from which he financed and made the works' fortunes, and his own son became a 'rich West India merchant'.[37] By 1800 Cyfarthfa was both the largest and technically the most advanced iron works in the world.[38]

The Scottish Carron iron works founded near Falkirk in 1759 drew heavily on finance and expertise from the midlands through Samuel Garbett and John Roebuck and the Scottish merchant William Cadell. This large iron works established during the Seven Years War expanded on munitions and navy contracts. But the Scottish tobacco elite, and later the Scottish West India merchants, diversified readily into the industries of the Glasgow hinterland, including its iron industry. Cotton manufactories and sugar refineries were their most popular investments,

[37] Birch (1967: 77, 80).
[38] Evans (2010: 58–65).

but they also financed iron, mining, brewing and glassworks on the back of their profits from sugar plantations and the sugar trade.[39] Long before the Carron works a number of smaller iron works financed by Glasgow merchants produced for the West Indies trade. The Smithfield Iron Company in Glasgow, from 1732, produced nails, adzes, axes, hoes and spades for the plantations. This was among a number of iron works, such as the Clyde iron works in Glasgow's immediate hinterland. The partners of some of these works then went on in a co-partnership to establish the large Muirkirk and Omoa iron works (both built 1787), to produce bar iron and cast goods.[40]

Scottish iron depended heavily on the development of Scottish iron and coal mines; these in turn were often developed on the estates of 'improving' landlords repatriating their wealth from the plantations. James Dunlop drew on a fortune made in colonial trade to invest in mineral and coal in land near Glasgow. He invested in association with Andrew Houston, son of the founder of the West India House of Alexander Houston and Company, the greatest of the Scottish West India houses, and most powerful member of Glasgow's 'sugar aristocracy'. Andrew Stirling, together with another plantation trade inheritor, Andrew Buchanan, ran the Faskine colliery in the early 1790s. Another tobacco merchant, John Glassford, leased the Banton ironstone mines near Falkirk in 1774.[41] William Forbes, the London coppersmith who made his fortune in making sugar refining vessels, returned to his native Scotland in 1782, and on his estate in Callender, Stirlingshire, exploited coal resources, selling the output on to the neighbouring Carron iron works.[42]

Tobacco and sugar plantations and their trade not only financed a proportion of Scotland's development of heavy industry, but provided markets for its products. The Americas and the West Indies took only 25% of Scotland's exports in the 1770s, but this included not only the ubiquitous linens and herring, but all manner of iron goods; Scotland sent 657 tons of wrought iron goods to the British Atlantic colonies in 1771. This added to Scotland's rising export trade in cotton textiles and

[39] Hamilton (1963: 193–7); Hamilton (2005: 202–4); Devine (1976: 1–13).
[40] Hamilton (1963: 202, 204).
[41] Hamilton (1963: 211); Hamilton (2005: 84); see also Devine (2015a: 225–45).
[42] Zahedieh (2021: 804).

to its largest exports at the time: colonial re-exports of tobacco, sugar, raw cotton and rum.[43]

The iron goods produced in the northeast and the midlands, and in Scotland, varied from heavy castings to holloware, the full range of ironmongery and hand-wrought nails: all expanded to meet the dynamic growth of markets not just in the colonies of North America, but in the West Indies and South America. Chapter 4 investigated technological innovation in plantation tools. It was small workshops in the Black Country and elsewhere that mass produced these hand tools for planting and harvesting plantation crops. Ambrose Crowley's iron works near Newcastle had 54 hoe shops with 162 hammer men who turned out 11,000 hoes a week for Virginia, the Carolinas and the West Indies. Crowley's hoes were ranked first in the hierarchy of plantation hoes; the Carron company in Scotland produced the second in the rankings. Another classic product was knives for cutting sugar cane; steel blanks for these were made, for 1½d a dozen in wages, '12 inches long with both the edge proper and the back steeled and sharpened and provided with a socket'. Angerstein found them being manufactured at Crowley's iron works near Newcastle and at the Brockmill factory near Wigan as well as in the midlands. Angerstein also visited Crowley's Winlaton manufactory, which produced nails, hinges, fire tongs and 'chains of all kinds'. Three ships were constantly occupied in transporting the goods from nearby Swalwell to London.[44]

Putting-out ironmongers in the west midlands organized production of similar products in the myriad small iron works and forges of the Black Country. Other great iron capitalists of early to mid-eighteenth-century Shropshire and Staffordshire typically employed 300 to 500 workers in highly developed capitalist enterprises. The rich among them became bankers, including John Barker, Thomas Attwood and Richard Spooner.[45] The west midlands metalworkers had access via tributaries of the River Severn that reached to Wolverhampton, on to Bristol and from there to rapidly growing markets in the West Indies and the American colonies. Even long before the canals that made the transportation of heavy iron goods to the ports much easier, it was well known in Barbados

[43] Hamilton (1963: 264–5).

[44] Evans (2012: 81, 84); Berg and Berg (2001: 262, 295, 265–6).

[45] Court (1938: 177–203).

that 'nails of all sorts with hooks, hinges and clamps of iron are to be had at Birmingham in Staffordshire much cheaper than in London'.[46] By the eighteenth century Atlantic colonies took four-fifths of the total export of nails and half the export of wrought iron. Ships left Bristol every week for Virginia, Barbados or Jamaica with nails, hoes, bills, scythes and other wrought iron work. The midlands metal manufactures by this stage were highly diversified and specialized. At Willenhall 138 locksmiths produced nineteen different types of lock. Sketchley's Directory in 1770 listed over seventy different metal trades in Wolverhampton, Walsall, Bilston, Willenhall and Dudley, including a 'Negro collar maker' in Wolverhampton.[47] 'Metal instruments of domination' manufactured in England also included 'the thumbscrew', the 'iron necklace', the iron ring 'boots' and 'spurs, the chain, the padlock'.[48]

Guns

Gun manufacture has a classic historical connection with the slave trade. Its rapidly growing concentration by the beginning of the eighteenth century within the Birmingham metal trades contributed to a special regional metals-based industrialization. While the Board of Ordnance and the London-based gun sector with its proof house had controlled the pre-industrial manufacture of armaments, the centre of the industry shifted northwards in the later seventeenth century. Guns became important commodities to exchange for the enslaved in the rapidly advancing trade to West Africa. This coincided with the end of the Royal African Company's monopoly and with changing warfare methods along the Gold Coast.[49] The trade in slaves by private merchants made for new opportunities for private gun merchants and manufacturers based in Birmingham. Formerly a trade led by the Dutch, the West African market was dominated by the English by the 1750s.

Birmingham did not get its own proof house until 1813 and was forced to send a proportion of its guns to London for the Woolwich

---

[46] Rowlands (1975: 127).

[47] Rowlands (1975: 127, 131–2, 180–1).

[48] Letter from an Antiguan resident, 1787, quoted in Robinson (1987: 122–40, esp. 125).

[49] Richards (1980: 43–59, esp. 45).

proof house, where at least 20% were rejected. Its manufacturers engaged in a long dispute with the Board of Ordnance and the London gunmakers, but the Africa trade provided the opportunity for the rapid rise of major gun manufacturers and merchants, like Farmer and Galton (who later became bankers), Alexander Champion, George Hayley and John Whately. All kept large warehouses, gathering their arms through outsourcing contracts in a concentrated locale: 'the gunmaking quarter' of Birmingham. Guns passed through many stages of manufacture in the separate households and workshops of highly specialized craftsmen.[50] The output thus produced was staggering: Farmer and Galton provided 25–30,000 guns a year for the West African market in 1754. Whately had 50,000 guns in his warehouse in 1750. It has been estimated that, in the period 1750–1807, there was a minimum import per annum into West Africa of 283,999 guns with the standard slaving vessel carrying 610 guns. Guns and gunpowder made up a third of the value of cargoes to New Calabar and the Windward Coast.[51]

Whately argued to the Council of Trade in Birmingham in 1788:

> According to the best calculation I have been able to make on the subject, the gun trade, in which I am considerably engaged, affords subsistence to between four and five thousand persons, who, in time of peace, are almost entirely supported by the African trade, a business so very different to any other, that their whole existence may be said to depend on it.[52]

There has been much debate among African historians over the 'gun–slave' cycle, one of the concepts underpinning the case made by slavery abolitionists. Abolitionists condemned a trade in poor-quality, unproofed Birmingham guns made by increasingly degraded and poorly paid subcontracted labour. Historians of Africa, however, have elaborated the differing demands of African warfare, not just in militarized slave-exporting states, but in communities seeking protection from slave raids.[53] Nor were the guns supplied by Birmingham as well as by

---

[50] Allen (1966: 17).

[51] Inikori (1977: 349); Richards (1980: 43, 45–9).

[52] Cited in Inikori (2002: 339–68, 458).

[53] See Thornton (1999: 132–51); Satia (2018: 184–90); Richardson (1979: 49–51); Inikori, (1977: 351); Richards (1980: 44–7); Shumway (2011).

Liverpool and London all low-quality muskets. African gun merchants imported many different types of guns, and these had to meet a quality standard recognized by them. The taste for different types of guns changed over time and place, and the guns also functioned as a currency. There was a shift from matchlock muskets early in the eighteenth century to more reliable flintlock muskets. Asante and the Gold Coast sought the more accurate long-barrelled musket first from the Danes, then from Birmingham's quickly imitated versions. Farmer and Galton traded in eight different types of better-quality guns, sought out for prestige and power.[54]

This quickly evolving African slave-based market for guns also generated innovation in organization and technology. The gun sector, often dismissed as a technological backwater weighted down by the restrictions of craft traditions, in fact drew on the significant knowledge spillovers of the allied hardware trades in the town, improving gun barrels, applying the town's brassworking expertise in gunlocks and fittings, developing its own unofficial proofing system, and responding nimbly to large orders suddenly placed by slave traders. Farmer and Galton met orders for 15,900 guns for the African market in 1772; one order alone from Liverpool was for 6,410 guns.[55]

In addition to guns there was gunpowder. To the long-established gunpowder mills in southeast England five companies added several new powder mills and magazines outside of Bristol and Liverpool between the 1720s and 1760s. All focused on supplying the slave trade. All were capital-intensive and drew capital from Atlantic merchants and trade, and all produced the specific types and grades of gunpowder demanded on the African coast. The companies were successful and long-lasting, shifting their markets after slave abolition into explosives for mining and the wider African trade.[56]

The gunmakers' trade included significant supplies to the East India Company and to other European colonial powers for their slave trades. Farmer and Galton exported especially to the Portuguese, notably Angola muskets, and to the French, filling regular orders from slave merchants

---

[54] Richards (1980: 53–5); Satia (2018: 188–90).
[55] Richards (1980: 53–5).
[56] Radburn (2023).

in Nantes, Bordeaux and Dunkirk.[57] Gun merchants also traded direct to Africa, to the West Indies and southern American colonies, and some invested in the plantations. There was close integration in the trade to Africa of the major copper and brass manufacturers and the gun trade. Traders in Montserrat paid for their guns with shipments of sugar, cotton and indigo; in 1757 Galton received sugar and a bag of silver from a South Carolina customer.[58]

Copper and iron masters, metalworkers and gunmakers all sought out and gained lucrative contracts with the navy. Thus the navy and the state also underpinned their markets. This was nowhere more true than in the West Indies. Though the navy's key priority in the later eighteenth century was the defence of Britain in home waters, it was still the case that the West Indies accounted for more naval ship days than the Mediterranean, North America and the East Indies. Britain demonstrated the strategic value of the West Indies in its deployment of ships, men and resources, including guns and cannon. In 1781 21% of the navy's ships and 26% of its manpower (25,600 men) were deployed in the Caribbean, far higher than anywhere else in the Empire. Only 34 more ships and 2,600 more men were deployed in home waters.[59]

Conclusion

Britain's heavy mining and smelting industries, coal, iron and copper, in England, Wales and Scotland, were stimulated by the demands of Atlantic markets and frequently drew on capital derived from sugar and tobacco plantations and, in some cases, from the slave trade. Large-scale enterprises demanding long-term investment in fixed capital and infrastructure transformed the industrial landscapes of south Wales, southern Scotland, the west midlands and the northeast of England. West India merchants and banks, based in London, Bristol and Glasgow, made substantial investment across these industries and regions. The export trade in iron was closely tied to Britian's mercantilist hold in the Caribbean and the American colonies before the American

---

[57] Richards (1980: 43).
[58] Satia (2018: 91, 190, 196).
[59] See Rodger (1986: 352; 1998: 169–71); Williams (1938/2014: 38).

Revolution.[60] Sugar refining and, later, copper sheathing rescued the copper industry from its doldrums in the early seventeenth century and helped to stimulate the prescient industrial development of the Swansea Valley. The lighter metal industries, including guns, innovated, specialized and expanded in line with growing Atlantic and slave trade demands. Regional and local specialization and concentration added to the accumulation of commercial and technical knowledge. Expanding orders placed by slave traders, plantation managers, ship owners and the navy, in addition to the specialized demands of the northern American colonies, were a major force in the innovative development of the mining and metalwares industries that lay at the heart of the wider industrialization process.

[60] Harris (1988: 51–3); Evans (2005: 15–28).

CHAPTER 7

Textile revolutions

Huge imports of raw cotton from the slave-plantation states of the USA enabled Britain to become the leading world producer of cotton cloth in the nineteenth century. By the early 1820s, cotton goods accounted for 48% of British exports. But the links between Britain's textile industries and slavery started at least a century earlier. New Atlantic raw material supplies – cotton from the Caribbean colonies, Atlantic dyestuffs (indigo, logwood, cochineal) and Iberian wool stimulated expansion and innovation across the textile sector in the eighteenth century. At the same time, changing European tastes in favour of lighter and brighter textiles were joined by new demands from fast-growing transatlantic and West African markets. Humid-tropical and warm temperate climates, as well as specific needs and tastes, buttressed demand for light, colourful wool, silk and linen fabrics, as well as 'cottons',[1] and for an array of fashionable textile accessories and haberdashery from handkerchiefs and ribbons to lace and hosiery. New demands and imported raw materials together spurred innovation in the commerce, design, colour and finishing of cloths, and in the use of mixed fibres.[2] This changed the products, markets, organization, location and technologies in most branches of the industry over the course of the long eighteenth century.

Textiles accounted for up to two-thirds of all commodities traded from Europe to Africa and more than 50% of goods traded from Europe to the West Indies and North America in the eighteenth century.[3] In the 1680s half the value of British exports to the West Indies and almost two-thirds of exports to North America and Africa comprised clothing and textiles. Silk then accounted for 25% of the value of British

---

[1] Until the last two decades of the eighteenth century domestically produced 'cottons' were most often made from other fibres or fibres mixed with cotton, particularly cotton wefts with linen warps.
[2] Riello (2013: 110–59; 187–21); Styles (2020; 2022b).
[3] Riello (2022: 92).

Atlantic textile exports.[4] Silk was a relatively small industry in Britain, an expensive luxury trade, centred on London. But silk exports were of high value, and silk 'waste' and silk threads were used in mixed fabrics and in ribbons and trimmings, adding to the range of colour and texture in goods made for fashion-conscious markets.[5] There were also mass exports of woollens, cottons, lace, linens, ready-made clothing, stockings, hats, wigs and haberdashery throughout the eighteenth century.[6] The demands and needs of West African consumers, colonists, enslaved and First Nations people were all important in determining the direction of the industry.[7]

Much of Atlantic demand for colourful cottons in the first half of the eighteenth century was satisfied by re-exports of Asian cottons in a trade that linked the slave-based Atlantic system to the Indian Ocean via the activities of the East India Company and the London entrepôt.[8] Between 1721 and 1774, in order to protect British worsted and silk manufacturers, the Calico Acts banned Indian all-cotton printed fabrics from British markets, and imports of plain calicoes and muslins were heavily taxed. Almost all coloured cotton fabrics were also banned, including Indian checks and stripes. But there were no obstacles to supplying these goods to Africa or the colonies. Both regions provided substantial and buoyant markets for re-exported Asian textiles but also, increasingly, for the varied British textiles that attempted to imitate them.[9] Over the course of the eighteenth century, aided by protective tariffs, improvements in quality and product ranges and, eventually, by technological innovations, British textile products were to a large degree substituted for Asian cloths in both export and domestic markets.[10]

[4] Zahedieh (2010: 263–4).
[5] Styles (2022a); Styles (2022b: 48).
[6] Riello (2022: 100–14); Davis (1979: 15); Smith (1998); Zahedieh (2010: 260–70); DuPlessis (2016); Breen (2004); Haggerty (2023: chapter 7).
[7] Riello (2022: 91).
[8] See table 2.4.
[9] See discussion below and table 7.2.
[10] This accelerated after the 1750s. Joseph Inikori was the first to emphasize the role of slavery and the Atlantic trade in import substitution (IS) industrialization, which also involved export substitution: Inikori (2002: 476–86); Inikori (2015: 239–42). Riello (2013: 147–51). For the structure of tariff protection that supported this see O'Brien, Griffiths and Hunt (1991: 395–423). The substitution was only partial in African

Table 7.1: Proportions of exports of British domestically produced wool, cotton and linen textiles going to the Americas and West Africa, % of total values.

Years	Wool Textiles	'Cottons'	Linens
1699–1701	6.1	80.0	Not available
1722–4	10.1	83.3	88
1752–4	9.5	94.0	90
1772–4	27.4	79.6	92
1784–6	26.1	57.2	83
1794–6	45.1	69.2	89

Sources and note: The percentages are three-year annual averages. Figures for 1699–1774 are for England and Wales, those of 1784–96 are for Great Britain. Derived from Inikori (2002: 414, 426, 448), compiled from Davis (1962: 120) and Davis (1979: 94–101). 'Cottons' include all cloths described as such, including Indian all-cottons printed in Britain.

The impact of Atlantic demand: linen

Export-oriented linen industries in south Lancashire, Scotland and Ireland supplied sailcloth, twine and durable fabrics for work-wear, gradually supplanting European sources. Linen use also grew as a component in mixed-fibre cloths, especially cotton-linens. Linen warps with wefts of other fibres, especially cotton, enabled production of loom-patterned checks and stripes that provided a cheap, lower-quality substitute for Indian all-cotton checks and stripes, popular in both domestic and Atlantic markets. Linen relied on imported flax and ready-spun yarn from Ireland and northern Europe; these came to rank alongside sugar as the most significant import into Britain in the second half of the eighteenth century.[11]

Cheap, undyed linens called 'Osnabrigs' or 'Osnaburgs' (after the Osnabruck area in Germany from which many originally came) were made in Britain, largely for slave clothing. State-sponsored expansion of

markets (Indian cottons remained as much in demand as their British substitutes) but almost total in the Americas by the 1780s: Riello (2022: 96–8, 118–23, 136–9); Kobayashi (2019: 9–11); Morgan (2000: 89): Inikori (1989: 343–79, 354–5, 369); Maw (2010: 734–68).

[11] Zahedieh (2014: 405).

the linen industry in Fife, Angus and Perthshire, and especially around Dundee, may have employed 230,000 men, women and children by 1780 with 90% of output going to America and the West Indies. Colonial demands were also important for Irish linen producers, whose exports were confined by the Navigation Acts to British shippers and ships.[12] The USA and the West Indies together took well over 80% of total British domestically produced linen exports in the 1780s and 1790s.[13] Almost the same value of manufactured linens from central Europe and Ireland was re-exported to Atlantic markets over the century.[14]

Sailcloth manufacture employed large numbers of rural workers over areas of Lancashire and Somerset. Warrington developed a major industry to satisfy Royal Navy contracts, drawing linen warp yarns and flax from Ireland and the Baltic. In 1781 21% of the navy's ships and 26% of its manpower (25,600 men) were deployed in the Caribbean, far higher than anywhere else in the Empire.[15] The proportion of British merchant shipping in trade with the West Indies and the Americas was also high: over 40% in the later eighteenth century with a further 15% employed in trade with West Africa.[16] The fortunes of the linen sailcloth industry were thus closely connected with the slave-based Atlantic trading system. One Warrington sailcloth manufacturer around 1750 was said to employ 5,000 people in domestic and workshop premises.[17]

The impact of Atlantic demand: woollens

Wool textiles were the most important of the textile industries of Britain until after 1800. A third of exports went outside Europe by the early 1770s. By 1794–6 over 60% of production was exported, most to the Americas and West Africa.[18] Export products included durable plain cloths geared to slave clothing but, above all, new bright woven designs, especially worsteds, for the middling and higher end of the market.

[12] Devine (2015a: 235–6); Durie (1979: 148); Nash (1985: 331, 350).
[13] Davis (1979: 94–7, table 41).
[14] Inikori (2002: 426).
[15] Williams (2016: 38).
[16] Inikori (2002: 280).
[17] Walton (1989: 41–68).
[18] Davis (1979: 21); Inikori (2002: 414); Hudson (1986: 155–67).

'Welsh plains', Yorkshire 'Penistones' and 'Kendal cloths' from Westmorland were all repurposed as basic fabrics for slave clothing. 'Welsh plains' were preferred among planters especially in the North American plantation colonies (later the southern states of the USA) through to the 1830s.[19] They were produced by thousands of otherwise underemployed rural domestic workers. Some Welsh plains were also traded to West Africa. In 1716 8,600 yards of Welsh plains were sold to the RAC by the London merchant Samuel Monck.[20] Plains destined for West Africa were dyed bright colours in London by contractors employed by the RAC but were often unravelled and rewoven by their purchasers, to produce African patterns for ceremonial and elite dress.[21] The commercial manufacture of Welsh plains for slave use gradually undermined the old Drapers' monopoly of the trade via Shrewbury and London, in favour of west-coast Atlantic ports. In the later eighteenth century Liverpool merchants and their agents extended their credit and control over the domestic manufacture of Welsh plains, reducing independent weavers to dependent wage labourers and collecting their products for export via Liverpool.[22]

The transformative power of transatlantic demands on the wool textile industry was even stronger in Yorkshire. Yorkshire woollens, particularly worsteds, found favour with white settlers, especially in the mainland American colonies. The African market was smaller but also buoyant: between the mid-1760s and early 1780s the value of British woollens exported to Africa was almost as high as the value of British 'cottons' exported there.[23] As in Wales, Yorkshire merchants increasingly bypassed the domestic and export trade through London. Liverpool had become the major port of shipment for all textiles from the north by the early 1790s, at the expense of both London and Hull.[24] Merchants in Manchester as well as in Yorkshire, dealing in 'cottons' as well as

[19] For the takeover of the US slave cloth market from the 1820s and 1830s by North American manufacturers see Rockman (2018: 170–94).

[20] Evans (2010: 47).

[21] Kriger (2009: 105–26); Evans (2010: 47–8).

[22] Evans (2010: 52); Jenkins (1969: 126–7).

[23] Kobayashi (2019: 10).

[24] Wilson (1971); Maw (2010: 734–68); Hudson (1986: 155–81); Kobayashi (2019: 10).

wool textiles, dislodged London exporters from their leading role in the trade. They did this by working directly with their US principals and responding to their needs, by specializing in textiles rather than consignments of mixed manufactures and by using international commercial travellers and pattern books.[25] Northern textile merchants in the later eighteenth century profited from improvements and innovation in local textile finishing and printing, and from new regional banking and discounting services, which had earlier existed only in London.[26]

Foreign wools (from Spain, Portugal and Germany) came increasingly via Bristol and Liverpool rather than London. Spanish and Portuguese raw wool imports into Liverpool were exchanged for exported manufactures suitable for Iberian re-exports to their own Atlantic colonies. In 1810 John Jowitt and Sons, woolstaplers of Bradford, were buying Spanish wool from half a dozen suppliers in Bristol.[27] By the 1830s Liverpool had a wool brokerage and auction system, geared increasingly to high-quality southern-hemisphere merino wools. These mainly came from Australia but some came from South Africa.[28] £1 million pounds was paid in compensation when 38,000 enslaved workers were freed in the Cape Colony in 1833. This money helped to launch a sizeable wool export trade which supplied the factories of Yorkshire, alongside wools from New South Wales. The share of wool (by value) in Cape Colony exports reached 62% by 1850.[29] From the early nineteenth century cloths made with imported merino wool wefts and machine-spun cotton warps created a new synergy between the wool textile and the cotton textile sectors of the north.[30]

Atlantic demand for wool textiles pushed the Yorkshire industry into some new products. By the 1750s a trade in worsteds of a strong blue shade was developed for the Africa trade by the manufacturers and merchants of Halifax Parish in Yorkshire. They 'were packed in

[25] Maw (2010); Smail (1999: 113–32).

[26] Smail (1999: 138); Maw (2010: 745–61); Hudson (1986: 217–34).

[27] Hudson (1986: 118–19).

[28] The auction system was fully developed in Liverpool with the advent of mass imports from Australia after the 1830s but facilitated by the fact that Liverpool was already central to the importation of fibres of all descriptions.

[29] Keegan (1996). We are grateful to Chris Evans for pointing out this source.

[30] Hudson (1986: 131–2); Hudson (2009).

pieces of 12 and a half yards in length, and wrapped in oilcloth painted with negroes and elephants to captivate the natives'.[31] Information flows between buyers in North America, the Caribbean and Africa and their suppliers dictated preferences for particular colours, designs and qualities. In the 1780s Daniel Glover, a Leeds merchant, supplied his brother, a merchant in New York, with a pattern card that included over 300 swatches of different colours and designs of broadcloth.[32] Robert Heaton of Haworth followed several of his contemporaries in dramatically changing the types of cloth he produced in the 1780s in response to Atlantic demands, conveyed via northern merchants, as well as to growing domestic markets. In the 1770s he made only shalloons but a decade later he was making denims, lastings, rolls, plain and ribbed deroons, ribbon figures, stars and posts, and russells in different grades.[33]

At the other end of the spectrum, putting-out clothiers around Barnsley mass-manufactured cheap durable 'Penistones', suitable for coats and blankets for the enslaved. The Crossley family of Penistone held estates in Jamaica in the eighteenth century. In 1833 Luke Thomas Crossley and his family were major claimants of emancipation compensation, receiving over £12,631 for 696 slaves on several Jamaican plantations.[34] In 1830 Crossley had interests in textile mills, print and dye works in Leeds.[35]

As more British wool textile production came to be concentrated in west Yorkshire (20% at the beginning of the century, growing to about a third of national production in 1772 and to 60% by 1800), the proportion of west Yorkshire woollens and worsteds going abroad rose: from 40% in 1700 to 72% in 1771–2 (amounting to £3.5 million per annum).[36] The proportion of Yorkshire's textile exports going to Europe may have declined to 30% or less by the 1780s. The value added in the

---

[31] Pennant (1776: vol. 3, 362), quoted in James (1857: 290).

[32] Smail (1999: 75–132).

[33] Smail (1999: 121). For the richness of Caribbean and mainland colonial textile demands see: DuPlessis (2016); Breen (2004); Baumgarten (2012); Haggerty (2023: chapter 7).

[34] https://www.ucl.ac.uk/lbs/search/.

[35] https://www.ucl.ac.uk/lbs/commercial/view/2146006233; *London Gazette*, 4 May 1830, 896.

[36] Deane (1957: 207–23, esp. 215, 220); Wilson (1973: 228–30, n15).

wool textile sector remained greater than in cottons until after 1800, and as late as 1831 the sector had an output value two and a half times that of iron and steel.[37] The bulk of output of this major industry went to Atlantic markets.[38]

The impact of Atlantic demand: cotton

Atlantic demand had the greatest impact on the cotton sector. British output of 'cottons' rose from £600,000 in 1760 to £5.4 million in 1784–6 (annual average) to £11.1 million in 1798–1800 and £30 million in 1815–17. West Africa and the Americas together absorbed between 79 and 94% of total British 'cotton' exports between 1700 and 1774. Between 1784 and 1806 more than half of cotton textile exports was sent to Atlantic markets, including West Africa. Spain and Portugal took additional exports of cottons, much of which was re-exported to Spanish America.[39] When south Lancashire experienced massive growth of cotton production in the early nineteenth century, stimulated by technological innovation, the bulk of the industry's exports continued to be directed to Atlantic markets.

Table 7.2 gives a breakdown of the values and shares of British-made textile exports (of all kinds) and Asian re-exports (almost all cottons) in different Atlantic market zones in 1771, distinguishing between 'plantation colonies' and those with mainly 'free' and settler populations. At this date 'plantation colonies' absorbed 43% of domestically produced textile exports. If we add the textile trade to Africa, it is clear that the slave trade and slave-based British colonies together accounted for most of Britain's Atlantic textile exports. Some of the demand from the northern colonies of the mainland was also underpinned by slavery, as these colonies (later the northern states of the USA) were partly dependent upon the sale of provisions and shipping services to the southern slave states and (even more so before 1776) to the British Caribbean for the currency to purchase consumer-goods imports.[40]

---

[37] Crafts (1985: 22).

[38] See estimates of Thomas Wolrich, Leeds merchant, 1772, quoted in Bischoff (1842/1968: 187–9); Hudson (1986: 66, 156).

[39] Inikori (2002: 436); Pearce (2007: 194–202 esp. 197).

[40] Harley (2015: 171–2) suggests that more than 50% of trade income of the northern

Domestically produced textiles far exceeded re-exported textiles in African as well as transatlantic markets by 1771.[41] The population figures in Table 7.2 demonstrate that although the market for basic clothing for almost 861,000 enslaved workers was extensive and important, the thriving white settler population, numbering almost 2 million (doubling in the USA by 1800), with much more varied sartorial demands, was clearly the main stimulus behind British textile markets in America.[42]

As early as the 1750s cottons accounted for 43% of all cargoes to West Africa and 63% of all textiles traded there. Cotton exports to Africa increased twenty-two-fold over the century compared with woollen exports (four-fold) and linen exports (3.4-fold). The African market was sophisticated, regionally varied, competitive and already used to Indian imports from the trans-Saharan route operating long before the transatlantic slave trade. In the 1750s 62% of cotton exports to Africa from Britain were from Asia; by the 1790s this had fallen to 54% as British cottons became more competitive, but the total value of the trade had also risen more than seven-fold.[43] Demand was driven by tastes for colourful and geometric patterns. The taste for checks and stripes, also popular in the Americas, placed pressure on the industry in Britain to improve the quality of such loom-patterned cloths by increasing the amount and type of cotton they contained so that they would take dyes better.[44]

American as well as African textile consumers developed preferences that were often distinct from European tastes. By the 1750s cotton handkerchiefs and bandanas were far more popular in New England, Pennsylvania, Virginia and parts of the Caribbean than in Europe, for example.[45] Turkey-red dye, incorporating French techniques, was introduced in

---

colonies came from exports plus the provision of shipping and mercantile services for the West Indies in 1768–72. See also Kimball (2016); Pellizzari 2020).

[41] Although Indian cotton re-exports still accounted for more than 50% of all cottons arriving in West Africa from Britain. Kobayashi (2019: 10).

[42] O'Shaughnessy (2000: 9); Riello (2022: 19); Smith (1998: 676–708); DuPlessis (2016); see also Breen (2004).

[43] Riello (2022); Kobayashi (2019: 81–126; 165–93).

[44] Styles (2022b: 52–5).

[45] Riello (2022: 96–9, 108, 114); Inikori (2002: 427–51); Kobayashi (2019: 53–63; 81–153).

Table 7.2: British domestic textile exports and Asian textile re-exports to British colonies in the Americas and to Africa, 1771, by value and %, and colonial populations, *c.*1770.

	British colonies in the Americas*	Mainland: 13 colonies	Mainland: 8 northern colonies	Mainland: 5 southern plantation colonies	West Indies plantation colonies	All British plantation colonies	Africa
British-made textiles	£2,291,354 (100%)	£1,959,434 (86%)	£1,311,596 (57%)	£647,838 (28%)	£311,920 (14%)	£979,758 (43%)	£270,635 (Africa: Americas 1:8.5)
South and East Asian textiles	£176,909 (100%)	£155,433 (88%)	£123,575 (70%)	£31,858 (18%)	£21,476 (12%)	£53,334 (30%)	£168,106 (Africa: Americas 1:1.05)
Total population	2,540,619 (100%)	2,090.619 (82%)	1,096,185 (43%)	994,434 (39%)	450,000 (18%)	1,444,434 (57%)	
Enslaved population	860,742 (100%)	460,742 (54%)	49,546 (6%)	411,196 (48%)	400,000 (46%)	811,196 (94%)	

*13 mainland colonies plus West Indies.
Sources: The National Archives CUST 3/71. We are grateful to Karolina Hutkova, John Styles and Giorgio Riello for the use of these data, and John Styles for assembling them. Population figures from O'Shaughnessy (2000: 9); Berlin (2003: table 1).

Glasgow in the 1780s partly to meet these demands.[46] First Nations people in the riverine and Great Lakes area had pronounced tastes for blue, red and black woollens, flowered serges and colourful striped calicoes. A surviving sample book of Benjamin and John Bower of Manchester from 1771 contains 500 samples of 'cotton' cloths going to Africa and the Americas, with a preponderance of fashionable and complicated checks and stripes for both markets.[47] Atlantic consumers were as articulate as their European counterparts, if not more so, and they readily purchased British-made substitutes for Indian cottons, as these improved in quality. The substitution accelerated in the middle decades of the century, when the supply of Indian cloths was unstable and their prices relatively high.[48] These circumstances created incentives to mechanize spinning.

[46] Mullen (2022: 276–7); https://glasgowmuseumsslavery.co.uk/2019/05/09/turkey-red -and-the-slave-economy/.
[47] Riello (2022: 99, 112).
[48] Styles (2022b: 51); Riello (2022: 123).

The impact of Atlantic supply: cotton

Alongside Atlantic demand, Atlantic raw materials played a crucial role in driving the transformation of the British cotton industry. Caribbean raw cotton imports exceeded those from the Levant from the 1710s, partly the result of a 1660 tariff of 4d per lb imposed upon cotton from outside the British colonies. Its use expanded rapidly from the 1740s. By 1777–9 Atlantic cotton imports were over three times those arriving from the Levant (see table 7.3).[49] Dominica, Grenada and Jamaica accounted for over 65% of such imports before the 1780s. For a crucial decade, between 1791 and 1801, finest-quality slave-grown Brazilian raw cotton accounted for 40% of imports, via a re-export trade from Lisbon. Supplies from Britain's own West Indies colonies remained dominant into the nineteenth century, with increased amounts coming from captured French and Dutch plantation possessions, particularly Demerara, Surinam and the Grenadines. Imports of cotton from the southern USA were negligible before 1800. Only after 1820 did the US share rise above 70% and consistently thereafter provide between 50 and 90% of British raw cotton imports.[50]

British cotton spinning, well before 1750, had developed a unique production system, geared to the quality of Atlantic raw cotton supply, as well as to rising demand especially for yarn-dyed checks and stripes, and for plain cloths that would take colourfast printing. This system differed markedly from the rest of Europe and created a propitious environment for spinning innovation. Soft yet strong and long-stapled Atlantic cotton (a strain of *Gossypium Barbadense*), which had first been developed by generations of Amerindians, facilitated the drive to produce higher-quality yarns in which the preparatory processes were vital.[51] Cotton was washed with soap, carded with specialist flexible cards, then loosely 'spun' into rovings, which in turn were spun more finely. The coarser,

[49] Wadsworth and Mann (1931/1968: 520–21).
[50] Olmstead and Rhode (2018: 1–17, figures 2, 4); Riello (2013: 202–3); Pereira (2018: 919–48, esp. 925). For details on the distribution of cotton exports and imports from the individual islands see Pereira (2018: table 6, 943, table 7, 944, 947); Rydén (2013: 539–70).
[51] Russell (2011: 103–31).

Table 7.3: Sources of British raw cotton imports % and totals in lbs, 1698–1780.

Year	Levant	West Indies	Misc. Europe and Africa	Total lbs (%)	Re-exports as % of imports
1697–9	37%	57%	6%	2,615,082 (100%)	18%
1717–19	30%	70%	<1%	5,604,553 (100%)	16%
1737–9	21%	78%	<1%	6,462,161 (100%)	6%
1757–9	17%	65%	18%*	7,482,896 (100%)	20%
1767–9	24%	73%	2%	12,159,748 (100%)	6%
1777–9	22%	67%	11%+	19,473,798 (100%)	9%

* 94% of the 1757–9 total came from Prizes seized, i.e. captured ships.
+ 73% of the 1777–9 total came from Prizes.
The weight of cotton imported via Prizes seized in other years listed here was none or negligible.
Source: Wadsworth and Mann (1968: 520–1).

shorter-stapled and cheaper Levant raw cotton would not have repaid the cost of the British preparatory processes.[52]

Carefully prepared *Barbadense* cotton was ideal as weft in the higher-quality cotton/linen mixes produced in Lancashire, such as Blackburn Greys, which were produced to be printed with colour-fast dyes in imitation of Indian products. By the 1760s it was estimated that Blackburn Greys (a new product that had not existed before 1700) accounted for 18% of Lancashire textile output. Yarn-dyed loom-patterned, as well as printed, 'cottons', made with wefts of *Barbadense* cotton and linen warps, also had a much better finish than cloths using coarser raw cotton.[53]

The French cotton industry (principally in Normandy and especially Rouen) also began to use Caribbean cotton after the mid-1730s. Cotton was cultivated in Saint-Domingue as well as in Martinique and Guadeloupe, but the French suffered severe interruptions of supply during the eighteenth-century wars, and Levant cotton remained as important as Atlantic supplies. There was also a dramatic *rise* in its use in the 1780s, as it was purchased in return for the French wool textiles that

[52] Styles (2020: 9, 25–6).
[53] Styles (2020: 16–18).

dominated Ottoman markets.[54] In contrast, it was estimated that 82% of raw cotton used in Lancashire was from the Caribbean as early as the 1760s. A growing proportion of the Atlantic cotton used in Britain was imported via Liverpool. This helped to set the Lancashire cotton industry on an innovative path, while its more limited adoption in France was a factor inhibiting an equivalent development there.[55]

New World cotton and technological innovation

Atlantic cotton made a difference not only to the quality and type of fabric produced, but also to the mechanization of spinning. Hargreaves' spinning jenny was introduced in 1764/5 specifically to aid the production of Blackburn Greys. The preparatory processes used on *Barbadense* cotton produced rovings that the jenny was able to handle. Without these processes and the long-stapled strength of *Barbadense* cotton, it is doubtful whether the jenny would have been developed or widely adopted at this time.[56] Arkwright's water frame (patented 1769) likewise relied on sharply increased supplies of *Barbadense* cotton, applied in this case to the mechanization of warp spinning where its longer staple worked to achieve the required twist.[57] Hargreaves' jenny produced yarn suitable only for wefts. The Arkwright machine produced a high twist yarn suitable for cotton warps. This technology enabled mass production of cloths with 'cotton both ways' (warp and weft), cloths that were well suited to printing. Aided by the 1774 repeal of the Calico Act of 1721, which prevented the use and sale of domestically produced all-cotton cloth in England (as well as such imported cloth), the water frame allowed the cotton printing industry of the northwest to take off. Before the Arkwright invention, textile printing, whether on plain

[54] Styles (2020: 1–43).

[55] Styles (2020).

[56] The shortage and cost of spinning labour also played a part in encouraging labour-saving innovation, especially its timing and location, but the nature of Britain's raw cotton supply was likely the key factor: Styles (2020).

[57] The role of biological innovation via plant breeding, on the part of Amerindians in particular, and its implications for inventions such as the frame, is emphasized by Russell (2011: 103–31), and in the later US plantation context by Olmstead and Rhode (2008).

imported Indian calicoes or on British-made mixed cloths, was almost entirely a London industry.[58]

All-cotton fabrics produced with mechanically spun wefts and warps solved the problem of producing cloths that could take washable printing dyes; they could now compete better with Indian re-exports. This was a giant step in export and import substitution. As North America was the largest export market for Indian calicoes printed in Britain in the mid-century, it provided a strong spur to the innovation and spread of the water frame.[59] By 1788, there were 340 Arkwright-type mills in Britain, most of which were in Lancashire. By 1800 a third of cotton spinning factories used the water frame.[60] Hosiery manufacturers also benefitted from this technology, as strong yarns facilitated the production of knitted cotton stockings and further innovatory development of the knitting frame. Nottingham stocking manufacturers were Arkwright's main financial backers. Manchester velvets (which mimicked silk velvets) and muslins, both with growing fashion demands in overseas and domestic markets, also gained from Arkwright's technology.[61]

Crompton's mule (1778–9) was a third major spinning innovation closely linked to Atlantic raw material supplies. The mule increased the fineness and tightness of yarns and allowed the production of both warp and weft yarns using the same machine. High-quality and carefully prepared *Barbandense* cotton facilitated the operation of Crompton's mule, which enabled British manufacturers to produce high-profit, high-price muslins that could compete with finely spun Indian imports.[62] By 1811 the mule had become the dominant technology in spinning in Lancashire. The jenny and the water frame remained common, however, because all three technologies produced yarns of different specificity

---

[58] Hahn (2020: 64–75).

[59] Styles (2022b: 65).

[60] Hahn (2020: 67–75); Chapman (2004); Cookson (2018: 12–21).

[61] Fitton and Wadsworth (1986, esp. 31–7); Styles (2022b: 58–65).

[62] Brazilian high-quality, slave-grown cotton supplies were also important in this. While calicoes required yarn counts between twenty and forty, muslins needed yarn counts above forty: Pereira (2018: 919, 925, 932–7); Riello (2013: 200–1); Styles (2022b: 60–1).

that could be used in combination, and with different fibres, to create distinctive products dictated by diverse markets.[63]

The innovations of the jenny, the water frame and the spinning mule relied heavily on cotton from the West Indies and later Brazil. Raw cotton imports into Scotland alone rose thirty-two times in 1783–1800.[64] Imports of cotton into Britain rose from 8,100 tons in 1781–90 to 54,800 tons in 1815–24, doubling again by 1834.[65] But as the industrial revolution in the cotton industry advanced, the demand for high-quality, long-stapled cotton outstripped supplies. Sourcing this cotton in the West Indies faced challenges in harvest failures, soil depletion and the competing demands of profitable sugar and coffee cultivation. Expanding production of cotton in the southern plantation states of the USA during the first decade of the nineteenth century started seriously to compete with Caribbean and Brazilian supplies. The different bushier US upland cotton (*Gossypium Hirsutum*) became a viable alternative to *Barbadense*, with improvements in the cotton gin (enabling easier harvesting), and with developments in spinning technologies that enabled use of a greater variety of staple lengths. From the 1820s the USA became the dominant supplier. It was cotton produced by enslaved workers that fuelled the cotton factory era of the nineteenth century, but now this came from the slave plantations of the southern states of America.[66]

Capital investment and sources of capital

Arkwright technology drove the early centralization of cotton spinning into large factories on water power sites. This transition to centralized, supervised, capital-intensive processing was a hallmark of industrialization. Arkwright mills commonly employed 500 or more workers with others engaged on a putting-out basis using other technologies, particularly jennies and mules. Many water-powered Arkwright mills brought a return of between 50 and 100% per year on investments. By 1786

---

[63] Hahn (2020: 74–86). For use and spread of spinning technologies using different fibres see Cookson (2018: 12–21).

[64] Devine (2015a: 231).

[65] Allen (2009: 211).

[66] Olmstead and Rhode (2018: 1–17, figures 2, 4); Riello (2013: 202–3).

Samuel Oldknow became a major fine muslin and calico manufacturer using Arkwright technology, with profits of around £17,000 a year.[67] His new mill at Mellor in Derbyshire, southeast of Manchester (built 1787–95), employed 2,000 workers. By 1790 he had a steam-powered mule spinning factory in Stockport, Lancashire, producing muslins of the highest counts.

These new factories demanded heavy capital outlays on excavating reservoirs and dams, waterwheel construction and purchasing an Arkwright licence (which generally cost £500 per thousand spindles a year).[68] One important source of funds was profits from the slave trade and plantations. Wealth gained in the West Indies contributed to financing the textile revolutions, especially in Scotland. More than a quarter of Scottish West Indian traders who made industrial invest-ments in the mid- to late eighteenth century were partners in cotton firms, including two investors in James Findlay and Co., Scotland's largest cotton concern in the early nineteenth century.[69] Robert Owen, cotton spinner and early utopian socialist, drew nearly half the capital in 1810–12 for his famed extension of David Dale's New Lanark cotton works from partners of major West India merchants, John Campbell Senior and Co. and Dennistoun, Buchanan and Co.[70]

In the 1780s Samuel Greg established one of the largest cotton-spinning and weaving complexes in Britain, Quarry Bank Mill at Styal in Cheshire. The mill cost £3,000 to set up. Some funds came from his father and uncle, who were Atlantic merchants and ship owners in Belfast with plantations in the Caribbean and North America. He also inherited £10,000 from the cotton textile merchanting business of his Manchester uncles. In 1795, with his brother Thomas, he inherited, and continued to operate, the Hillsborough plantations in Dominica, along with other estates.[71] Peter Ewart, a cotton spinner of Manchester in the 1820s, was in partnership with William and John Ewart, Liverpool

---

[67] Unwin (1968: 69–84, 162).

[68] Chapman (2016: 15–38); Fitton and Wadsworth (1986: chapter 2).

[69] Devine (1976: 4–5, 11; 1978: 40–67); Hamilton (2005: 203).

[70] Devine (1996: 299–312); Mullen (2022: 253–92). On Owen's social theory see Taylor (1983/2016).

[71] Hahn (2020: 73); Rose (1986: 13–20); https://www.ucl.ac.uk/lbs/person/view /2146644249.

merchants. William was co-mortgagee with John Gladstone of the Belmont Estate in Demerara from 1803, whilst John Ewart (William's son) was mortgagee of the Long Lane Delap's estate in Antigua, for which he received emancipation compensation in 1839.[72] The affairs of the Hibbert family illustrate the direct links between West Indies trade and the growth of textile manufacturing in the northwest. The Hibberts were prominent slave factors and plantation owners in Jamaica. They were also important in the sugar commission business in London and in the manufacture of cotton cloth in Manchester in the 1740s and 1750s. The investments and enterprises of Samuel Touchet, slave trader and textile entrepreneur of the mid-eighteenth century, provide another good example.[73] Compensation monies also contributed to the growth of Liverpool's cotton-broking activities: four partners of the Liverpool cotton-broking firm of Nicholas Waterhouse and Sons applied for compensation relating to the Clonbrock estate and other plantations in British Guiana in the 1830s.[74] Capital investment from slavery was as prominent in textile manufacturing in Bristol as in the northwest. Eleven partners in the Great Western Cotton company of Bristol, including slave owners in Barbados, Nevis and St Kitts, received the benefits of compensation for owning slaves in the Caribbean in the 1830s.[75]

In the absence of more systematic study, the multiplication of examples of investment funds flowing from slavery to the textile industry can only be indicative of its importance. But circulating capital from the Atlantic trades was vital and must be added to any assessment of the flow of funds from slavery into industry.[76] Investment monies arising from slavery found their way into the establishment of a growing number of provincial banks that were key players in providing credit to manufacturers. The Heywood Bank in Liverpool (established in 1773), which had a Manchester branch from 1788, was founded by merchants with capital amassed in the African trade and privateering. Leyland and Bullins

[72] https://www.ucl.ac.uk/lbs/person/view/465; https://www.ucl.ac.uk/lbs/person/view/2146651793; https://www.ucl.ac.uk/lbs/firm/view/2144929187.
[73] Williams (1944/1994: 71); Riello (2013: 152). For Touchet see chapter 2, p. 73; Kidd (2008); Wadsworth and Mann (1931/1968: 444–5).
[74] https://www.ucl.ac.uk/lbs/firm/view/-2021176976.
[75] https://www.ucl.ac.uk/lbs/firm/view/1543992380.
[76] For further discussion of this see chapter 8.

(established in 1807) was founded by Thomas Leyland, one of the biggest slave traders in Liverpool in the last quarter of the eighteenth century. William Gregson, banker, was a slave trader and ship owner; another banker, Francis Ingram, was a slave trader and member of the African Company in the 1770s.[77] These banks and their counterparts across the northwest, Yorkshire, lowland Scotland and around Bristol were a conduit for the flow of credit from Atlantic trading into manufacture.[78]

Textiles and regional industrialization

As outlined in chapter 5, a major shift occurred in the regional distribution of textile manufacture in Britain between the late seventeenth and the early nineteenth centuries. Older centres in East Anglia and the West Country stagnated or declined whilst west Yorkshire, south Lancashire (extending into northern parts of Cheshire, Staffordshire and Derbyshire), mid Wales (for a time) and parts of Scotland came to the fore. Some of the most economically backward parts of Britain became the most important and innovative centres of production of woollens, linens and cotton/linen mixes. They all directed much of their trade through Atlantic ports. Already by the 1690s Liverpool imported Irish wool and linen yarn, West Indian cotton, and dyestuffs from Africa and the Caribbean for the industries of its hinterland, exporting woollen goods, linens and 'cottons' to Africa and the colonies.[79] By the later eighteenth century and into the nineteenth century, Atlantic markets absorbed about two-thirds of the total cloth output of Lancashire and Yorkshire combined, but a much smaller proportion of the output of the older textile regions of East Anglia and the West Country.[80] At the same time the northern textile regions, including Scotland, grew more dependent upon imported Caribbean cotton, plantation-grown indigo, African logwood and Senegalese gum (used in textile printing). Aside from the direct impact of exports and imports, profits made in the slave

[77] Williams (1944/1994: 99–101).

[78] For the importance of West Indian finance in Scottish banks and links between Scottish banks and industry see Mullen (2022, esp. 65–87, 271–4, 295–6). Bank credit is more fully explored in chapter 8.

[79] Wadsworth and Mann (1931/1968: 72).

[80] James (1857: 286–7); Wilson (1973); Inikori (2015).

and plantation trades were finding their way into these regional industrializing economies both via direct investment and by credit flows.

Maps 7.1 and 7.2 show the geographical distribution of male employment in textiles in England and Wales in 1710 and 1817 respectively, demonstrating the success of the textile industries of Lancashire and west Yorkshire in the eighteenth century compared with the declining specialization of other regional producing areas (especially East Anglia and the West Country), and also of domestically oriented production that had been scattered through most counties at the beginning of the century.[81] Dense face-to-face networks of credit and information flow and a large range of specialist commercial, technological and mechanical engineering services grew close to hand: these included textile machinery makers, banks, brokers, insurers, shippers, social institutions (clubs, coffee houses), commercial exchanges and a commercial press. All of these contributed to the evolution of dynamic, urbanizing, industrializing regions.[82]

Lancashire and west Yorkshire led textile-patenting activity throughout the eighteenth century; the older cloth centres such as East Anglia had low patent numbers, similar to southern arable counties.[83] Patents before the 1790s were mostly about new designs or fibre combinations in cloths; textile patents of the period 1790 to 1830, by contrast, were about inventiveness in manufacturing processes and textile engineering.[84] The 1831 census for England and Wales shows that male textile factory employment exceeded retail trade and handicraft sectors only in Lancashire, the West Riding of Yorkshire and Stafford. Lancashire had almost a third of the factory employees in England and Wales and a further 24% were in west Yorkshire.[85] Lancashire and west Yorkshire exhibited the key markers of industrial transformation: centralized

---

[81] Similar figures for Scotland are not yet available.

[82] Hudson (1989: 5–40); Stobart (2004); Cookson (2018).

[83] Inikori (2015: 224–65, esp. 232–3). The geographical origins of patents are difficult to ascertain because the prevalence of London addresses reflects the location of agents, financial backers and temporary residences. Inikori relies here on MacLeod's estimates: MacLeod (2002).

[84] O'Brien, Griffiths and Hunt (1996: 167); Griffiths, Hunt and O'Brien (1992: 896).

[85] By 1850 west Yorkshire had 65% of England's factory employment, whilst Lancashire had much of the rest, including 70% of Britain's power looms. Census Enumeration Abstract II, Parliamentary Papers, 1833, 36, 832–3, summarized by Inikori (2015: table 9.4, 249–50); Timmins (1993: 20).

Map 7.1: The regional concentration of adult males employed in the textile sector, *c.*1710.

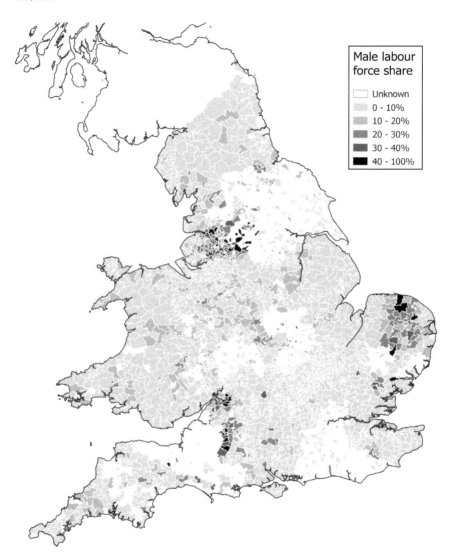

Source: based on probate data and parish register information collected as part of the CAMPOP project on Occupational Change in England and Wales. Map drawn and supplied by Sebastian Keibek and Leigh Shaw-Taylor. For full details of sources and more detailed maps see www.economiespast.org.

Map 7.2 The regional concentration of adult males employed in the textile sector, 1817.

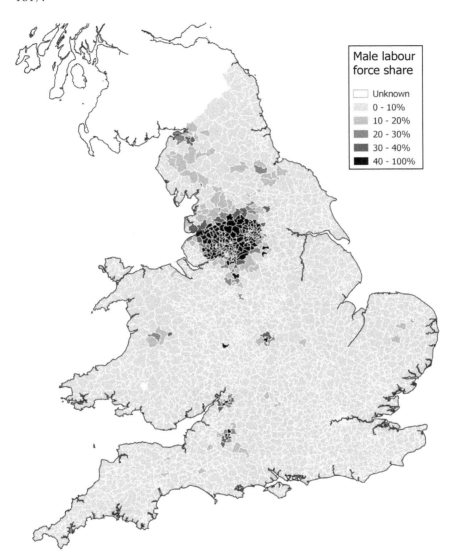

Source: based on parish register and census information collected as part of the CAMPOP project on Occupational Change in England and Wales. Maps drawn and supplied by Sebastian Keibek. For full details of sources and more detailed maps see www.economiespast.org/.

manufacture in integrated production units or factories using wage labour and new technologies.

Explanations for the textile revolutions

Most historians focus on high wages or access to coal to explain technological advance during the industrial revolution. These factors were certainly in play but a regional perspective points to other explanations. As late as 1767–70 Lancashire and Yorkshire were among eleven counties with the lowest wages in England; by 1794–5 they were among the eleven counties with the highest wages, even though they also had among the highest population growth rates in the country.[86] These wage shifts, caused largely by rising demand for textile workers, generally postdated the major textile product and raw material revolutions and the early mechanization of spinning. They could also be countered by using low-cost child labour, including pauper apprentices who were drawn from lower-wage parts of the country. Pauper apprentices were used by Arkwright himself, by Samuel Greg and by many other employers, especially of the Arkwright system. The shift from low to high wages seems to have occurred *because* of the initial success of product changes and export-oriented Atlantic-port hinterlands, rather than being the cause of inventiveness or primacy.[87]

Cheap coal is another causal factor that is rightly emphasized in explanations of Britain's industrial lead and the changing location of manufacturing.[88] By 1813–20 over 75% of wool textile weavers in England and Wales lived in parishes where coal miners also resided, suggesting the importance of cheap coal, but spinning labour (largely female) was scattered much more widely.[89] The application of steam power to textiles was limited before the 1840s.[90] Most mill owners,

---

[86] Hunt (1986: 965–6); Inikori (2015); Kelly, Mokyr and Ó Gráda (2014: 363–89); Shaw-Taylor and Wrigley (2014: 53–88). Wages for spinning labour were not high: Humphries and Schneider (2019: 126–55). Compare Allen (2011, 461–4; 2015).

[87] Kelly, Mokyr and Ó Gráda (2014: 363–89); Shaw-Taylor and Wrigley (2014: 53–88); de Vries (2008); Honeyman (2007); Humphries (2010).

[88] See chapter 5, pp. 117–18.

[89] Sugden et al. (2023).

[90] Crafts (2004: 338–51).

including Arkwright himself, found coal too expensive. In 1800 the total number of Boulton and Watt engines sold to cotton mills was eighty-four at a time when over 1,000 spinning factories were powered by water. 'All the major technical breakthroughs in cotton spinning (were) originally developed for other forms of power.'[91] No doubt access to cheap coal for domestic heating and dyeing helps to account for concentrations of textile manufacturing *within* the larger hinterlands of Atlantic ports. But the major spinning innovations were not simply the result of cheap coal or expensive labour. Above all, they depended upon markets and raw material supplies, stimulated by the transatlantic colonial and plantation trades. This was surely the reason why it was the Lancashire/Yorkshire coalfield areas and the Scottish coalfield rather than Northumberland or south Wales that saw textile industrialization in the later eighteenth century.

Conclusion

From the late seventeenth century the British textile industry had four combined advantages that its European rivals did not possess. First, it had one of the three largest East India trading operations in Europe, along with the Dutch Republic and France. This brought in Asian textiles crucial for the trade in enslaved peoples from Africa. Second, Britain dominated the slave trade and thus had key access to competitive African markets for innovative coloured and patterned cloths, especially cottons, which created pressure to develop domestically produced substitutes. Third, unlike France or the Dutch Republic, Britain established large, fast-growing and relatively prosperous white settler populations in the Americas. These discerning consumers bought textiles (alongside other manufactures) from the metropole. Finally, the rapidly growing and varied markets of the northern mainland colonies were well established before the 1770s at a time when they generated significant purchasing power from their trade to the West Indies. These markets were resilient enough to revive after the decade-long severe interruption of the American War of Independence. The textile revolutions in Britain

---

[91] Von Tunzelmann (1978: 183); Malm (2016: 55–6, 78, 89). This was less the case with the mule than with the frame.

before 1800 were primarily a response to changing markets, especially in the Atlantic. But they would not have occurred without the benefit of Atlantic raw materials, above all cotton, which encouraged innovation in preparatory processes and the early mechanization of spinning, as well as higher quality and greater variety in cloth output. It was the market and raw material supplies, rather than cost saving, that directed the industry and its regional concentration through the eighteenth century and that laid the ground for further technological advance.

CHAPTER 8

Financial capitalism

Finance drove the slave trade and the slave plantations. The financial needs of slave-related enterprise contributed to key financial innovations in national and international trade credit, bills of exchange, banking, mortgage lending, stock broking, insurance and public debt. All had spill-over effects on the rest of the economy but these are seldom addressed in assessing the economic contribution of slavery. Neither are the profits made by discount houses, commission agents, bankers, mortgagees, brokers, underwriters and others drawn into the orbit of plantation commerce and the slave trade. Innovations in financial institutions and practices, largely precipitated by trade with the Atlantic colonies, helped to make Britain a major financial, as well as industrial, power.

Political influence and financial innovations were closely related. The West India interest dominated parliamentary debates and policy-making on trade, protectionism and militarism in the Atlantic. Its influence was at its height during the half century following the 1730s. Many 'retired' West India planters became MPs, and some, such as William Beckford, Samuel Pennant and Slingsby Bethell, held office as Lord Mayor of the City of London.[1] By the 1770s there were sixty-eight 'West Indian' voting MPs, ten formal representatives of the Islands in London, dozens of merchants trading to the West Indies from Glasgow, Liverpool, Bristol, London and elsewhere, and up to 3,000 absentee planters or slave owners living in Britain.[2] Commission merchants, who by this time handled practically all of the sugar imports, also had power in the City and at Westminster.

Over the course of the eighteenth century the West India interest promoted legal changes that furthered the sale and profitability of sugar

---

[1] Sheridan (1957: 70).
[2] Hoppit (2017: 128–9).

and other plantation crops in protected markets.[3] It also influenced Parliament and colonial governments to enact laws and adopt policies that strengthened the hand of planters, slave merchants, parties in payments settlements, mortgagers and mortgagees of overseas land and property, insurance underwriters and traders in general.[4] Atlantic colonial trading interests were not the only force influencing the emergence of new forms of financial capitalism. The influence and needs of East India Company traders and investors, for example, also had an impact, not least via innovation in joint stock company organization and stock trading, but also in long-distance credit and investment arrangements. But the particular investment and trading requirements of slave-based transatlantic trade, and its powerful advocates, created significant new institutions, laws, precepts and practices that helped to revolutionize both private and public finance.

Credit and Payments Systems

From the late seventeenth century a new multilateral payment and credit system, based on bills of exchange, evolved to service the needs of the plantation and slave trades.[5] A bill of exchange is a binding agreement (on paper) to pay a fixed amount of money to another party on a specified date or on demand. Such bills had long been used in international trade but in the eighteenth century they were increasingly used as negotiable instruments in the months before their maturity and final payment: they were passed many times between traders and between traders and their banks to pay bills or gain credit. The increasing use of bills in this way speeded up payments and the circulation of credit in both internal and external trade. Assessments of the financial impact of slavery have concentrated on the flow of profits from the slave trade and plantations directly into industrial infrastructure. But easing payments and credit

[3] Sheridan (1957); Massie (1759). For earlier mercantilist policy and practice see Zahedieh (1999: 143–58).

[4] Though these laws were frequently ignored or subverted, the weight of legislation impacted significantly upon the terms and profitability of trade. Hoppit (2017: 123–30).

[5] Already in 1672–94 the RAC received around 1,500 planters' bills worth nearly £350,000: Sheridan (1958: 253).

dealings mattered more than fixed capital for most firms before the 1820s. The role of the slave and plantation trades in increasing credit supply in both international trade and in the industrializing regions of the country was pivotal.[6]

Bills of exchange, rather than produce or bullion, were favoured in purchasing enslaved people because planters demanded long credit in what was often a buyers' market.[7] The multilateral settlements of this trade, involving transactions on three continents, also favoured bills and the development of a clearing system. West India Houses, mostly in London, stood at the centre of the web of bills and credit; they were long established in the Atlantic trade and had considerable financial resources. Many were involved with sugar importing and processing, which secured their operations. These Houses came to accept final responsibility for the payment of slave trade bills. They gained from commission charges, discount rates and the interest charged on usance (the time allowed for the payment of bills). Plantation produce consigned to them was placed for sale with brokers in London, Liverpool and other Atlantic ports, and the proceeds were used to meet outstanding acceptances from the slave trade.[8]

By the 1730s, few merchants sold enslaved people directly to planters because the long credits demanded from them would have placed merchants out of funds for several years. Instead, the enslaved were sold to 'Guinea' or 'African' factors, resident in the colonies. These factors had the credit available to pay with long-dated bills. Many, such as Aspinall and Hardy, Lindo and Lake, Blundell and Rainsford, William Daggers and John Tailyour, all in Jamaica, were important and wealthy figures who formed an oligopoly of five firms responsible for around 50% of the trade. Tailyour, the second-largest slave factor in Kingston in the 1780s, was reputed to make an annual profit of £5–6,000, gaining around 9% return on sales of 17,295 enslaved people over his twelve-year career.[9]

---

[6] Hudson (1986: 51); Chapman (1979: 52, 66).

[7] Sheridan (1958); Price (1991: 293–339); Berendt (2001: 171–204).

[8] Sheridan (1958); Price (1980); Richardson (2022: 81–5).

[9] John Tailyour (b. 1755) moved to Jamaica in 1782 and became a 'Guinea Factor'. Between 1785 and 1796 fifty-four slave vessels were consigned to him from which 17,295 enslaved people were sold: Morgan (2016b: 337, 341); Radburn (2015a: 244, 255).

Factors issuing bills required bonds from planters so that payment could be enforced. Such bonds were underpinned and regularized by the Colonial Debts Act of 1732, which allowed creditors to seize not only crops in settlement of outstanding debts but also land, buildings and chattels, including enslaved workers. After the passage of the Colonial Debts Act the use of planters' bonds became almost universal in Virginia and the Chesapeake as well as in the West Indies.[10]

To underpin the security of long-dated bills, African factors in the Caribbean had to name a 'guarantee' in England upon whom the bills would be drawn and who would cover the factor for their payment. These were wealthy individuals, mostly in London or Bristol, who had links with the key West India merchant houses. William Miles, eminent and 'immensely rich' West India merchant of Bristol, sugar factor and owner of Jamaican plantations, acted frequently as guarantor for slaves sold by Tailyour Ballantyne and Fairlie in Jamaica.[11] The guarantee system was made possible only by such wealthy individuals, enriched by plantations and sugar. The 'guarantee' was relatively secure because he generally received payments before the long-dated bills became due and received a 0.5% commission for his services rising to 5% for late remittances. Payments to guarantors were made in planters' bills for supplies and from other bills originating from British traders buying produce in colonial ports.[12]

As this payment system developed there was a sharp rise in the number of slave trade ships returning from the Caribbean carrying ballast rather than produce and 'bills in the bottom' for four-fifths or more of the proceeds of slave sales. The credit terms of the bills varied at three- or four-monthly intervals to around sixteen months to stagger payments.[13] Because the bill-based immediate remittance system ensured that slave traders received payments at a specified time, it enabled them to sign off a voyage within twenty-four months, releasing funds to buy

---

[10] The enslaved (including claims on their future unborn offspring) could be seized and sold as payment for certain classes of their owners' debts until this provision was rescinded by Act in 1797: Price (1991).

[11] Morgan (2016b: 339); Radburn (2015a: 258); Bourne (1866: vol. 2, 17).

[12] Morgan (2016b); Haggerty (2012: 54–5).

[13] Checkland (1958a: 461–9); Morgan (2016b); Anderson (1977).

manufactured goods and ships' supplies ready for the next outward trip.[14] Instead of British merchants supplying credit to planters, the colonial factors and their backers in Britain now supplied the credit in an arrangement that involved enforceable guarantees. No other slave trading power had such institutionally based credit arrangements. Before the crash on the Amsterdam stock exchange in 1773, Dutch planters used bills of exchange drawn on the merchant houses in the Netherlands in order to pay captains of slave ships, but such bills were no longer honoured in the Netherlands after the crash. As a consequence, the shippers themselves were forced to collect the price of their slaves in cash or in kind from the planters. Full payment often took many years. This partly explains the rapid decline of the Dutch slave trade in the last quarter of the eighteenth century.[15]

French traders had no equivalent of the immediate remittance system, even though they were familiar with the assignment of bills and with discounting. French slave traders found it hard to find well-endowed factor correspondents in the Caribbean and more often had to sell through their ship captains or through branches of their own firms. They were thus burdened with the responsibility of ensuring planters' payments.[16] Without the guarantee system, French slave traders generally operated with higher debt levels than their British counterparts. In 1785, for example, eight large firms in Nantes were owed 8 million livres in the West Indies, and some French ventures took between five and ten years to be settled. Another problem for French slave sellers was the more ambiguous legal position over the security of property underlying planters' bonds. The integrity of the plantation was upheld by French colonial legislatures. Thus creditors could seize crops if debts were unpaid but were prevented from reducing the productive capacity of the plantation. Together, these factors gave British slave traders an edge in dominating the Atlantic slave trade.[17] They also meant that the proceeds, as well as the risks, of the British slave trade were spread through a chain of intermediaries.

British innovations in financing the slave and West Indies trades

[14] Morgan (2005; 2016b).
[15] Emmer (2005).
[16] For the French slave trade see Daudin (2004).
[17] Price (1991: 335).

benefitted the wider economy in the development of its financial institutions and payment systems. Slave trade bills, with their lengthy credit terms, required not only acceptance houses but also discounting specialists, particularly in the slave-trading ports and their industrial hinterlands. In the late eighteenth century a growing number of provincial banks in the industrializing regions concentrated their activities on the brokerage and discounting of bills.[18] In 1750 there were only twelve banks in England and Wales outside London; by 1801, there were more than 383, and by 1824, 660.[19] Most had a London correspondent bank that, in discounting their bills and accepting their notes, linked them to the London money market. The Scottish banking system was separate and dominated by the operations of the two public banks, the Royal Bank and the Bank of Scotland. The latter set up branches in the provinces (eighteen by 1790), and provincial banks also grew in number to reach twenty-four by 1824. From the early 1780s this structure, working largely through the agency of the Royal Bank, operated 'the greatest discounting business outside London'.[20]

Bills originating in the slave trade were brought back to the ports of Liverpool, Bristol and Glasgow. As negotiable instruments, they were then used as a means of payment, endorsed each time they changed hands. They circulated in the industrializing hinterlands of the ports. By the end of the century bills with only a short time left to maturity were increasingly accepted, at a discount, by banks when cash was needed. Bills from overseas trade were common in Lancashire in the 1760s, and as provincial merchants became used to dealing with external trade bills, they turned to bills in internal trade as well from the 1780s.[21]

Bills, especially in south Lancashire and Scotland, but also in west Yorkshire and the midlands, boosted the money supply, became the basis of a pyramid of credit and oiled the wheels of trading before being sent at maturity to London for final payment. In 1795 a Liverpool trader

[18] Unlike in Scotland, deposit banking was slow to develop in the industrial regions of England. Not many banks issued notes or drafts because payment in bills was preferred. They thus did not have to hold large fiduciary reserves: Pressnell (1956).

[19] Pressnell (1956: 116).

[20] Checkland (1975: 145–6, 711–28).

[21] Pressnell (1956: 435–6); Anderson (1977). See also Ashton (1945: 25–35); Checkland (1954: 129–42).

wrote that 'these bills are numerous in the town of Liverpool and, in general circulation on a discount, therefore answer the purpose of the receiver in the first instance, being taken in payment on the faith of the acceptor and indorser without hesitation or indifference'.[22] Bills of exchange were regarded as more secure than private bank notes and they were not subject to stamp duty, giving them an edge over bankers' drafts. As late as the 1820s some 90% of the trade of Manchester may have operated in bills.[23] Only in the 1830s with changes in the regional and national banking systems did this means of payment decline. The industrial revolution in the northwest and in central Scotland was largely dependent upon it.[24]

The ability of Liverpool merchants to buy manufactured goods for export from south Lancashire, Yorkshire, the midlands and elsewhere on much longer credit than they in turn advanced in the transatlantic trades was a product of the guarantee system and the developed nature of the bill discount market.[25] Liverpool merchants used slave-trade bills as security for advances of goods and services on credit to outfit new slaving voyages.[26] Few slave traders' bills were drawn on London, but most of their foreign bills were paid there. As London gradually succeeded Amsterdam as the leading centre of international finance, this allowed the inter-regional and international flow of funds via London, from areas of capital surplus to those in need of funds. The external trade of Liverpool and Glasgow in particular was thus largely responsible for sucking vital funds northwards from London into the manufacturing regions.[27] This underpinned the expansion of trade and of productive capacity, combining the resources of the provinces with those of the London money market and contributing to the national and international role of the City of London.

---

[22] Sheridan (1958: 262).
[23] Ashton (1945: 27); Pressnell (1956: 435).
[24] Checkland (1958a: 461–9; 1975: 145–6).
[25] Edwards (1967: 111–13, 119–22); Inikori (2002: 333); Morgan (2007: 14–42); Richardson (2022: 84–93).
[26] Richardson (2022: 89).
[27] Checkland (1958a: 461–9); Sheridan (1958: 249–63); Morgan (2005: 415–49); Pressnell (1956); Anderson (1977: 59–97).

Caribbean mortgages

The heavy fixed capital requirements of Caribbean investment (in land, slaves and processing equipment) greatly extended the mortgage market. Tens of millions of pounds were raised on mortgage, buoyed by anticipated high profits of sugar planting.[28] Borrowing was further encouraged during the mid-century decades, when the terms of trade favoured plantation producers and the value of West Indian estates and plantations was rising, increasing their potential as collateral.[29] Where an estate and its contents appreciated in value, the creditor gained, making Caribbean mortgages an attractive investment. Sugar plantations tripled in value in Jamaica in this period, rising up to ten-fold in some cases.[30]

Plantations were also attractive to British investors because of the interest rate differential between London and the Caribbean. Interest rates in the colonies avoided some of the legal restraints of the metropole. This created a peacetime gap of between 3.5 and 4% in the mid- to late century and a larger gap early in the century.[31] By 1750 George Hibbert, a leading sugar merchant suggested that £20 million of West Indian debt was owed to British creditors, and a contemporary estimate from the 1780s placed the value of Caribbean mortgages alone at £70 million.[32] Mortgage loans in the British islands increased further after the peace of 1783, after the Saint-Domingue rebellion in 1791, and in the decades of mixed fortunes that followed the ending of the slave trade in 1807. Foreclosures and remortgaging occurred after each wave of expansion, and many merchants became plantation owners by default, often having

[28] Mortgages do not figure prominently in the 1802 debt claims under the American Loyalist Claims Commission (set up to repay debts to British traders and investors following the American War of Independence). This suggests they were less important in the mainland colonies than in the West Indies, perhaps because planters did not have to buy replacement slaves as urgently as did their West Indian counterparts: Price (1991).
[29] For colonial terms of trade and their relationship to mortgage debt see Smith (2002: 434–65).
[30] Sheridan (1974: 229–31; 1960: 163).
[31] Smith (2002).
[32] Pennant, MP for Liverpool 1767–90 and chair of the Standing Committee of West Indian Planters and Merchants, House of Commons, 1789, quoted in Anstey (1975: 311); Smith (2002: 459); Sheridan (1960: 165–6).

to take out a new mortgage on the estate to make it viable.[33] Frequent defaults, in addition to sales, inheritances and remortgages, created hefty commissions for financiers and lawyers and meant that 'the whole value of the West India colonies was paid for over and over again, and the proceeds quietly deposited in Britain.'[34]

The Lascelles family, slave traders, plantation owners and collectors of customs for the Port of Bridgetown, Barbados, extended £226,772 to West Indies planters in the period 1723–53, of which £95,000 was on mortgage of these planters' estates. Failure and foreclosure on these loans made the Lascelles major plantation and slave owners by mid-century. Henry Lascelles was involved in winding up the affairs of many non-residents and deceased planters; he was granted nineteen powers of attorney for this purpose in the period 1716–36. By 1787 the family held more than 27,000 acres in Barbados, Jamaica, Grenada and Tobago, mostly bought or acquired by defaults following the Caribbean credit crisis of 1772–3.[35] Attorneys, like Simon Taylor (1739–1813) in Jamaica, became immensely wealthy sugar tycoons partly through facilitating the turnover of plantation ownership and the transfer of colonial wealth to Britain.[36] Where London commission houses and sugar importers were the creditors, they often insisted on securing the commission business as a condition of a loan. The Pinneys allowed £2–3,000 of debt in return for handling 100 hogsheads of sugar per annum. Lascelles and Maxwell allowed £5,000 of debt for 500 hogsheads of sugar business. Such arrangements were not legally enforceable but they generally worked to the advantage of the mortgagee.[37]

Eighteenth-century mortgages had no fixed provision for repayment but always specified the security and the interest payable.[38] The Colonial Debts Act of 1732 was hailed as 'the Palladium of colony credit and the English merchant's grand security' as it offered improved determination of collateral.[39] A legal precedent in 1745 demonstrated the flexibility of

---

[33] Price (1991: 293–339, esp. 330).
[34] Sheridan (1971: 285–96, esp. 296).
[35] Smith (2002).
[36] Sheridan (1971: 296).
[37] Pares (1950: 210, 253–5); Smith (2002).
[38] Smith (2002: 435 n8).
[39] Commissioners for Trade and Plantations (1920–38: vol. 1728–34, 347).

adjusting interest rates on colonial mortgages, and further acts in 1772–4 gave extra security to non-British mortgagees and regularized lending on mortgages at 6% in the West Indies and in Ireland. The 6% rate made the mortgage attractive at a time when the yield on government funds hovered around 3.5%.[40]

It is likely that the use of the mortgage domestically during the industrial revolution was strengthened by its ubiquity in the Caribbean. The mortgage of land and property to raise finance for industrial and commercial investment became well established, particularly in the north of England and in London in the early eighteenth century, aided by the activities of intermediaries, particularly attorneys, and by the establishment of county deeds registries.[41]

Dutch and French capital and mortgages

Eighteenth-century capital markets were not national but international. It is impossible to study finance in the British economy in isolation from European and particularly from Dutch capital. Most of the large finance houses of London were Anglo-Dutch before the Napoleonic War period.[42] The mid-century move towards higher-risk speculative investments including mortgage loans on overseas plantations was European-wide. Between 70 and 80 million guilders (around £7–8 million) is estimated to have been invested by the Dutch in plantation mortgages in the second half of the eighteenth century.[43] The Dutch market was more sophisticated than the British but also more risky, because mortgages were often pooled and sold off to investors who had no ties to the slave economy. Dutch investors were unusual in placing

[40] Price (1991).
[41] Five county deeds registries were established early in the century to create security for such transactions in the commercial and industrializing regions. Hudson (1986: 96–8); Tate (1944: 97–105).
[42] Ormrod (2003: 332); Ormrod and Rommelse (2020: 22–3); Wilson (1941). The integration of European capital markets via joint Dutch and English broking came to an end during and after the Napoleonic Wars: Neal (1990: 5–9, 229–30).
[43] Emmer (2005); Van der Voort (1981: 85–105). This was only around 10% of total Dutch overseas investments and dwarfed by the amount of Dutch acceptance credit in international circulation: de Vries and van der Woude (1997: chapter 4).

most of their highest-risk investment in the West Indies, a move that became a mania in the early 1770s with many loans 'sub-prime'. In 1773 a wave of Dutch bankruptcies and a stock market crash in Amsterdam wiped out much of the invested capital. Investment fell dramatically, hampering development of the Surinam plantations.[44] The Amsterdam stock exchange did not recover from the 1770s crisis and suffered marked decline, especially during and after the Napoleonic Wars.[45]

In reaction to the crisis of the 1770s, Dutch investors increasingly put their money into the British Caribbean commodity trade rather than its Dutch equivalent, further aiding the British advantage.[46] Dutch investment failings in the later century reflected political instability and the outbreak of the Fourth Anglo-Dutch War in 1780. Between 1785 and 1805 the value of Surinam exports of sugar, coffee and cotton declined by 20% despite rising sugar prices, and the Dutch slave trade fell by 80% in the last quarter of the eighteenth century, at a time when the British trade was at its height.[47] Dutch failure in the Caribbean was a failure of both the mortgage and the bill market.

France similarly raised large sums on mortgage for both domestic and overseas investment, including West Indian investment. It did so via notaries outside of the formal banking system which was emerging in the early nineteenth century. By 1840 outstanding mortgage debt in France amounted to 28% of GDP but it was never highly focused on plantations in the eighteenth century as in the Dutch and British cases.[48] British mortgages on her sugar plantations were underpinned by the uniquely prodigious growth and social spread of British sugar consumption within the protected home market. Dutch and French sugar traders had to compete for European markets, which meant that the plantation mortgage was a less secure form of investment than its British counterpart.

---

[44] Hoonhout (2013: 85–99); De Jong, Kooijmans and Koudijs (2021); https://sites .google.com/view/peter-koudijs/research?authuser=0.

[45] Neal (1990).

[46] Ormrod (2003).

[47] Onnekink and Rommelse (2019). For recent debate about the economic impact of the Dutch slave trade on Holland see: Fatah-Black and van Rossum (2015: 63–83); Eltis, Emmer and Lewis (2016: 724–35).

[48] Hoffman, Postel-Vinay and Rosenthal (2014: 13–41).

Insurance

The slave trade, colonial commodity trading, and the processing and storage of plantation produce were risky ventures which prompted the insurance industry to emerge as a major financial player in the eighteenth century. Fire insurance of industrial premises and warehouses increased markedly in the late century, hastened by the risks of highly inflammable colonial raw materials, most prominently sugar and cotton, and their associated processing in textile scouring and dyeing and in sugar refining, which required naked flames and high temperatures. The Phoenix company, the first new insurer in London for 60 years, was founded by 84 of the 100 sugar refiners active in the capital in 1782 to extend their ability to get cover.[49] Most importantly, however, by the mid-eighteenth century Britain emerged as the most prominent marine insurance centre in Europe.[50] Lloyd's of London was established in 1688 in Edward Lloyd's Coffee House and became a centre for shipping news, risk assessment and underwriting. By 1810 there were 1,500 subscribers to Lloyd's, of whom two-thirds were underwriters.[51] The state significantly aided London's rise in the marine insurance business, including the creation of two chartered companies in 1720, the Royal Exchange and London Assurance. These were, however, slow to capture the trade from private insurers partly because of heavy losses they sustained from investments in South Sea Company stock.[52] More important was the evolution of a common law framework, promoted by Lord Mansfield, that established sound precepts for the industry. Among other things, this endorsed cheap and rapid dispute resolution using panels of merchants rather than recourse to the law.[53]

Marine insurance expanded to reduce risk in many branches of trade, but the high value of human cargoes and the high risks of the slave and Caribbean trades made them a focus of eighteenth-century business, even though premiums on a round trip were commonly between 10 and

---

[49] Pearson (2004: 76, 149, 194–5, 213).
[50] John (1958: 127); Inikori (2002: 338–61).
[51] Pearson and Richardson (2019: 431).
[52] Leonard (2022: 154–5, 161). For more on the South Sea Company see p. 181.
[53] Leonard (2015: 137–60); Leonard (2022: 161–211).

20% of the value of the ship plus its cargo.[54] By the mid-century slave traders regularly insured their ventures. Of seventy-four slaving voyages operated by William Davenport of Liverpool between 1757 and 1784, all were insured, as were all of the fifty-five slaving voyages of James Rogers of Bristol between 1784 and 1793. Six underwriting ledgers of Abraham Clibborn provide details of 330 policies on slave ships issued between 1769 and 1775, mostly departing from Bristol.[55]

By the 1790s over 40% of marine insurance covered by the London chartered duopoly is estimated to have derived from the slave and West Indian trades.[56] In addition, groups of merchants acting in mutuality as private underwriters undertook marine insurance especially in outports such as Liverpool, establishing 'a virtual pool of contingent capital' that enabled them to maximize their investments in cargoes and ships. The British insurance sector also covered much trade in Caribbean re-exports and had increasing business in brokering and underwriting policies for North American clients and for other Europeans trading in slaves and plantation commodities.[57] The slave-based trades in total therefore drove a large part of the insurance business, accounting for well over half of overseas voyage insurance.[58] The East India Company covered its own risks at this time.[59]

Unsurprisingly the connections between the African and West Indian interests and the burgeoning marine insurance industry were close. Off the coast of Demerara in 1804 Robert Hall, captain of the *Fame*, defeated an attack from a French corvette: the reward for saving his insurance company the cost of capture was a silver tea service, currently held by Lloyd's. Sir Francis Baring (1740–1810), one of the two leading operators at Lloyd's in the Napoleonic War period, was a member of

---

[54] Inikori (2002: 346–50).

[55] Pearson and Richardson (2019: 419).

[56] Pearson and Richardson (2019, 417–46, 431). Slave voyages themselves accounted for 7%.

[57] Leonard (2015: 160); Pearson and Richardson (2019: 418, 432).

[58] This is consistent with Inikori's rough estimate that around 63% of the British marine insurance market derived from the slave trade and West Indies trades in the 1790s (which might have exceeded 70% if the North American and re-export trades are included). Inikori (2002: 356–7).

[59] Inikori (2002: 357).

the Company of Merchants trading to Africa. In 1834 the Barings firm (via a son, Francis Baring, 1796–1866) claimed for ownership of 1,079 enslaved people across eight plantations in British Guiana.[60]

Slave trade insurance was profitable because policies evolved to exclude costly elements, such as 'natural wastage' at sea.[61] Losses from suicide or shipboard revolts were treated as uninsurable in the same way as cattle panicking during a storm. Slave merchants themselves had to find ways to mitigate risks associated with their human cargoes. This kept premiums on the Atlantic trades modest compared with the East Indian and north European trades.[62] A 'safety revolution' also occurred in British Atlantic shipping in general between the 1780s and the 1820s such that shipping losses and insurance rates almost halved. Improvements in navigation and in ship construction, including copper sheathing and iron reinforcements, drove the reduction in premiums.[63]

The *Zong*, owned by James Gregson and captained by Luke Collingwood, set sail from Liverpool in September 1781, boarded 470 enslaved people in West Africa and headed for Jamaica. Storms and navigational problems extended the voyage well beyond the eight weeks expected. After twelve weeks, and still at sea, seven of the seventeen crew had died, and Collingwood had ordered over sixty of the enslaved (dead and dying) to be thrown overboard. Slave deaths on board were not covered by insurance, but the value of any slaves thrown overboard 'in order to protect the safety of the ship' was recoverable. Within a few days 122 Africans were forced overboard with a further ten choosing to end their own lives in the same way, once unchained.[64] These practices were not unusual, but more is known about the *Zong* because the insurance claim was disputed, leaving court records. A murder charge levied against the captain and crew of the *Zong* was rejected on the basis that the slaves

---

[60] Wright and Fayle (1928: 212–13); Orbell (2004); Inikori (2002: 360).

[61] The case of Tatham v. Hodgson, 1796, confirmed that natural wastage of slaves was exempt from insurance even when caused by starvation because of hold-ups: Pearson and Richardson (2019: 422).

[62] John (1958: table 2, 442).

[63] Kelly, Ó Gráda and Solar (2021: 239–75).

[64] Walvin (1993: 17); Walvin (2011).

were not human but property: the incident was 'the same as if horses had been thrown overboard'.[65]

Insurance reduced risk and encouraged the expansion of distant trades. It also eased balance of payments arrangements between world regions (through invisible earnings). Furthermore, the wider economy benefitted because insurance brokers invested their premiums in order to underwrite future claims.[66] Accumulated premiums provided a pool of capital. The premium income on all British insured maritime risks was said by the chairman of Lloyd's, J. J. Angerstein, to be over £10 million by 1809, having increased from around £2 million per annum in the mid-century decades.[67] The annual average of premiums was perhaps £6 million in the period 1793–1807.[68] Insurance brokers, earning 5% fees, had by then become key players in financial markets including investment in public debt as well as in private enterprises.[69] Reinvestment of premiums was only part of the story; the insurance industry also created profits and commissions for a growing number of brokers and underwriters.

Public and private finance

Britain's 'financial revolution' of the eighteenth century has largely been seen as a revolution in public finance, but innovation in private finance was part and parcel of the changes. Increased trade due to developments in private finance facilitated the conversion of government debts into tradeable assets and increased 'fiscal capacity' (the tax base). Heavy capital investments in plantation development brought changes in long-term capital markets and in asset trading already pioneered by trading in government and royal charter company stocks. Multilateral payments systems, especially those developed for the slave and plantation-commodity trades, expanded the use of paper credits,

---

[65] Assessment of Judge Mansfield, quoted by Walvin (2011: 20). The Dolben Act, 1788, precipitated partly by the *Zong* case, placed limitations on the number of enslaved people that could be transported on each ship, related to their tonnage, and contributed to a reduction in slave voyage mortality.

[66] John (1953: 137–58).

[67] Inikori (2002: 341–2).

[68] Marryat (1810), quoted by Pearson and Richardson (2019: 430, 442).

[69] Leonard (2022: 22).

increased the money supply, speculation and volatility tying the London money market to the provinces and increasingly prompting intervention by the government and the Bank of England to avert crises.

The development of financial services in the eighteenth century would have been impossible without the fiscal and financial operations of the state. It is often argued that state borrowing, and public finance in general, occurred at the expense of private investment. But the two reinforced and complemented each other, as demonstrated by their interconnections in Atlantic trade.[70]

The national debt fluctuated between 5 and 20% of GDP during the eighteenth century but reached unprecedented heights of over £800 million towards the end of the Napoleonic Wars, around twice the level of GDP.[71] Most war finance was raised on the London capital market from Dutch and later metropolitan and southern English investors. Servicing government stock holders with their interest payments absorbed 40–50% of peacetime tax revenues. Between 1660 and 1815 there was an eighteen-fold increase in taxes in real terms, and the share of national income appropriated in taxation doubled.[72] The capacity to raise taxes was thus the foundation stone of the national debt and all the state activity that arose from it. Fiscal capacity set Britain aside from her contemporaries: the English tax burden far exceeded that borne much more reluctantly in other countries such as France, Spain and Austria.[73] Greater efficiency and less corruption in tax collection aided acceptance of taxation in Britain, but more important was the fact that between two-thirds and three-quarters of eighteenth-century tax revenues were indirect, rather than direct taxes on wealth or income. Their burden fell most heavily on sugar, tobacco, tea, wines and spirits along with malt,

[70] O'Brien and Palma (2020a).

[71] Quinn (2008); Neal (1990: 225); Mitchell (1988: 600–3); O'Brien (1988); O'Brien and Hunt (1999).

[72] O'Brien (1998: 3). For the differential burden between England and Scotland see Hoppit (2021: 35–85).

[73] As a proportion of national income per capita, taxation in Britain was between 40 and 50% higher than in France in the eighteenth century. Only in the Netherlands before around 1780 was it higher: Mathias and O'Brien (1976); O'Brien (2011: 408–46); Brewer (1989: 91); Karaman and Pamuk (2013).

beer, salt and soap.[74] The colonial trades thus contributed to Britain's increased fiscal capacity.

The slave-based trades influenced the state's ability to borrow as well as to tax. Slave trading to South America and the Caribbean underpinned a key development in the process of converting state debt into more liquid and tradeable private assets. The biggest debt for equity swap occurred in 1710, when the South Sea Company was established and took over almost £10 million of outstanding state debt.[75] Buoyed by the promise of high slave trade profits and by the 1715 award of the *Asiento* to supply slaves to Spanish America, Company shares experienced a speculative surge that created the South Sea Bubble, which collapsed in 1720. The reorganization of the company in 1723 has been argued to be 'the defining moment' in securing the system of public finance, merging public and private financial developments to bring down debt-servicing costs and to secure the credibility of the national debt.[76] To bail out some of the individuals who had converted their state debt into South Sea shares, around £4 million of the capital stock of the Company was transferred to the Bank of England, and the remaining £38 million was split equally into equity in the Company and perpetual annuities. This was a vital precursor to the further restructuring of the national debt in the 1750s, when annuities were consolidated into 3% consols.[77]

Many historians have argued that the 'credible commitment' necessary for sound public finance (based on belief that sovereign debt constituted an accessible, safe and liquid investment vehicle) resulted largely from the shift of power to Parliament following the Glorious Revolution of 1688–9.[78] But convincing public creditors that sovereign debt was safe and liquid involved a range of private as well as public developments. These were worked out through successive refinancing experiments, over several decades, in which the South Sea Company and the expectations

---

[74] O'Brien (1988: 11).

[75] In the case of the South Sea Company, the expected high profits never materialized, but the expectation was enough to float the Company and the speculation; Neal (1990); Paul (2011).

[76] Carlos et al. (2013: 147–68, esp. 154–5).

[77] Carlos et al. (2013: 147–68).

[78] The influential initiators of this view were North and Weingast (1989: 803–32).

of profits from the slave trade played a part.[79] Corporate projectors and financial intermediaries, many of them involved in the colonial trades, expanded the secondary market. This transformed state debt into investment choices attractive to a range of investors, thereby encouraging the mobilization of savings in the wider economy.[80]

Crises, the state and the Bank of England

Transatlantic colonial investment, credit and payments systems stimulated developments in financial institutions and practices, but this must be set alongside the systemic threat that they repeatedly posed in periods of crisis. The conditions for rapid long-distance trade expansion were created, but the system was precarious, especially with the arrival of more avaricious and speculative planters in the 1790s. Crises, such as that in 1793, exposed how overleveraged many investors were and how dependent overall credit was on relatively illiquid and increasingly over-valued plantation mortgages. West India finance was the first major extension of City financing beyond government funds and the chartered companies.[81] When under threat, it had the potential to undermine large areas of the economy. Under pressure, West India Houses would persuade holders of maturing bills to accept new bills at longer dates, and they took increasing risks knowing that they could generate 'accommodation bills', unrelated to real transactions. The mutualism between merchants, agents and finance houses, and between London and the outports, was constantly under strain and insufficient to avoid crises that were threatening enough to demand increased state and Bank of England interventions.[82]

The Bank of England's main private business in the eighteenth century was the discounting of bills for its merchant and banker clients in London. As a 'bankers' bank' it often propped up private traders, and

---

[79] Coffman, Leonard and Neal (2013: 1–20).

[80] Neal (1990); Dickson (1968: 39–156, 407–15, 486–520); Sheridan (1960: 161–86); Paul (2011); Carlos et al. (2013: 147–68); For a case study of the earlier secondary market, involving Caribbean investors, see Graham (2018a: 685–704).

[81] Checkland (1958a: 461).

[82] Checkland (1958a: 468); Morgan details a case study of cooperation between Kingston, London, Bristol and Liverpool which depended on local intelligence networks, mutual support and confidence: Morgan (2016b: 336–45).

liquidity in general, from the middle decades of the century through its provision of discount facilities.[83] It began to underpin the north European financial system by bailing out Dutch merchant banks and by increased discounting in both the 1760s and the 1770s.[84] The practice grew in the crises of the late eighteenth and early nineteenth centuries. Between 1787 and 1823 outstanding Bank discounts varied between £5 million in 1797 and £21 million in 1810.[85] In 1793 the government extended its own role in sustaining credit in difficult times by issuing Exchequer bills (promissory notes bearing interest).[86] Exchequer bills were then discounted at the Bank, generating much-needed liquidity.[87] This averted serious crisis, particularly in Scotland.[88]

Credit in transatlantic remittances was the cause of waves of bankruptcies in particular years (such as 1793, 1799, 1811) and responsible for the spread of crises from the provinces to London and vice versa. Protested bills became a feature of the trade.[89] The shaky but vitally expansive pyramid of credit built up in the industrial regions is illustrated by a snapshot of Liverpool merchant John Leigh's business at the time of his bankruptcy in 1811. Leigh was heavily involved in both Brazil and the Caribbean. His failure was precipitated by the bankruptcies of his London bank, Brickwood and Co., and his Brazilian correspondent. He reported £800 lost in West Indies bills and over £6,000 in protested bills from Demerara. Leigh owed over £139,000 to some sixty-five creditors; 63% to banking houses on bills of exchange.[90]

---

[83] The Bank became more exclusively a bankers' bank, discounting mostly for merchant bankers only in the Napoleonic War years. This change was completed after the suspension of cash payments in 1797, when the Bank determined that, in order to be discountable, bills must be payable at a bank: Sissoko (2022); O'Brien and Palma (2020a); Sissoko and Ishizu (2023). For longer context see: Clapham (1945); Kynaston (2017).

[84] Ormrod (2003); Wilson (1941).

[85] Sissoko and Ishizu (2023).

[86] Checkland (1975); Sissoko and Ishizu (2023); Ishizu (2013); Hudson (2014).

[87] Sissoko and Ishizu (2023).

[88] Checkland (1975: 712).

[89] In the early decades of the nineteenth century a nationwide and transnational commercial intelligence industry developed largely because of the need to assess the creditworthiness of bill signatories, and for banks to decide on discount limits.

[90] Ishizu (2013).

The instability and weight of West Indian trade led the Bank of England directly to intervene further, in new ways, in order to steady the system during periods of crisis. The Society of West India Merchants had close connections with both the government and the Bank of England from at least the 1760s and could influence Bank policy. By the 1790s almost 50% of Bank directors and governors were connected either directly or through family to the West India interest, and 30% of directors were West India merchants.[91] In 1799, to avert a broader financial collapse, the Bank supported Caribbean traders with a nine-month loan of £1.5 million organized by the West India Merchants Committee. Such loans continued during the subsequent crises of 1810, 1816, 1825 and into the 1830s, involving tens of thousands of pounds loaned to a range of Houses.[92] The innovation in emergency lending occurred during the 'Restriction period' 1797–1821, when the convertibility of bank notes into gold was suspended because of the financial requirements of the Napoleonic Wars.[93] These requirements, and the suspension, boosted financial activity and credit throughout the economy and generated 'a hothouse' for the rapid development of loan contractors, who became pacesetters in the post-war economy.[94] Emergency lending, first precipitated by the instabilities inherent in the payments systems and credit involved in the Caribbean and plantation trades, later became a cornerstone of the British financial system.[95]

The state also intervened directly in attempts to stabilize the West Indian economies, fearful that their importance to the rest of the economy would make it impossible to avoid transatlantic contagion in times of crisis. A series of substantial grants and relief loans was made in 1780, 1795, 1831 and 1832 in the wake of slave revolts and natural disasters.[96]

---

[91] Sissoko and Ishizu (2023); Checkland (1958a: 464).

[92] Sissoko and Ishizu (2023). The Bank also occasionally stabilized international trade in the Atlantic by lending to non-British firms that had become too big to fail. During the panic of 1837 a loan was extended to the US bank Brown Brothers (forerunners of Brown Brothers Harriman), which was deeply involved in transatlantic commerce, especially in shipping cotton to Britain from the slave states. Karabell (2021).

[93] Sissoko (2022).

[94] Chapman (1984/2006: 4).

[95] Sissoko and Ishizu (2023).

[96] Mulcahy (2005); Smith (2011; 2012); Draper (2015b); Burnard and Graham (2020).

Conclusion

An effective financial system is the foundation for economic growth. An efficient network of financial institutions and intermediaries creates incomes and wealth in itself. It also reduces transaction and information costs, facilitates trade, mitigates risks and mobilizes savings. The institutional underpinnings of financial development in both the private and the public sectors were partly set in train by Britain's involvement with slavery and plantations. Complex supply chains and long credits were not the sole preserve of Atlantic commerce. The East India trades also required credit and investment innovations to cover long voyages, for defence, and to develop trade in spices and textiles. Much of this, including insurance, however, was internalized through the corporate monopoly of the East India Company. The evolution of joint stock organization and finance was a vital innovation that must be included alongside the impact of the Atlantic trades in any assessment of the causes of Britain's financial and commercial development. But, only in the early nineteenth century, with the rise of agency houses in India, and when new territories such as Sri Lanka and Mauritius were being developed for tea and sugar, did East Indies investment start to engage with British financial markets in the same way that the Caribbean had throughout the eighteenth century.

Key changes in the insurance and mortgage markets, spurred by the slave trade and slavery, drove the development of financial institutions and an accumulation of business and profits across the financial services sector. The credit and payments system based on Atlantic bills, and their related trading, discounting and clearing practices, underpinned the liquidity of industrializing regions and gave them access to the resources of London. This expansive credit system was so unstable that the Bank of England's first forays into supportive lending (beyond emergency discounting) were necessarily focused on the West India trade. Innovations also occurred in direct state intervention to stabilize the plantation economies. All of these developments created the financial infrastructure that enabled merchant banking firms to invest in slavery and coerced labour beyond the Caribbean in the nineteenth century: in Cuban and Brazilian sugar and coffee and in the formal and informal British Empires, especially after the downfall of the East India Company in 1834. The financial capitalism that arose from slavery set in place a pattern of state-promoted financialization of Britain's global economy, centred on London, that became even more marked in later centuries.

CHAPTER 9

Slavery after slavery: legacies of race and inequality

The abolition of the British slave trade in 1807 did not end British investment in the transatlantic slave trade nor direct involvement in trading enslaved people, especially between different colonies in the Caribbean. Similarly, the abolition of slavery in British territories in the 1830s was long drawn out, with full emancipation a distant or impossible prospect for most of those formerly enslaved. The plantation system was not abolished. Indeed, 'it went viral in the aftermath of abolition' based upon the labour of indentured servants, largely from Asia, and spreading to other British colonies throughout the world, predicated upon various forms of coerced labour.[1] The plantation system was also extended for sugar and coffee production in Cuba and Brazil, and, principally for cotton, in the southwest of the US (following the Louisiana Purchase). This ensured a 'Second Slavery' in the Americas in the early and mid-nineteenth century in which British investment played an important role, in turn affecting the trajectory of British industrial development, not least through the import of US cotton. In this chapter we examine the longer-term British involvement with slavery and its socio-economic consequences. We then turn to the impact of the slave trade and the African diaspora on the modern history of Africa, the Caribbean and other parts of the Americas. Finally, we examine the economic, social and political legacies of slavery that remain in Britain today and consider restorative justice.

Britain's continuing involvement with the slave trade after 1807

Eight years after the abolition of the British slave trade a bill was presented in Parliament to forbid the investment of British capital

---

[1] Beckert and Desan (2018: Introduction, 1–35, 24); Manjapra (2018: 370–87, esp. 382); Tomich (2004); Kaye (2009: 627–50).

in the slave trade of other nations, where it was continuing to reap rewards. Alexander Baring warned that every commercial organization in Britain would petition against the bill, and indeed the Lords threw it out.[2] Anti-slave-trade voices after 1807 were generally loudest where they aligned with British economic interests. Such 'lucrative humanity' lay behind the setting-up of the West Africa Squadron in 1808 to prevent slave trading by other nations after British abolition.[3] It was also prominent in British debates about Brazilian independence in the 1820s. Fearing restriction of the ballooning South American market for British manufactures (which depended upon the slave trade and slavery in Spanish and Portuguese colonies), British exporters began to campaign against suppressing the slave trade.[4] After various high-level bribes had failed to end Spanish and Portuguese slave trading, the Duke of Wellington, at the Congress of Verona in 1822, proposed that Prussia, Austro-Hungary and Russia should boycott Spanish and Portuguese goods. But he was asked if Britain would reject sugar imported from Spanish plantations for re-export and why British merchants were the dominant carriers of slave-produced goods from Brazil, Cuba and elsewhere.[5] Two decades later British firms still handled three-eighths of the sugar, half of the coffee and five-eighths of the cotton exported from Pernambuco, Rio de Janeiro and Bahia.[6] Lord Brougham pointed out to Parliament in 1841 that Liverpool and Manchester traders were still sending cottons, fancy goods and metalwares, including fetters and shackles, direct to the coast of Africa, or indirectly via Rio de Janeiro and Havana from where they were used to purchase enslaved people. And as late as 1845 Peel was unable to deny that British subjects were engaged in the slave trade. In 1848 it was said that seven-tenths of the goods used by Brazil for slave purchases were still British manufactures and, at

---

[2] Williams (1944/1994: 171).

[3] The term 'lucrative humanity' was coined in the 1840s by William Hutt during a Parliamentary debate: Hansard Third Series XCVI, 1096, February 22 1848, quoted by Williams (1944/1994: 170). Between 1808 and 1860 the Squadron captured 1600 slave ships and freed 150,000 slaves. Olusoga (2016: 289–308).

[4] Williams (1944/1994: 171).

[5] Williams (1944/1994: 169–70).

[6] Figures quoted for 1843: Manchester (1933: 133).

the same time, British banking firms in Brazil financed slave traders and insured their cargoes.[7]

Closer to home, British trade in enslaved people within the Caribbean continued. At least 20,000 enslaved workers were shipped between the colonies of the British Caribbean in the three decades after 1807. The urgent need for enslaved workers on the labour-hungry sugar frontiers, especially in Demerara, Essequibo and Trinidad, resulted in major shipments largely from colonies producing cotton, coffee and provisions.[8]

The slow and incomplete emancipation of slavery in British territories

Under the Slavery Abolition Act of 1833, over 800,000 slaves in the British West Indies, Mauritius and the Cape of Good Hope were to be freed, but the Act stipulated that enslaved people had to work for their former owners as apprentices for a further six years in the case of field hands and for four years in the case of house workers. Apprenticeship was seen as part of the compensation package for owners of the enslaved.[9] It was also seen as necessary to inculcate work-discipline, to assist planters to adjust to a different labour supply and to soften the impact of abolition on West Indian plantation output. The unpaid work of apprentices was formally limited to forty-five hours a week, in return for provisions and shelter, but practices varied and were often severe. Fearful of a breakdown in law and order, Crown-appointed magistrates oversaw the new labour system, and the colonial authorities created police districts to this end with houses of correction and workhouses. These institutions quickly became harsh tools of social discipline, including use

---

[7] Hansard LIX, 609, 20 September 1841 (Lord Brougham); XCVI, 1,101–2, 22 February 1848 (Sir William Jackson); Williams (1944/1994: 172); Eltis (1979: 211–27).

[8] Higman (1995: 76–92).

[9] The enslaved may thereby have paid between 20 and 50% of the cost of their freedom: Draper (2010: 106). The value of a six-year apprenticeship amounted to around 47% of compensation: Fogel and Engerman (1974: 377–401). The enslaved were freed immediately in Trinidad, Antigua and Bermuda, where the apprenticeship system was opposed, but the majority of freed slaves in the British Caribbean were subject to apprenticeship, unless they could buy their freedom which some masters encouraged in order to maximize their income.

of corporal punishment and treadmills. The state had effectively replaced the individual slave owner or overseer as the source of coercion.[10]

Strikes and other widespread opposition to the terms of partial freedom were repressed, but the anti-apprenticeship movement grew, supported by abolitionists in Britain. Parliament investigated apprenticeship conditions in Jamaica, and the findings led to formal emancipation in 1838.[11] The political and social status of emancipated slaves was much debated in colonial assemblies and in Parliament, including the reform of colonial laws in order to increase the social and economic opportunities of ex-slaves and to encourage their political participation. In practice, however, planters and their representatives, with a near monopoly of power and influence in the colonies, were reluctant to allow extensive rights to freed slaves. Their social and political position was further hampered by the racialized beliefs that had attended the institution of chattel slavery. Forms of social control were exercised by missionaries and magistrates intent upon reforming former slaves spiritually and morally including promoting (often inappropriate and socially destabilizing) European gender and family structures, forms of social behaviour and dress.[12]

The British West Indies economies remained dependent upon the export of sugar and other labour-intensive staples but, unsurprisingly, many ex-slaves were reluctant to work for very low wages on plantations where they had been enslaved.[13] Many sought employment in skilled trades or as independent cultivators, despite the shortage of available cultivable land. But colonial officials often barred or discouraged freedmen from landownership and destroyed the crops of squatters. Some local regulations classified freed slaves, who were not engaged in paid agricultural work, as vagrants subject to imprisonment.[14] The black right to vote that came with legal emancipation was also deliberately restricted by the imposition of high poll taxes, as in Jamaica. The

---

[10] Fergus (2013); Altink (2001).

[11] Altink (2001: 41); Turner (2004: 303–22).

[12] Kenny (2010: 130); Scully and Patton (2005: 254–5).

[13] Kenny (2010: 79). For more on wages and the transition to wage labour see essays in Turner (1995).

[14] Brereton (2005: 153); Fergus (2013: 80).

movement towards full emancipation in the British Caribbean was thus very slow and marked by racism, violence and exploitation.[15]

Emancipation in the British West Indies also took place when the British Caribbean island economies were faltering economically due to slave rebellions, soil exhaustion, falling sugar prices and new competition in sugar supplies from Cuba, Brazil, Europe and Asia. Between 1807 and the abolition of preferential sugar import duties for British colonies in 1846, however, planter and mercantile fortunes continued to be made from Caribbean business, especially in the newer colonies, Guiana in particular.[16] Booker Brothers, for example, came to dominate the Guyanese sugar industry until its nationalization a century later. The firm transformed its position from agent to large-scale plantation proprietorship in the period following emancipation.[17] But by the 1840s and 1850s plantations in the Caribbean were no longer a source of clear or reliable profits for British investors, and a high proportion of the 3,000 or so absentee plantation owners disinvested in the West Indies. By 1865 sugar production in Jamaica, and in some of the other older colonies, was half of what it had been in 1834. This brought high unemployment and high taxes, exacerbating the problems of low wages, poverty and outbreaks of cholera and smallpox. Social unrest was countered with extreme and violent repression, exhibited most starkly in the actions of Governor John Eyre following the Morant Bay rebellion of 1865 in Jamaica: 439 were killed, and over 600 men and woman were summarily executed or punished with whipping and long-term incarceration. Morant Bay was the most severe single incidence of repression of unrest in the history of the British West Indies.[18] Morant Bay pushed Britain into formalizing Jamaica as a Crown Colony, the most direct form of British colonial rule.[19] Living conditions on all the islands, particularly for freed slaves, were very poor and stagnated for the rest of the nineteenth century.

[15] Beckles (2013: 22).
[16] Draper (2010: 269); Draper (2021: 65–83).
[17] Draper (2010: 266).
[18] Heuman (1994).
[19] Koram (2022: 122).

British involvement in chattel slavery and indentured labour after 1838

British investors, banks and businesses continued beyond the 1830s to invest in enterprises run with chattel-slave labour. Some businesses already owned plantations in the colonies of other European powers. Baring Brothers, for example, owned plantations with some 500 slaves in the Danish colony of St Croix between the mid-1820s and 1848.[20] Barings and other British banks also invested in slave businesses in the US South through to the Civil War period.[21] So fundamental to southern US slavery was British capital that in 1857 *The Times* declared 'we are partners with the southern planter; we hold a bill of sale over his goods and chattels, his live and dead stock, and take the lion's share of the profits of slavery'.[22] An attempt in 1843 to prevent the ownership of enslaved people by British subjects anywhere in the world proved ineffectual. British investors and entrepreneurs also engaged in slave-labour mining and manufacturing industries, as well as plantations in other parts of the Americas. Copper mines in Cuba and gold mines in Brazil, owned by London-based companies, were in the 1840s the largest slave enterprises in the Western hemisphere. Such enterprises, often technologically and organizationally advanced, continued to attract British capital and management until at least the 1880s.[23] Their success contributed to the financial infrastructure that enabled merchant banking firms to invest further afield in Africa and Asia as well as in Latin America.[24] Apart from direct connections via investment, British trade and industry continued to thrive on markets underpinned by slavery in Spanish America and the USA and to deal in raw materials that were a product of slavery in Brazil (coffee and cotton), Cuba (copper and sugar) and the United States (cotton and tobacco).

The plantation system expanded across the British Empire after the 1830s, creating the conditions for slavery and near slavery in new

---

[20] Dresser and Hahn (2013: 9); Orbell (2004). For more on Barings and slavery see https://www.ucl.ac.uk/lbs/firm/view/-1735259225.

[21] Ziegler (1988).

[22] *The Times*, 30 January 1857, quoted by Williams (1944/1994: 172).

[23] Evans (2013: 118–34).

[24] Chapman (1984/2010: 16–69).

forms.[25] Planters, as they had in the sixteenth and seventeenth centuries, turned to indentured servants, this time from all over the globe but especially from India. Coerced and semi-coerced labour spread rapidly in the wake of both British and later American slave abolition. Indentured labour systems re-emerged and large-scale migrations proceeded across the world's oceans from India, Southeast Asia and China to work a new global economy of plantations that formed a belt around the Global South by the 1890s. Between 1846 and 1932 an estimated 28 million South Asians embarked, largely upon British ships, as indentured servants. Many went to the Caribbean, especially to Guiana, Surinam, Trinidad and Tobago, but also to Jamaica, Grenada and Barbados. Between 1833 and 1917 Trinidad imported 145,000 South Asians and British Guiana 238,000.[26] £1.5 million of compensation was paid to banks in the colonies by the British government in 1834 to help finance the transition to 'free labour': in the sugar islands it was largely used to finance the shift to indentured labour.[27]

Given the continuities and similarities between the trade in slaves and that in servants, it is no surprise that British ship owners and merchants, alongside Caribbean planters, were prime movers in the global indentured labour trade throughout the nineteenth century. A number used their slave ownership compensation monies to embark on the business. Andrew Colvile, West India merchant, plantation owner (in Antigua, Guiana and Jamaica) and sugar broker, was one of the leading mercantile beneficiaries of slave compensation money and became a major figure in the Hill Coolie importations into British Guiana from the late 1830s.[28] Sandbach Tinne, a Liverpool shipping firm, the second-largest mercantile beneficiary of emancipation compensation monies, became one of the biggest players in the indentured labour trade between the 1830s and the 1920s.[29] Founded in 1782 in Demerara, Sandbach, Tinne and Co. were ship owners, produce brokers, general merchants and plantation owners, exporting sugar, coffee, molasses and rum from the West Indies to Liverpool and Glasgow. The other giant in the

[25] Manjapra (2018); Stanziani (2014: 175–203).
[26] Hay and Craven (2004); Williams (1944/1994: 28).
[27] Graham (2021: 473–87).
[28] Draper (2010: 242); https://www.ucl.ac.uk/lbs/search/.
[29] Draper (2010: 235, 237, 252).

indentured labour trade in the nineteenth century was the Nourse Line. Founded in Glasgow in 1861, the Nourse Line specialized in shipping Indian labour from Calcutta to the West Indies, principally Guiana, and to the new sugar frontier in Mauritius, in specially designed ships. Conditions on such ships were little better than those on the slave ships that had preceded them. Men and women were segregated and confined below deck for most of the voyages, which took three to four months.[30] Despite closer regulation and more state-enforced medical supervision than occurred with the slave trade, the longer voyages and overcrowded conditions brought mortality and disease rates comparable to those in the slave trade.[31]

Well-established trading institutions and practices enabled the relatively easy shift from African slavery to its Asian counterpart. Planters sought to replicate the conditions of the slave plantations in the Caribbean and the American South in new environments where slavery was formally illegal, but debt bondage and indenture were not.[32] Tea and coffee plantations in India and Ceylon became new centres for coerced indentured labour. Large numbers of indentured servants, mostly 'blackbirded' from Vanuatu, the Soloman Islands, Melanesia and Micronesia, were taken in British ships in the nineteenth and early twentieth centuries to work on plantations in Fiji, New Caledonia, the Samoan Islands and Australia.[33] Plantations in Java, Malacca, Cape Colony and Mauritius as well as in Trinidad and Guiana followed the model of the slave plantations. Indeed, many former West Indian planters established new estates in the East.[34] John Gladstone sold most of his property in the West Indies in the 1830s and invested in Bengal sugar. He also invested in Ogilvy and Gillanders, which became one of the chief agency firms in Calcutta. The firm organized the import of eastern plantation commodities into Britain and Europe, including coffee, indigo, sugar and later jute, and managed

[30] Steamships, which would have reduced the journey time by half, were not in general use in the trade until the end of the nineteenth century. The Nourse Line appears not to have employed steam until 1904: https://en.wikipedia.org/wiki/Nourse_Line.
[31] Tinker (1974: chapter 5).
[32] Harvey (2019: 66–88, 75–6, 83); Beckles (2013: 3); Anderson (2014: 113–27); Stanziani (2014: 175–203).
[33] Tinker (1974).
[34] Manjapra (2018: 370–87, esp. 382).

investments across the Indian subcontinent.[35] New phases of capital- and resource-intensive industrialization in nineteenth-century Britain, Europe and the US relied on key primary products and foodstuffs, found across many other parts of the British and wider European empires, and extracted with racially based coerced labour.

British slave ownership compensation

Compensation of £20 million was paid by the British state to over 45,000 individual slave owners, accounting for around 800,000 enslaved people. Over 80% of these were in the West Indies, with the remainder in Cape Colony (South Africa) and in Mauritius. £20 million amounted to 40% of annual government expenditure at the time, which equates to around £220 billion as the same proportion of state expenditure today (2019–20).[36] In relation to the size of GDP in 2019 the £20 million compensation would be the current equivalent of around £128 billion.[37] This was the largest single financial operation undertaken by the British state to date. £15 million of the £20 million was raised for the government by Nathan Rothschild and Moses Montefiore, from UK and European creditors. The debt incurred was only finally settled in full in 2015, as part of government debt restruc- turing.[38] Until then regressive taxation ensured almost two centuries of subsidy from British wage earners and consumers of basic commodities to the elite holders of public debt, to the ex-slave owners themselves and their descendants.[39]

---

[35] Manton (2008); Webster (2008: 35–54).

[36] We have compared with 2019–20 to avoid the distortion of Covid-related state expenditure in 2020–1: https://www.measuringworth.com/calculators/ukcompare/. Unless otherwise stated, all conversions to contemporary values in this chapter use this source and the simple purchasing power calculator.

[37] Calculated on the basis of 2019 (pre-Covid) GDP of £2.17 trillion and 1831 GNP of £340 million: Mitchell and Deane (1962: 366).

[38] HM Treasury tweet, 9 February 2018: https://www.taxjustice.net/2020/06/09/slavery -compensation-uk-questions/; 'How the Government only finished paying off the UK's slavery debt in 2015', *Telegraph* 17 June 2020, https://www.telegraph.co.uk/news/2020 /06/17/government-finished-paying-uks-slavery-debt-2015/.

[39] https://eu.usatoday.com/story/news/factcheck/2020/06/30/fact-check-u-k-paid-off -debts-slave-owning-families-2015/3283908001/.

In the debate on compensation the sanctity of property rights overrode any notion that the enslaved themselves might be compensated. Even most abolitionists accepted that emancipation without compensating slave owners would be equivalent to theft.[40] It was also feared that a wider threat to property and prosperity would descend if slave owners were not properly compensated. John Horsley Palmer, former governor of the Bank of England, argued that, because slavery was at the heart of the credit system, emancipation without reparation would undermine the credit and confidence of the country.[41]

Slave owners received around 40% of the value of their slaves.[42] It has been estimated that over £27 million (in 2018 equivalence) was paid to the average slave owner with around 200 slaves.[43] Many planters owned several thousand slaves and received far higher compensation. The largest number of enslaved people in the West Indies colonies was in Jamaica (311,070). Barbados had 83,150, Demerara-Esquibo 64,185, Antigua 28,130 and Grenada 23,645.[44] Owners of the enslaved in Jamaica alone received over 30% of the entire compensation package of £20 million.[45] Enslaved people valued highest per head, in terms of productiveness foregone, were in British Honduras, British Guiana and Trinidad.[46] Plantation owners receiving compensation monies were able to pay off debts and refinance their businesses, often enabling them to recover from excessive credit consumption in the years leading up to emancipation. This had the effect of encouraging planters to hold on to their West Indian estates; such rigidities in the land market blocked off access to landownership by free blacks. Compensation added to capital in the Caribbean directly through ownership compensation but also indirectly by injecting liquidity into the economy of the British West Indies and boosting the value of West Indian estates.[47] The investor class and plantation owners benefitted, but the black population of the Caribbean

[40] Draper (2010: 272); Piketty (2020: 210–13).
[41] *The Times*, 28 May 1833, 5, quoted in Draper (2010: 82); Piketty (2020: 208–13).
[42] Draper (2010: 268).
[43] Piketty (2020: 208).
[44] Higman (1984/1995: 418).
[45] Draper (2010: 139).
[46] Higman (1984/1995: 79).
[47] Draper (2010: 268); Butler (1995: 74–91).

experienced 'a period of intensive policing, racial division and increased hostility to their demands for justice.'[48]

Apart from bolstering plantation agriculture and plantation-related trades and investment throughout the Empire, about half of the £20 million stayed in Britain, adding to the wealth already accumulated by many families in the slave trade and in plantation agriculture.[49] It contributed to the build-up of large landed estates and aided the mid-Victorian investment boom in British and overseas railways and public utilities. Some was invested in industry, particularly in the cotton industry and in railways. But the compensation programme mostly reinforced the long-held interests of slave owners in urban and rural land ownership, commerce and finance, including international finance.[50] Compensation extended the capital of the commercial and financial sector, especially in the City of London, but also in the other Atlantic ports. The 1830s and 1840s were decades characterized by trade crises, but also by a widening of the industrial, commercial and financial base of the British economy. The share of textiles in exports and GDP declined; the shares of producer goods industries, international investment, insurance and shipping in the economy grew. Compensation money helped to underpin this transition to a wider economic base in the mid-Victorian economy.[51]

Nowhere was this more apparent than in the capital that flowed from compensation into the mercantile and financial sectors in London.[52] London merchants and bankers were deeply involved in Caribbean profits and wealth. Not surprisingly, over 150 London merchants were slave owners at the time of emancipation, and dozens more acted as agents of slave and plantation owners. Around £2 million of the £20 million compensation was paid directly to London merchants in 1838. Many used their compensation to invest in trade and finance in other parts of the Empire.[53] Many London banks also benefitted from being

[48] Beckles (2013: 159).
[49] Draper (2010: 272); Legacies of British Slavery: https://www.ucl.ac.uk/lbs/; Hall, Draper, McClelland et al. (2014).
[50] Draper (2010: 166–203, 232–69); Read (2003: chapter 4).
[51] Draper (2010); Hall, Draper, McClelland et al. (2014: 78–126).
[52] Draper (2010: 242–51).
[53] Draper (2010: 242).

trustees of major slave owners or from being mortgagees for West Indian planters where enslaved people had been used as collateral for loans. Coutts and Co. managed the accounts of many Scottish West Indian proprietors. James Blair MP, the largest individual beneficiary of West Indian slave ownership compensation and owner of 1,598 slaves on the Blairmont estate in Guiana, was among their clients.[54] Of twenty-one London predecessor banks of the Royal Bank of Scotland group, six were mortgagees, three others were trustees for Caribbean slave owners and six more were the bankers of West Indian planters.[55] Other banks that benefitted were Barings, Rothschilds, Barclay Bevan and Tritton (forerunners of Barclays PLC), and four predecessor banks of Lloyds TSB.[56]

Because London was the administrative centre of the compensation process, many London law firms and other representatives of owners earned fees for negotiating disputed settlements. London was also the centre for 'farming' compensation claims: a number of firms, such as Pitcairn and Amos, made significant profits from systematically purchasing the smaller claims of slave owners resident in the colonies.[57] The mercantile and financial sectors in other Atlantic ports also benefitted, with Liverpool the provincial vanguard. Descendants of several Liverpool slave traders such as the Tarletons and the Backhouses were compensation recipients. Fifteen merchants of the city were awarded a total of £450,000 (£44 million 2019) for slaves owned in Guiana alone. John Bolton received over £24,000 (£2.3 million). William Shand received £58,000 for slaves in Guiana and Jamaica (£5.5 million 2019).[58] By the 1840s many Liverpool merchants in receipt of compensation had invested in railway shares including John Moss and Robertson Gladstone.[59] Compensation also had an important impact upon the regional financial system centred on Liverpool. The *Circular to Bankers* noted in 1836 that it had resulted in a 'great accession to the floating capital of Liverpool' which oiled the wheels of trade with

---

[54] He received £83,530 8s 11d (over £8 million 2019): Draper (2010: 243).

[55] Draper (2010: 244).

[56] https://www.ucl.ac.uk/lbs/firm/view/-2030672549; Draper (2010: 243–51).

[57] Draper (2010: 263).

[58] Draper (2010: 252).

[59] Draper (2010: 253); Williams (1944/1994: 105).

its hinterland.[60] Compensation monies eased the diversification of Liverpool mercantile enterprise away from the Atlantic towards the Indian Ocean and assisted the development of Liverpool's nineteenth-century role as a centre of shipping, insurance, banking and cotton broking.

Bristolians in 1833 registered ownership of 15,553 slaves in total and received over £500,000 compensation.[61] Charles Pinney (mayor of Bristol in the 1830s) invested much of his proceeds (totalling £44,458: £4.3 million in 2019) in railway stocks, dock and canal shares and in the Great Western Cotton Works. Compensation recipients were particularly prominent in financing the construction of the Great Western Railway.

Glasgow merchants received a total of £400,000 in compensation for slaves owned mostly in the newer territories of Trinidad and Guiana (almost £39 million 2019). Four of the five original directors of Glasgow's West India Association (set up in 1807) were beneficiaries, as were new participants in the West Indian business, including the Eccles family, who owned slaves in Trinidad.[62] Unlike in London, few Scottish banks had loaned directly on mortgage to planters but many heavily invested in, or were offshoots of, Atlantic mercantile firms in the city who in turn had financed slave owners. These firms provided a foundation for the growth of new Scottish financial institutions, particularly life insurance and banking in the early nineteenth century.[63]

Whether in landed estates, transport or financial infrastructures, the Empire, trade or industry, investments made with compensation monies strengthened the hand of wealthy landed and commercial families, some of which continue to dominate British elite society and politics to this day.[64] The Lascelles family, for example, made one of the greatest fortunes from slave plantations owned in Barbados, Tobago and Jamaica from the mid-seventeenth century. In 1753 Henry Lascelles left a fortune of £392,704 (£59.5 million 2019). His descendants from

[60] *Circular to Bankers*, 11 March 1836, cited in Reed (1975: 268).
[61] Draper (2010: 257 n87, Appendix 15); Marshall (1975: Appendix 1); Morgan (1993b: 185–208, esp. 193).
[62] Draper (2010: 258–9).
[63] Draper (2010: 259–60); Mullen (2022: 271–4).
[64] https://www.ucl.ac.uk/lbs/; Piketty (2020: 209).

the late eighteenth century became the Earls of Harewood, hereditary peers who married into the royal family. Belle and Mount plantations in Jamaica remained in the family's hands until the 1970s.[65] Other names signalling the continuity of slave ownership in the mainstream of modern British life include the McGarel-Hogg family (Viscounts Hailsham), which produced two twentieth-century lord chancellors, the Akers Douglas family (Viscounts Chilston), the Holland Hibberts (Viscounts Knutsford) and the banker Robert Cooper Lee Bevan (whose firm was one of the predecessors of Barclays bank).[66] Aristocrats, business elites, the established church, the clergy, judiciary, universities, banks, MPs and the royal family were all claimants of compensation. There were also many beneficiaries much lower down the social scale. This spread the stimulus of compensation far and wide within British society and the economy. Just as slave ownership had done, compensation benefitted more people than the direct owners of slaves because many had indirect dependence upon slave ownership via annuities, marriage settlements and legacies and also through incomes earned from managing, financing and settling claims.[67]

Wealth derived from slave ownership significantly shaped British society and culture, as well as the economy, in the nineteenth century and beyond. Slave owners receiving compensation figure prominently in the mid-Victorian philanthropic boom, in financing museum and art collections, in church building and especially in the foundation and development of universities in England and in Scotland.[68]

The injection and disposition of £20 million in the British domestic and imperial economy of the mid-Victorian period was important, but this should not detract from the fact that this was only a coda in the long series of financial transfers involving slavery over the previous two centuries. Slave owners and merchants in Britain were likely making similar sums in real terms every decade or so from the early 1700s

[65] Beckles (2013: chapter 9); https://www.measuringworth.com/calculators/ukcompare /result.php?year_source=1753andamount=392704andyear_result=2020.
[66] Hall, Draper, McClelland et al. (2014).
[67] Draper (2010: 114–37; 204–31ff.).
[68] Hall, Draper, McClelland et al. (2014: 50–56); Draper (2010: 303–15); https:// www.ucl.ac.uk/lbs/search/.

through to the 1820s from the expropriated labour of enslaved people and from high sugar prices in protected markets.[69]

The impact of slavery on Africa and the Caribbean until today

The long-term social and economic development of West Africa was subverted by the slave trade. The trade over more than four centuries removed a significant proportion of the population of the continent, especially of its younger men.[70] It also created political instability and encouraged warfare and conflict. From Senegal to Angola client states sprang up or were created from old states with the support of European slave traders. A purpose of these states was to displace those polities and leaders (the majority) that opposed the slaving business.[71] The demographic impact alone upon West Africa was far larger than the figures of the slave trade itself suggest. Hundreds of thousands of Africans died during capture and awaiting shipment. These mortality rates were exacerbated by mixing captives from different disease environments and by exposing them to European pathogens. Other enslaved people, well over a million, died, were killed or committed suicide in the Atlantic crossing.[72] It has been estimated that Africa as a whole, as a result of Indian Ocean as well as the transatlantic slave exports, lost close to 20 million people. According to the best estimates, by 1800 Africa's population was half what it might have been had the slave trades not occurred.[73]

It is no accident that the countries from which most of the enslaved were taken (as a proportion of the total populations of those countries) are the poorest in Africa today and have the greatest inter-ethnic conflict. It has been estimated that, had the slave trades not occurred, around 72% of the average income gap between Africa and the rest of the

---

[69] We are grateful to Nick Draper for discussing this point with us. For 105 Scottish West India mercantile fortunes generated between the mid-eighteenth and the later nineteenth century (amounting to almost £5 million) see Mullen (2022: 256–7).

[70] Inikori and Engerman (1992: 2–7); Inikori (2014); Manning (1992: 117–41).

[71] Manning (1990); Lovejoy (2000); Nunn (2008: 139–76).

[72] Beckles (2013: 47).

[73] Nunn (2008); Manning (1990). For early surveys of gainers and losers from the slave trade see Inikori and Engerman (1992, esp. 1–24).

world and 99% of the income gap between Africa and other developing countries would not exist today.[74] The slave trade impacted in the longer term upon the transition from slavery and debt-bondage to hired labour and agricultural indebtedness in Ghana and elsewhere in the nineteenth and twentieth centuries.[75] A recent survey of research concluded that the slave trade affected a wide range of important outcomes in Africa 'including economic prosperity, ethnic diversity, institutional quality, the prevalence of conflict, the prevalence of HIV, trust levels, female labour force participation rates and the practice of polygyny'.[76]

In the Caribbean today there is widespread poverty, illiteracy and ill health, which can be directly related to the economic legacies of slavery.[77] Colonial locations with good agricultural potential and natural resources in the Caribbean and large parts of Latin America developed institutions, pre- and post-slavery, that strongly favoured narrow landholding elites and encouraged the extreme inequality that persists today.[78] Social and economic marginalization amongst descendants of the enslaved endures throughout the former British colonies of the Caribbean.

At the same time, descendants of slave owners and their mercantile backers and partners continue to be enriched. One major source is the profits they draw from the lucrative tax haven business that dominates the economies of several of the former British possessions.[79] Race, class and gender hierarchies of colonial domination have left a legacy of high levels of wealth inequality. Poverty rates average 30% of the Caribbean population, with Belize, Dominica, Grenada and Surinam badly affected, but the once most wealthy plantation economies of Jamaica and Haiti are now the poorest states. There is much evidence of intergenerational transfer of poverty, stigmatization and discrimination.[80] Low worker productivity, low education and skill levels, limited economic diversification and scarcity of productive investment beyond a few economic enclaves have historically restricted economic growth and

[74] Nunn (2010: 142–84).
[75] Austin (2008); Inikori (2000). For a broader perspective see Rodney (1972/2018).
[76] Nunn (2017); Teso (2019: 497–534).
[77] Piketty (2020: 203–51); Pons (2007).
[78] Engerman and Sokoloff (2012).
[79] Bowen (2007: 150–58); Ogle (2020: 213–49).
[80] Bowen (2007).

curbed employment in the region. Most states, including Jamaica, rely heavily on imports of basic necessities, including food and clothing. This creates an increasing trade deficit, endangering the economy and keeping people below the poverty line.[81]

Lasting discrimination in Britain and restorative justice

Slavery has also had a lasting social and cultural impact on Britain, entrenched in key British institutions, as well as in the economy, through to the present day.[82] Racially based discrimination and inequality, with its roots in slavery, fed into and were endorsed by the ideas and beliefs surrounding imperial conquest and global exploitation in the nineteenth and early twentieth centuries. The post-Second World War and post-colonial immigration of black and Asian labour forces from the West Indies, West and East Africa, India and Pakistan to work in factories, infrastructure and hospitals during Britain's years of expansion between the 1950s and the 1970s further ties contemporary race-based inequality to the long legacies of empire and coerced labour. The substantial economic growth of the past half century has come with increased inequalities of wealth and income, including those based on race, as well as social class.[83]

During the era of slavery the British legally defined Africans as non-human and kept slaves violently subordinated by local militia, imperial troops and legal machinery. Denial of African humanity, in the eyes of white Europeans, and fear of African insurrection were driven deep into popular culture, creating a lasting legacy of racism. Not only did the dehumanization of Africans in British law, philosophy and religion enable slave trading and chattel slavery, but indigenous populations such as the Kalingos were defined as savages not fit to have their lands, in order to justify their expulsion or genocide.[84] Similar attitudes drove the violence perpetrated upon indigenous peoples in other parts

---

[81] https://www.macrotrends.net/countries/JAM/jamaica/trade-balance-deficit. For the impact of sugar slavery in the Caribbean in the nineteenth and twentieth centuries see Pons (2007); for Jamaica and Haiti in the nineteenth century see Smith (2014).

[82] Hall, Draper, McClelland et al. (2014: 50–6); Draper (2010: 303–15); https://www.ucl.ac.uk/lbs/search/.

[83] Piketty (2014: 304–76, esp. 316, 319, 344).

[84] Blackburn (1997: 259–60); Beckles (2013: 57–8).

of Britain's imperial world in the nineteenth and twentieth centuries; in Asia, Africa, Australia, New Zealand, Canada and elsewhere.[85] Britain's white elite, and much of her white population, prospered from this violence, from slavery and from coerced labour, and continued to prosper from their legacies. Many Africans, Caribbeans and their descendants in Britain are still paying the price. Afro-Caribbeans in Britain are twice as likely to be unemployed as whites, earn 60% less on average, and (among men) are more than twice as likely to be in prison.[86] Households that have more debts than assets are twice as likely to be 'black African' and 'other Asian' than white families.[87] The legacy of slavery and the deeply entrenched racism that accompanied and survived slavery impacts upon everyday life in Britain today through discriminatory cultural, as well as economic institutions and through institutionalized racism within the policing and the justice system.[88]

Many now seek reparative justice for the impact of historic slavery upon the Afro-Caribbean population in Britain and upon the economic, social and political circumstances of the Caribbean and West African states.[89] Among these is the CARICOM Reparations Commission, set up in 2013 by Caribbean member states. The Commission draws its case for reparations from international law, which clearly states that redress for crimes against humanity should take account of the continuing harm suffered by persons and populations.[90] Yet restorative justice for slavery has yet to become a subject of serious public or political debate in Britain. Because African chattel slavery was a foundational element within the

[85] For graphic illustration see the film *Exterminate All the Brutes*, dir. Raoul Peck, 2021.
[86] https://www.ethnicity-facts-figures.service.gov.uk/work-pay-and-benefits/pay-and-income/income-distribution/latest#by-ethnicity-after-housing-costs; https://researchbriefings.files.parliament.uk/documents/SN04334/SN04334.pdf; https://assets-global.website-files.com/61488f992b58e687f1108c7c/61bca661b8abd33d2f6f579c_Runnymede%20CERD%20report%20v3.pdf.
[87] Koram (2022: 17–18).
[88] For recent data see the Runnymeade Trust Report to the UN on Racial Discrimination in Britain 2021: https://assets-global.website-files.com/61488f992b58e687f1108c7c/61bca661b8abd33d2f6f579c_Runnymede%20CERD%20report%20v3.pdf.
[89] For an early survey of this see Beckles (2013: 163–230).
[90] Gifford (2007: 243–54; 2000); For detailed treatment of the mix of benefit, entitlement and responsibility involved in rectifying international injustice see Butt (2008).

domestic economy of the USA, discussions there about within-country racial reparations have been more prominent.[91] The legacy of slavery and lasting racial discrimination in the USA since 1865 means that today the average black family has only 10% of the wealth of the average white family. Jim Crow legislation (lasting a century following the Civil War), anti-black housing policies, red lining in the mortgage industry and other discriminatory policies in transportation, business, criminal justice and education contributed to long-lasting racialized capitalism that has denied black Americans opportunities to build wealth.[92] It has also led to calls for a revolution in educational and equal opportunities policies. But only in April 2021, following the Black Lives Matter protests, did Congress pass a bill to set up a commission to discuss reparations as a way to underpin the necessary reforms.

The idea that the slave trade was the province of private businessmen working outside of Britain and had little to do with the British polity itself is sometimes used as an argument against the need for the British state to get involved with restorative justice. But the state played a key role in the slave trade and slave plantations from an early stage through to both abolition and planter compensation.[93] It did not confine itself to the regulation or fiscal management of slavery. The state set up royal chartered companies to further the expansion of the trade and implemented legal frameworks for financing and administering the slave-based colonies and their commerce. The Royal Navy policed the seas, protected convoys and oversaw the gains that came through warfare. The British

---

[91] Early calculations, restricted to the value of the slave labour expropriated between 1620 and 1865, suggested that the 1983 value of the debt to the black population would amount to between $96.3 billion and $9.7 trillion. Calculations of L. Neal cited in Munford (1996: 428–9) and cited in Beckles (2013: 171). More recent and comprehensive reparations estimates suggest compensation of about $12 trillion would be needed: https://www.cnbc.com/2020/08/12/slavery-reparations-cost-us-government -10–to–12–trillion.html.

[92] Policy 2020 Brookings: https://www.brookings.edu/policy2020/bigideas/why-we -need-reparations-for-black-americans/; Darity et al. (2018): https://socialequity.duke .edu/wp-content/uploads/2019/10/what-we-get-wrong.pdf; Institute of Policy Studies, *The Road to Zero Wealth: How the Racial Wealth Divide Is Hollowing Out America's Middle Class*, 2017, https://prosperitynow.org/sites/default/files/PDFs/road_to_zero_wealth .pdf; Robinson (2000).

[93] Daunton and Halpern (1999: 12).

state also sanctioned a divide between the common and civil law over chattel slavery. It was illegal in Britain to treat an employee as a chattel, but chattel slavery was legal in the colonies.[94] In the final years of the slave trade the government professed abolition yet made thousands of slave purchases largely to raise troops for the West India Militia.[95] Finally, the emancipation settlement marked acceptance of the view that slavery had been sanctioned politically and legally by the state and that the nation should therefore bear the cost (to slave owners) of the policy change.

As in the USA, there have been some attempts in the UK to place a monetary value on the losses and the debt.[96] Such calculations are a first step and a useful tool in acknowledging the extent to which enslaved (and colonized) people, and their descendants, subsidized the British economy in the past and the losses they suffered as a result. But acknowledgement of the debt owed to the enslaved and their descendants among the white British public and politicians is muted, and its impact upon social, employment, educational and health-care policies is small. Neither has discussion of the debt entered to any degree into debates about overseas reparations or even overseas aid. The case made for reparative justice views aid payments as a matter of international justice and restitution, not charity. Progress is being made, albeit often cloaked in the secrecy imposed by non-disclosure agreements, in recent payments of educational and social grants to black social foundations, by private institutions, including banks and big businesses, whose roots go back to profits made from slavery and where commercial reputations have been damaged by Black Lives Matter and similar campaigns.[97]

---

[94] This statement distils a complicated pattern of civil and common law which was only partially clarified by Lord Mansfield's decision in Somerset v. Stewart in 1772. There were between 10,000 and 15,000 people of African descent in Britain in the later eighteenth century, many in states of near slavery. Chater (2009: 21–136); Olusoga (2016/2017: 113–98); Walvin (1993: 15); Beckles (2013: 56–67).

[95] Rawley (1981: 146–7, 168); Lambert (2018: 627–50).

[96] Beckles (2013: 170, 24–36). One attempt in 2004 calculated restorative justice for the Caribbean alone at £7.5 trillion for unpaid wages, unjust enrichment and pain and suffering: *The Empire Pays Back*, https://www.youtube.com/watch?v=MzctBXOHewk.

[97] These developments are discussed in https://www.tortoisemedia.com/thinkin/racial-privilege-can-white-debt-ever-be-repaid/.

Conclusion

British involvement in the slave trade and slavery continued well into the nineteenth century. Commerce and investment in other forms of coerced labour throughout and beyond the Empire remained central to Britain's nineteenth- and twentieth-century imperialism. The slave trade and slavery, including the monies distributed as compensation to slave owners, impacted on British capitalism and on inequality and discrimination over the longer term. Finally, it is important to set the gains to Britain from slavery alongside the negative impact of the African slave trade and diaspora on the societies of West Africa and the Americas, especially the Caribbean. Understanding the afterlife of slavery, as well as transatlantic slavery itself, is fundamental to addressing and repairing the harms that they have created.

CHAPTER 10

Slavery, capitalism and the economic history of Britain

Capitalism in Britain in the late eighteenth century had features in common with many other countries: a regime that endorsed private property rights; the search for profits based on the exploitation of labour as well as technological change; growing capital investment in manufacturing plant and equipment as well as in trade; and the power of rising economic interests exercised through monopolies and the state as well as through markets.[1] Neither was Britain unique in benefitting from the transatlantic slave trade and from the labour of enslaved millions in the Americas. European powers – Portugal, Spain, Sweden, the Netherlands, France, Denmark – participated in transatlantic slavery in different ways, at different times, to different degrees and from different economic and political circumstances and starting points. These meant that the impact of slavery would be different in each case.

We have argued that Britain was able to gain disproportionately from the slave trade and from plantation colonies, compared with her European rivals, for several decades, in the mid- and late eighteenth century. This arose from her military and protectionist successes, her relative political and financial stability and her dominance of the slave trade. Protected trade with uniquely prosperous and populous white settler colonies and ex colonies, driven by both domestic and colonial consumption, and underpinned by the exploitation of enslaved labour, gave Britain an advantage. Together with internal factors, this ensured that capitalism in Britain developed some particular and distinctive characteristics over both the short term and the long. In the short term, as we will argue in this chapter, Britain's early success in commerce and

---

[1] For debate about the history of capitalism, various conceptualizations of capitalism and its re-emergence as an analytical term since the 1990s, see Kocka and van der Linden (2016: 1–7; 207–66); Kocka (2016). For economic practices that generate profits see O'Sullivan (2018: 754, 775, 778–9); Levy (2021: xviii–xxi).

colonialism, shipping and financial services, arising from slave-based global trade and investment and supported by the state, provided both a context and a driver for a particular kind of industrial revolution. In the longer term, this set the British economy on a path where industrialization was shaped within empire, and where commerce and empire, shipping, international investment and financial services became and remained as important as Britain's manufacturing power.

Economic historians on a narrower quest for the sources of economic growth have largely denied connections between economic development and slavery. This was easy because slavery was something that happened elsewhere, not on home soil. But sidelining slavery was also easy because economic growth is conventionally analysed at the level of the nation state and studies are generally preoccupied with internal factors. Overseas trade and colonies are little considered as independent sources of stimulus. Study of capitalism, by contrast, necessitates a global perspective in order to understand the full scope for profitable investment. During the eighteenth century, global trade and colonies were an attractive source of profits. Although risky, the returns could be far higher than those available in the domestic economy. Profitable investment possibilities at home escalated only in the nineteenth century with the capital demands of large-scale industries and the expansion of new domestic and global markets for their products. Inducements to make profitable investments are as much a part of the story of capitalist development as the removal of domestic institutional obstacles. For Britain and other parts of western Europe in the eighteenth century inducements came especially from the Atlantic colonial project based on slavery.[2] Slavery introduced a uniquely elastic and harshly exploitable supply of labour to European colonies in the Americas that quickly allowed a huge expansion of their output and trade. It enabled Britain and other European colonial powers to gain greater investment opportunities, it demanded sophisticated commercial institutions and increased factor, commodity and capital flows globally. These raised the rate of return on the investment of European capital. Slavery made British capital investment more profitable, as well as increasing national output.[3]

[2] Levy (2021: xiv–xv, 1–38).
[3] Solow (1987: 72–4).

A recent body of research and writing, emerging from the different circumstances and legacy of slavery in the USA, places slavery and coerced labour at the heart of the formation of modern capitalism. The New Histories of Capitalism (NHC) began as seminar debates, at Harvard in the late 2000s, on many aspects of world as well as US history. The aim was 'to draw out the character and varieties of modern global capitalism and their roots in the past' using insights from cultural history, legal history, social history and political history, rather than conventional economic history methodologies. Historians pursuing this approach connect the sources of modern economic growth in markets, property rights and money with the part played by violence, coercion and war, especially as these connect with slavery. They emphasize that the celebrated roots of capitalism in the rise of free markets, democracy and inclusive institutions, had illiberal underpinnings: slavery, imperialism and bellicose and powerful states, giving rise to 'war capitalism'.[4]

The research of the NHC has rejuvenated debate about slavery and economic development, transcending old discussions about whether or not slavery is compatible with capitalism. They have been joined in the US by a public-history/educational movement, the 1619 Project, an initiative led by the *New York Times*. The Project rejects the common starting point of US history in the War of Independence, instead selecting 1619, the date of first landing of African enslaved peoples in Virginia. Alongside the NHC, the 1619 Project reframes the narrative of US history, emphasizing the proactive role of enslaved people and black Americans in that history and centring the consequences of slavery in debates about contemporary racial inequalities.[5]

The NHC have helped to anchor the economy as a subject in US history faculties, but there is disagreement and often mutual incomprehension between historians of slavery and economic historians in the US.

---

[4] Beckert and Desan (2014: 503–36); Beckert and Desan (2018: 1–35); Beckert (2014); Baptist (2014); Baptist (2016); Johnson (2013). For critiques of NHC see Wright (2020), Vries (2017) and Burnard and Riello (2020). Also see the wider discussion of American capitalism in Levy (2021).

[5] *New York Times* (2019): https://www.nytimes.com/interactive/2019/08/14/magazine /1619-america-slavery.html; https://www.nytimes.com/2019/12/20/magazine/we -respond-to-the-historians-who-critiqued-the-1619-project.html; Hannah-Jones (2021); Wilentz (2019).

There is likewise little interaction between British and American debates about slavery and economic development.[6] This is regrettable because the NHC provoke questions about the relationship between earlier phases of Atlantic slavery and European capitalist expansion. Moving the focus from the US to Europe and specifically to Britain offers an opportunity to rethink some of the issues raised by the NHC.

In this final chapter we set out key differences in the relationship between slavery and capitalism in Britain compared with the US. These revolve around timing, geography, demography, crop regimes and, crucially, the support of the state. We also summarize our findings on the role of slavery in the case of British economic development. We stress three elements in particular: the dynamic created by new consumer tastes and markets for plantation groceries; the ecological relief provided by both food and raw materials produced by enslaved labour; and the role of the state, particularly in relation to both public and private financial innovations. We suggest that these distinctive features of 'slavery's capitalism', embedded during the eighteenth century, influenced the development of British capitalism thereafter and were formative in some of the major economic, regional and racial inequalities that characterize Britain and the world today.

Slavery and capitalism: the British experience

The place of African enslaved labour in British and, more generally, west European, history contrasts with its role in the US. Slavery in the US has an immediate presence because it occurred on domestic soil and left a demographic, racial and social legacy in plain sight. This legacy has generated a long and contested historiography of slavery and of race. By contrast, although it is estimated that there were between 10,000 and 15,000 black slave-servants and other black people in Britain in the eighteenth century, British enslavement of Africans remained largely out of sight and it was under-researched, as a component of British history, until relatively recently.[7] The distorting effect of geographical distance on

---

[6] Olmstead and Rhode (2018); Wright (2020: 353).
[7] Chater (2011: 25); Sanghera (2021: 71); Olusoga (2017: 113–42); Otele (2020); https://www.runaways.gla.ac.uk/.

approaches to slavery has been compounded by foregrounding the story of Britain's role in abolition. This has tended to divert historical attention away from Britain's leading part in the operation of the slave trade and in the development of the plantation system.

Over a period of three centuries, millions of Britons experienced the Atlantic slave system through running plantations, managing and working in shipping, dock work, trading in plantation commodities and enslaved peoples, employment in commercial finance, processing and manufacturing with Atlantic raw materials and in consuming colonial produce. But this did not find its way into the mainstream story of Britain's past. Where slavery was studied in any detail in universities it tended to be separated from British history and located in Caribbean or African Studies centres. The history of British involvement in slavery was largely divided off from Britain's own, predominantly white, island story.[8]

The impact of distance on British perceptions of plantation slavery, compared with approaches in the US, is magnified by chronology. The cotton–slave nexus that dominates American history is a nineteenth-century story, even though the use of enslaved labour on the US mainland dates back to at least 1619.[9] The thirteen colonies were rich places well before 1775, largely on the back of slave-grown exports. Yet slavery's role in American capitalism has long been seen as largely a post-Independence phenomenon, centred on cotton plantations and the American South. Britain's use of enslaved labour in her colonies dates back to more than a century earlier. By the mid-seventeenth century enslaved Africans worked the plantation agri-business and capital-intensive industrial processing of sugar in the Caribbean. Enslaved peoples laboured on other plantation crops (principally tobacco, coffee, cacao, rice, indigo and cotton), in both the mainland colonies and in the Caribbean, but sugar dominated. Britain's earlier history of slavery and capitalism is thus a distinctive history based upon the early rise of consumerism, led by sugar; the associated extension of global mass markets for both groceries and manufactured goods; the integration of

[8] Walvin (2017: 1–10); Burnard and Riello (2020: 232).
[9] 1619 marks the first recorded landing of African enslaved peoples, but Amerindian slave labour was also important especially in South Carolina through the seventeenth century: (Davis 2010: xix).

the Atlantic with Indian Ocean trade; and the expansion of transcontinental financial and military power.

Britain's Caribbean sugar colonies also differed from the North American experience because they were 'slave societies' rather than 'societies with slaves'. Caribbean plantations, although they had started with indentured labour, quickly transitioned to slave labour in the seventeenth century. Sugar was a 'quintessential slave crop', cultivated on a large scale with intensively exploited African labour.[10] Because it was impossible to attract sufficient low-cost free labour to the harsh regimes of intensive sugar cultivation or white settlers to the high-disease environment of the Caribbean, West Indian plantation colonies had a very high ratio of enslaved to other workers and salaried managers. By the third quarter of the eighteenth century and into the nineteenth century, enslaved people accounted for around 90% of the population on several of the island colonies.[11] In Jamaica, by 1782, a white population of around 15,000 presided over an enslaved population of 240,000.[12]

The northern mainland plantation colonies (later USA) had more varied crop mixes and agricultural regimes, and higher ratios of white settlers. Tobacco, indigo, rice and cotton did not have the significant scale economies or capital requirements found in sugar cultivation. Cotton could be grown at any scale and in locations settled by free farmers. Early cotton growers on the mainland colonies as well as in the West Indies used enslaved labour because they were already slave owners and because land was extensive whilst labour was scarce and enslaved labour was cheap. Slavery was a 'pre-existing condition for the nineteenth-century American South'.[13] These were also 'societies with slaves', rather than 'slave societies'. Enslaved peoples made up 30–40% of the population, in parts of the Chesapeake, for example, rising to around 55% in Mississippi and other parts of the new slave frontier states of the deep South in the 1860s, but these ratios came nowhere near those found in the Caribbean.[14]

---

[10] Wright (2020: 354).
[11] Higman (1995: 77).
[12] Burnard (2015: 161).
[13] Wright (2020: 354, 353, 361).
[14] https://faculty.weber.edu/kmackay/statistics_on_slavery.htm; Finley (1980).

The slave societies of the West Indies inevitably relied on a more complex and expensive apparatus of management with physically harsh repression, and military backup deployed to stop slave flight or rebellion and to maintain output. Absentee owners, separated from their plantations for part or all of the time, required sophisticated accounting techniques and managerial hierarchies, involving the enslaved as well as white overseers. They also authorized violent and harsh regimes of labour discipline. Caribbean slave societies necessarily relied on backup from local militias, island assemblies and the military and navy of the British state for enforcement of labour regimes and for colonial protection.[15]

White dominion in the demographic context of the Caribbean meant violent racial subordination; an attempt to transform human beings into commodities. The dehumanization of enslaved captives, in the eyes of white Europeans, was embedded during passage on the slave ship.[16] This continued with stages of 'seasoning' on arrival on the plantation, enacted through complex hierarchies of managers and overseers, black as well as white.[17] Circumstances differed in the American South, where natural increase rather than importations of newly enslaved people was often sufficient to supply labour demands even before Independence. The huge internal slave trade in the mainland colonies (later USA) especially the movement of a million enslaved people to the new plantation frontier of the deep South in the decades before 1861, involved the routine and deliberate breakup of families of the enslaved and brought its own racial legacies.[18]

White European perceptions of black African enslaved peoples as sub-human became part of the ideas and legal codes used to justify Atlantic slavery, which in turn conditioned the nature of racism in Britain thereafter. The enslaved workforces in Britain's offshore plantation zones were racialized in British political philosophy and law from an early stage. England's 'free air' was declared by William Blackstone in the 1760s to be incompatible with slavery. The workforce brought from Africa to colonial zones half a world away was 'alien' and 'seasoned to

---

[15] O'Brien (1998: 53–77).
[16] Reddiker (2007); Morgan (2016a: 246–50).
[17] Rosenthal (2016: 62–86); Mintz (1985: 19–73); Radburn (2021).
[18] Tadman (1989): 136–54.

work' in an intensely commercialized and repressive system tied to 'free' Atlantic trade, an oceanic remove from the 'free air' of Britain.[19]

A revolution in consumption

Slavery was not only a labour system. It connected vitally in Britain's case to making new consumer markets in colonial groceries. Britain's story, like that in other parts of western Europe, was one of the power of consumption, as well as production, in transforming capitalism. Slavery, directly and indirectly, promoted the expansion of new consumer demands and mass markets in Britain, Europe, Africa, the Americas and worldwide. European consumer tastes, habits and ways of life were entirely transformed by slave-produced tobacco, sugar, rum, molasses, coffee, cacao, and by hot sweet beverages, alcoholic drinks, desserts, biscuits and preserves. New products not only included a range of derivatives of sugar and tobacco, but also an array of manufactured accoutrements, first desirable, then necessary, from snuff boxes and pipes to sugar basins and tongs. These changed the focus and processes of British manufacturing. Colonial consumer goods, alongside growing varieties of cloth and clothing, household textiles and utensils, spread down the social scale, and encouraged the shift from household self-sufficiency to wage labour. This 'industrious revolution' constituted a fundamental change in household and consumer behaviour that marked the process of industrialization.

The demand for new manufactured products, especially those geared to sugar consumption and rituals of tea drinking, stimulated production, not just in Britain but across Europe and in Asia, encouraging Asian and European trades in ceramics and silverwares. Britain's most important import from China in the eighteenth century was tea. In China and Japan tea was largely consumed in bitter black or green forms. The west European taste for black tea rose rapidly only after the introduction of Caribbean sugar as a sweetener. The burgeoning import trades in sugar and tea, from opposite ends of the globe, thus became co-dependent.[20]

---

[19] Blackburn (2015: 1–15, 2); Morgan (2016a: 57–86); Richardson (2022: 97–117); Olusoga (2016/2017: 113–97); Taylor (2020).
[20] Ellis, Coulton and Mauger (2015: 144, 183–5).

This synergy, through the operations of the East India Company, aided by a reduction of the tea tax in 1784 and by improved design of specialized sailing ships, made Britain the monopoly tea supplier to Europe by the end of the eighteenth century (at the expense of the Dutch, and of other European East India companies and private traders). This unlocked the further expansion of British trade in Asia, including the expansion of the opium trade from India to China to pay for tea, porcelain and silk. It also later resulted in the great expansion of tea cultivation on plantations in British India, providing a source of tea under British control.[21]

New consumer markets both at home and in the Atlantic world drove British industrial expansion and innovation. Product innovation was the highway into rapidly growing Atlantic markets for new sorts of textiles, metalwares and other manufactures, in Africa, the Caribbean and especially in North America, as well as in Europe. The textile sector saw difference and novelty in the weight, colour, design and fibre-mix of cloth, not just in cotton, but in silk, worsted, linen and hosiery. Producers of lightweight luxury metalwares in iron, copper, steel and silver plate, and manufacturers of domestic paraphernalia, finessed products and designs for discerning Atlantic-world markets. Plantation requirements for shipping, supplies, equipment, new sorts of harvesting tools and the copper vessels, utensils, windmills and steam engines required for sugar processing, placed new demands on British manufacturing and changed its locations. New products brought new technologies, in turn generating higher profits for this Atlantic system of consumption and production.

Discerning consumption in West Africa fuelled further distinctive synergies between slavery and global trade. Trade to Africa was a trade in currencies as well as consumer goods. Manillas, produced in the west midlands, and 'voyage iron' from the Baltic were used as currencies as much as commodities. Between 1700 and 1790 ten billion cowrie shells (1,143 metric tons), found only in the Maldives, were traded via Rotterdam and London to Africa and used to buy enslaved people.[22] Trade with Asia also brought Europeans the key commodity exchanged for enslaved peoples on the West African coast: dyed and patterned cotton cloth. West African taste for expertly dyed and brightly patterned

---

[21] Nierstrasz (2015: 7–9; 190–8); Hodacs (2016: 43–80); Mackillop (2015: 294–308).
[22] Green (2020); Walvin (2017: 37–53).

cottons from India linked Asia and Africa together and stimulated imitative and innovative manufacturing in Britain.

Britain's slave trade and slave plantations underpinned an early complex multilateral trading system that stretched worldwide. It pre-dated by over a century the capitalist globalization that rested on US slavery and cotton, foregrounded in the NHC. Slave-mined silver in the Americas had first given European empires access to Asian markets and consumer goods. By the mid- to late seventeenth century the global trading system cemented the links between Eurasia and the Atlantic. Sugar was pivotal. It was part of a global trade that embraced commodities and people from India and the Indian Ocean, from the African interior, from the settled frontiers of the Americas, North and South, from the Caribbean as well as from many of the economies of Europe from the Baltic to the Mediterranean. Voyages of 16,000 to 20,000 kilometres or more were common in this globalized trading system by the early eighteenth century, transporting people and goods across more than one continent. These trades brought porcelain tableware and tea from China, cotton textiles and spices from India, cotton from the Levant, naval stores, timber and iron from the Baltic, guns, textiles and other manufactures from central and western Europe, tobacco, sugar, coffee, cacao, cotton, indigo and other plantation products from the North American colonies and the Caribbean. The slave trade to and from Africa did not exist in isolation: it lay at the heart of early capitalist globalization, based on a revolution in consumption as well as production.

Food and raw materials: escaping the constraints of the domestic economy

Slave-grown agricultural commodities revolutionized tastes and consumer habits. But these commodities also helped to release Britain from the environmental constraints imposed by domestic food and raw material supplies. Britain's slave colonies in the Americas contributed food calories that helped to maintain the nutrition of the rapidly expanding population at the end of the eighteenth century as domestic food supplies struggled to keep pace. Atlantic world colonies also provided raw materials that reduced constraints in particular sectors, from textiles to shipbuilding and furniture making. These raw materials also encouraged product and process innovations. The four largest British industries by 1801, in terms of value added (with estimates of the value-added percentage in brackets), were wool (18.7%), building (17.2%), cotton (17%) and leather (15.5%).[23] Wool-textiles and leather drew around 90% of their main raw materials from domestic supplies at that point. But timber and iron imports were important for building and shipbuilding, and the cotton industry was entirely dependent upon imported raw material mostly from the Caribbean. In the absence of cotton, it would have taken almost two-thirds of the arable acreage in Britain by 1820 to have supplied the wool necessary for the equivalent amount of woollen yarn.[24] The Caribbean and North American colonies (later the USA) supplied not only cotton but dyestuffs, timber, tobacco and sugar, all of which formed the basis of new processing and manufacturing industries.[25] At the same time, growing re-exports of colonial produce from Britain to Ireland and to continental Europe helped to pay for additional vital raw material supplies including timber, naval stores, iron, linen and foodstuffs.

Logwood and mahogany, used in dyestuffs and furniture making respectively, initially formed ballast in many returning slave ships but soon generated a rapidly rising trade in tropical timbers. The West India interest successfully lobbied for mahogany to be included in an Act of 1721 that removed duties on imported 'naval stores'. After this, mahogany from the Caribbean led the refurnishing of elite and middle-class domestic interiors. Thomas Chippendale's company of London produced highly polished rococo styles wrought from this timber, harvested by slaves. Gillows, elite furniture makers of Lancaster, traded slaves and imported large quantities of mahogany for their business.[26]

The contribution of imported colonial sugar and cotton alone from highly productive colonial 'ghost acres' may have 'saved' 1.5 million domestic acres in 1772, 2.6 million in 1790, 6 million in 1815 and 8.1

---

[23] Crafts (1985: 22, table 2.3).

[24] Riello (2013: 240–1, 356); Pomeranz (2000: 276).

[25] Kumar (2020: 297–9). Compare Wrigley (2018: 9–42).

[26] Walvin (2017: 82–103); Barczewski (2014: 164–79). For mahogany furniture manufacture and fashion in Europe and in North America see Stuart (2008); Anderson (2012).

million in 1820 out of a total arable British acreage of 17 million.[27] With the addition of timber and other products, colonial imports may have effectively doubled Britain's land resources by the 1830s.[28]

The extraction of slave-grown foodstuffs and raw materials brought with it extensive environmental destruction. Slash-and-burn techniques to clear the land for plantations destroyed the forest ecologies of the West Indian islands, depleting the soil of its nutrients and causing soil erosion, even before continuous cultivation also brought soil exhaustion. The tropical timber trade took out more forests in the Caribbean and continues to this day to do so in South America and Africa. Water-management projects in canals, reservoirs and irrigation ditches brought rising malaria and introduced yellow fever to the Caribbean.[29] Environmental damage caused by colonial and imperial monocultures is a recurrent and present feature of global capitalism.

Britain's story of slavery and capitalism demonstrates that sugar became a leading global commodity, long before cotton. Of course, cotton's place in the rise of industrial capitalism is fundamental: a commodity that connected Asia, Africa, Europe and the Atlantic world and that became the main fibre of the factory system in the industrial age.[30] But sugar, a foodstuff, cultivated, harvested and refined using both enslaved labour and technologically advanced industrial processes, deeply affected Europe, Africa and the Atlantic world up to two centuries earlier than did cotton. Its widespread economic and social impact was totally novel. Apart from its effects on labour systems, consumption, and manufacturing, it also made fortunes for traders along the commodity chain and drove innovations in shipping, international trade and payments systems, banking and stockbroking: the sorts of innovations that commodity historians and the NHC have generally reserved for the US-based cotton era a century later.

[27] Cuenca-Estaban (2004: 35–66; 2014); Pomeranz (2000: 264–85); Wrigley (1988: 54–5).

[28] This excludes cotton from the US. Pomeranz (2000: 274–6); Cuenca-Estaban (2004: 55).

[29] Engineer (2016: 207–16); Johnston (2020).

[30] Beckert (2014: xv–xxii); Riello (2013: 3–8).

Slavery and the state

The NHC stress the importance of the state in underpinning the slave system of the Atlantic, especially during the century of bellicose commercial rivalry that culminated in the Napoleonic War period. But they pay little attention to how states functioned to advance capitalist development. Approaching the subject from a west European and specifically British perspective allows a closer look at the functioning of the state in relation to 'slavery's capitalism'.[31]

Many historians of capitalism in Britain see the Glorious Revolution and the Settlement of 1688 as a turning point in the origins of parliamentary democracy and in the related spread of more inclusive economic institutions and a state that favoured competitive capitalist enterprise. But Britain's slave-based colonialism in the eighteenth century was founded on militarism, mercantilism, protectionism and monopolies in which the central state and colonial governments played a major role.[32] Fiscal and military support from the state was promoted by groups of financial capitalists, plantation owners, merchants, ship owners and entrepreneurs who vied for access to political power and to influence commercial policy in their favour.[33] The West India and East India interests, but particularly the former in the eighteenth century, wielded power through formal and informal political positions in local and central governments and in the institutions of public and private finance.[34] Policy-makers adhered to a vision of political economy based on slavery, plantations, global trade, shipping, consumption and taxation.

The state played a key part not only in maintaining and endorsing the slave-based Atlantic trading system, but also in wider global activities connecting the Atlantic with the African and Asian trades. There was an

[31] The phrase is from the NHC as used by Beckert and Rockman (2016).

[32] Compare, for example, Acemoglu and Robinson (2012); North and Weingast (1989), with Pincus (2009); Pincus and Robinson (2016: 229–61); Ashworth (2017: 105–44). See also Vries (2015); Tilly (1990).

[33] A characteristic of the early capitalist state first emphasized by Fernand Braudel, see Kocka and van der Linden (2016: 3).

[34] The historiography has often separated these two, but in practice many commercial and investing families had interests in both the East and West Indies trades: Jeppesen (2016: 102–25).

alliance of sovereign and capitalist power put to work through licensed corporations (the Hudson's Bay Company, the East India Company, the RAC, the Virginia Company, the South Sea Company and others), but also through legal and military support given to powerful groups of private traders. Britain's trade was enforced by high tariffs and shipping restrictions backed up by naval power, colonial acquisition and warfare to thwart other European trading nations.

State revenue raising via innovations in borrowing and taxation was key to maintaining the mercantilist-military state. Rising tax revenues to service the national debt lay behind the state's ability to borrow on the London capital market, to prosecute costly trade wars and to uphold the Navigation Acts. Political stability as well as commercial expansion rested upon 'credible commitment', which in turn depended upon the government's ability to pay interest on its loans out of tax revenue. It also depended upon the ease of convertibility of government stock into more liquid assets that were attractive to investors. The capacity to extract high levels of tax, 70–80% of which was raised through customs and excise, was vital. Colonial trade and colonial goods shouldered some of the tax burden, while speculation on the slave trade brought about a major reorganization of the Debt and its tradeability following the South Sea Bubble.[35]

Monopolies, protective tariffs and taxation meant that British and Atlantic consumers often paid higher prices for their sugar, textiles and other goods than their continental European counterparts. But these were prices that the market could bear yet still expand exponentially, essentially redistributing income from consumers to the state and to potential investors. The excise was also responsible for imposing quality standards on British-produced commodities, which benefitted their wider reputation and sales.[36] Local taxation required by colonial infrastructures of repression and coercion almost bankrupted some of the island assemblies, Jamaica in particular, by the end of the eighteenth century. British imperial state intervention, even its heavy taxation, was welcomed, however, in most of the Caribbean as necessary to secure the islands from both internal and external threats and to enforce the Navigation Acts, which protected planters from better and cheaper French sugar. The northern colonies, by contrast, with

[35] See chapter 8, pp. 181–2.
[36] Ashworth (2003: 209–79); Ashworth (2017: 119–44); Brewer (1989: 101–14).

very different demographic and economic circumstances, demanded fiscal and political autonomy, culminating in the War of Independence.[37]

The Atlantic trading system can be viewed as a state-sponsored colonial economic and political project, but in practice the way in which the British state worked in partnership with Parliament, with provincial and colonial interests and institutions and with private contractors was contingent and complicated. State policies were a product of negotiations at local, regional and international levels, with Irish and Scottish as well as colonial institutions, and with private commercial interests.[38] Such negotiations meant that the British state was less powerful than some accounts allow. It also became more interventionist than is generally considered, both in domestic social policies and in colonial projects that involved spending substantial monies to reinforce British non-military power and influence. Significant sums were spent in the colonies on civil development, specifically upon disaster relief (such as from hurricanes), infrastructural improvements in ports, harbours and transport and on bounties, drawbacks and other incentives for industrial development and technological innovation. The interventionist British state of the eighteenth and early nineteenth centuries was felt most keenly outside England, in the Atlantic colonies, Scotland and Ireland. Eighteenth-century slave-based colonial expansion thus helped to encourage a negotiated civil interventionism beyond the hegemonic power conveyed in the NHC's concept of 'war capitalism'.[39]

Slavery, the industrial revolution and the long-term development of British capitalism

Recent research on consumption, global history, technical innovation and occupational structures demonstrates a rapidly transforming British capitalist economy of the eighteenth century. Slavery was part of this

---

[37] Burnard and Graham (2020: 461–89); Graham (2020b: 184–205; see also 2023); Breen (2004).

[38] Post (2015: 581–3); Burnard and Riello (2020: 225–44, 236); Carey and Finlay (2011); Graham and Walsh (2016: 1–25).

[39] Mulcahy (2005); Smith (2011); Smith (2012); Draper (2015); Burnard and Graham (2020); Pincus and Robinson (2016: 229–61); Pincus and Robinson (2017: 9–34). For internal interventionism see: Hoppit (2011: 93–128); Innes (2009).

transformation. It was not the only part, but it sits centrally alongside, and it influenced, domestic agricultural transformation, capital formation, technological change, the transformation of financial and commercial practices and the revolution in public as well as private finance. The profits directly derived from slavery are only part of the story; economic benefits do not have to be measurable to be significant. This is especially the case with institutional changes that were spurred by the slave and plantation trades.

Eric Williams incorporated institutional change into his analysis of the industrial revolution. In particular, he argued that 'the rise and fall of mercantilism was the rise and fall of slavery and that once the West Indian monopoly became a hindrance to wider British trade, the anti-slavery lobby garnered mass support. The ending of preferential sugar duties in 1846, in his view, finally sealed the fate of the West Indian colonies in favour of 'free-trade'.[40]

Historians today rightly see the shift to free trade in the mid-nineteenth century as partial and complex. An ideology of free trade prevailed in the nineteenth century, encouraged by Britain's (short-lived) competitive superiority in manufacturing export goods, and by the need to import foodstuffs. Protectionism declined, and free trade was adopted in important spheres of commerce such as the grain trade, textiles and other export-oriented manufactures. But Britain also retained a substantial and growing formal empire and protected markets, through the era of free trade, an empire that continued to expand for another century. Although imperial government was loose and informal in the white dominions and exercised largely through pre-existing power structures in Africa, India and elsewhere, it often involved coercive military force. The state tightened its grip on India in this respect after taking over from the East India Company in 1858. Force was also exercised to impose bilateral 'free trade' treaties on reluctant trading partners, creating an 'informal empire', especially in Latin America and in Egypt, beyond the areas coloured red on the map.[41]

---

[40] Williams (1944/1994: 153).

[41] The classic article on this is Gallagher and Robinson (1953); See also Cain and Hopkins (1993a); Cain and Hopkins (1993b); Darwin (2012: 167–222); Gardner and Roy (2020: 151). For the history and role of company states as progenitors of globalization see Phillips and Sharman (2020). For state support for capitalism in the mercantilist era see Pincus (2012); Rössner (2020); Ashworth (2017: 105–44).

With the expansion of Britain's nineteenth-century Empire came the expansion of racial capitalism.[42] In the colonial period, and influenced by experience in the Caribbean, many believed that cash crops, especially those grown in environmentally hazardous conditions, could only be produced by slave labour. Racial justifications endorsed what was essentially an economic choice based on maximal labour exploitation and minimum cost.[43] New plantations of Britain's nineteenth-century Empire, after the abolition of slavery in most British territories in 1833, absorbed the structures of the old, including work discipline enforced by violence. Debt bondage, indenture contracts and share cropping placed colonial labour regimes on plantations (and in mining), far below low-paid independent wage labour in terms of exploitation and remuneration. The slave-based plantation model, passed on from sugar and cotton to indentured and share-cropping labour systems, endorsed an already deeply embedded racial capitalism. Highly racialized descriptions of 'negro' labour forces and techniques for controlling them were extended to Tamil and Chinese indentured workforces.[44] The slave trade and slavery in the seventeenth and eighteenth centuries thus initiated a pattern of the use of racially based coerced labour to extract key primary products found across many other parts of the British Empire in the following century. They also created the legal, commercial and financial infrastructure that made this possible.

The pattern and institutions of trade and investment, established in the era of slavery, were cemented by British trade and colonialism in India and Asia as well as the Atlantic but the two were closely integrated, as we have seen. The particular investment and trading needs of slave-based transatlantic trade helped to revolutionize the financial sector. This included the raising of tens of millions of pounds of capital on the security of land and moveable property across the global empire. It also involved new multilateral payments systems, credit transfers and stock trading. Transatlantic commerce, together with these capital flows, generated hefty commissions that lay at the heart of new trade, financial and legal fortunes. Britain's leading roles in global shipping, international

---

[42] For definition and debate on racial capitalism see Robinson (1983: 9–28); Bhattacharyya (2018); Jenkins and Leroy (2021).

[43] Williams (1944/1994: 9–20); Johnston (2020).

[44] Manjapra (2018: 370–87, 372–4); Stanziani (2014: 183–91).

investment and marine insurance at the end of the eighteenth century were retained through the era of empire-based globalization. Finance, stockbroking and insurance connected with the slave and colonial trades helped to lay the foundations for further financialization of the British economy in the centuries that followed. And the same laws of private property that had encouraged chartered companies and private traders to undertake colonial and imperial trading, in the seventeenth and eighteenth centuries, confident that the proceeds would belong to them to the exclusion of others, continued. It can be argued that they still serve as the underlying model for transnational financial and credit dealings and claims to intellectual property rights and debts today.[45]

The slave-based Atlantic trading system set the British economy upon a particular path in which commerce and empire, shipping and financial services were and remained more important than her manufacturing power, although they were complementary and interdependent.[46] Already in 1759 services (principally financial services, shipping, other transport and retailing) made the same level of contribution to GDP as did industry. By 1841 services accounted for around 41% of GDP, while industry contributed 36%.[47] Britain's service- and investment-oriented global role, through the Age of Empire and beyond, rendered the economy more dependent upon imports of food and raw materials and upon income from invisibles (shipping, insurance, investments and financial services), especially as other countries industrialized.[48] At its height around 1900 British shipping accounted for 48% of global tonnage and total invisible receipts accounted for between 37 and 40% of current account earnings as late as the 1970s, far higher than other OECD countries, apart from the US.[49] Slavery and colonialism thus laid the foundations for the type of service-oriented rentier economy, which Britain later developed, and the varieties of profitable imperial outlets

---

[45] Koram (2022: 76).
[46] Compare the concept of 'Gentlemanly Capitalism' as in Cain and Hopkins (1993a); Cain and Hopkins (1993b). For complexities and critique see Daunton (1989). Also see Dummett (1999) and Akita (2002).
[47] Broadberry et al. (2015: 194).
[48] Cain and Hopkins (1993a: 170).
[49] Sturmey (1962: 4–5); https://www.bankofengland.co.uk/-/media/boe/files/quarterly-bulletin/1977/some-recent-developments-in-the-uks-invisible-account.pdf.

for direct and portfolio investment that British financiers were largely to pursue in the nineteenth and twentieth centuries. Britain was not exceptional in exporting capital and managerial capitalism overseas; France, Belgium, Holland and Japan did likewise in the later nineteenth and twentieth centuries. But the scale of operations emanating from Britain, and the extent of British imperial power, was significantly greater.[50] This further extended the role of the City of London as an international focus of finance and capital flows and helped to perpetuate London's place as a major global financial centre.[51]

Between 1809 and 1879 90% of British millionaires were landowners, but the economic and social power of commerce rather than manufacturing ranked next.[52] There was significant turnover, interchange, movement and complementarity between these categories, but when a new dominant group of the wealthy rose in the late Victorian period it was merchants and financiers rather than industrialists who were most prominent. The plutocracy that took Britain into and through the twentieth century was formed from an integration of financiers (later joined by other rentiers) and landed magnates.[53] Wealth in land was not idle: it brought profits from rents and coal royalties and it underpinned credit, finance and imperial investment, rentier and industrial incomes, as it had in the eighteenth century.[54] Post-colonial development greatly internationalized Britain's global role as an investment centre, a focus now of multinational corporations, increasingly outside the fiscal control of individual states.[55] It is no coincidence that, in the 1950s and 1960s, some of the Caribbean islands under British control and hungry for inward investment became tax havens, set up to absorb capital fleeing the British and other empires at the time of decolonization.[56]

---

[50] Gardner and Roy (2020: 152–4).
[51] Darwin (2012: 178–84); Cain and Hopkins (1993a); Cain and Hopkins (1993b).
[52] Cannadine (1990: 91); Anderson (1987: 20–70, esp. 28); Rubinstein (2006: 74–128); but see discussion by Daunton (1989).
[53] Daunton (1989, 1991); Rubinstein (2006: 74–145); Anderson (1987: 34, 41, 57); Rustin and Massey (2014, 2015); Jones (2002); Christophers (2020: 1–48).
[54] Daunton (1989).
[55] Cain and Hopkins (1993a); Cain and Hopkins (1993b); Jones (2002).
[56] Ogle (2020: 213–49); Piketty (2014: 465–7); Koram (2022: 155–90).

Slavery thus had a long-term material influence on the British economy and a lasting social and cultural impact on the distribution of power and influence in British society. It also greatly affected inequalities of wealth and income based on class, geography and race. Caribbean profits and Britain's early industrialization in the eighteenth century raised her national income, but average British wages lagged behind overall growth for almost a century, and poverty increased. Coupled with regressive taxation and structural unemployment (caused by technological innovations and regional shifts), a distribution of income and wealth was created during the industrial revolution that favoured elites and the entrepreneurial classes at the expense of wage earners and the poor; a distribution that was slow to change until the middle decades of the twentieth century and which has since returned.[57]

The colonial determinants of Britain's industrialization also created a new regional orientation of the industrializing economy in favour of the economic hinterlands of the Atlantic trading ports, particularly Liverpool and Glasgow. This regional shift has influenced the geographical distribution of income and wealth inequalities in Britain ever since. The westward-facing heavily industrialized regions of the late eighteenth and early nineteenth centuries were the only regions that boasted significant millionaire and half-millionaire wealth outside London into the twentieth century.[58] But the industrial regions in the UK's northwest and midlands experienced deindustrialization in the twentieth century as the centre of gravity of the economy swung decisively in favour of finance and other services rather than manufacturing industry. This recreated and endorsed an economic divide in Britain between a wealthy and prosperous southeast, centred on London, and most of the old industrial areas of the north, the midlands and the west. Superimposed upon geographical and class divides and very noticeable within them are inequalities of income, wealth and opportunity based on race. These are the product of the long history of racism that was set in place by transatlantic slavery.[59] It was endorsed by the widespread use of racially based coerced labour and servitude in the nineteenth- and twentieth-century Empire and

[57] Feinstein (1998: 625–8); Allen (2009b); Piketty (2014: 316, 344); cf. Crafts (2021: 327–30).
[58] Rubinstein (2006: 130–32).
[59] Otele (2020: 67–94; 201–16).

reinforced by the immigration of imperial and commonwealth labour in the later twentieth century. This black British migrant population was largely funnelled into low-paid labour-intensive manufacturing or into low-tier service-sector employments and it has faced an extremely hostile environment.[60]

Britain's development was not a stage process of merchant capitalism to industrial capitalism and on to financial capitalism; these were combined in one process during the long eighteenth century and beyond. Slavery was one of the sparks that set the industrial revolution alight, but it also played a role in the longer-term economic orientation of the British economy to international trade, investment in empire, shipping, insurance and rentierism. Slavery had a long-term impact on the structure and nature of the British economy: industrialization, financialization, elite formation and embedded inequality. Slavery gave modern capitalism some of its fundamental structures of production and consumption and promoted inequalities of race, class and geography that have characterized Britain and the rest of the world for the past three centuries.

---

[60] For the afterlife of empire, racial hostility and discrimination in Britain see Olusoga (2016/2017); Sanghera (2021); Koram (2022); Ashiagbor (2021); Goodfellow (2020). For transnational aspects see Darwin (2012).

References

Acemoglu, D. (2002), 'Directed Technical Change', *Review of Economic Studies* 69: 781–809.

Acemoglu, D. and Robinson, J. (2012), *Why Nations Fail: The Origins of Power, Prosperity and Poverty* (London).

Akita, S. (ed.) (2002), *Gentlemanly Capitalism, Imperialism and Global History* (London).

Allan, D. G. C. and Abbott, J. L. (1992), *The Virtuoso Tribe of Arts and Sciences. Studies in the Eighteenth-Century Work and Membership of the London Society of Arts* (Athens, Georgia and London).

Allen, G. C. (1929/1966), *The Industrial Development of Birmingham and the Black Country 1860–1927* (London).

Allen, R. C. (2005), 'Real Wages in Europe and Asia: A First Look at the Long-Term Patterns', in R. C. Allen, T. Bengtsson and M. Dribe (eds), *Living Standards in the Past: New Perspectives on Well-Being in Asia and Europe* (Oxford), 111–30.

Allen, R. C. (2009a), *The Industrial Revolution in Global Perspective* (Cambridge).

Allen, R. C. (2009b), 'Engels' Pause: Technical Change, Capital Accumulation, and Inequality in the British Industrial Revolution', *Explorations in Economic History* 46, 4: 418–35.

Allen, R. C. (2011), 'The Spinning Jenny: A Fresh Look', *Journal of Economic History* 71, 2: 461–4.

Allen, R. C. (2015), 'The High Wage Economy and the Industrial Revolution: A Restatement', *Economic History Review* 68, 1: 1–22.

Allen R. C. (2019), 'Class Structure and Inequality During the Industrial Revolution: Lessons from England's Social Tables, 1688–1867', *Economic History Review* 72, 1: 88–125.

Allen, R. C., Murphy, T. and Schneider, E. (2012), 'The Colonial Origins of Divergence in the Americas: A Labour Market Approach', *Journal of Economic History* 72, 4: 863–94.

Alston, D. (2015), '"The habits of these creatures in clinging to one another"' in T. Devine (ed.), *Recovering Scotland's Slavery Past: The Caribbean Connection* (Edinburgh), 99–123.

Alston, D. (2021), *Slaves and Highlanders: Silenced Histories of Scotland and the Caribbean* (Edinburgh).

Altink, H. (2001), 'Slavery by Another Name: Apprenticed Women in Jamaican Workhouses in the Period 1834–8', *Social History* 26, 1: 40–59.

Anderson, B. L. (1977), 'The Lancashire Bill System and Its Liverpool Practitioners: The Case of a Slave Merchant', in W. H. Chaloner (ed.), *Trade and Transport: Essays in Economic History in Honour of T. S. Willan* (Manchester), 59–97.

Anderson, C. (2014), 'After Emancipation: Empires and Imperial Formations', in C. Hall, N. Draper and K. McClelland (eds), *Emancipation and the Remaking of the British Imperial World* (Manchester), 113–27.

Anderson, J. L. (2012), *Mahogany: The Costs of Luxury in Early America* (Cambridge, MA).

Anderson, P. (1987), 'The Figures of Descent', *New Left Review* 161: 20–70.

Andrew, J. (2009), 'The Soho Steam Engine Business', in S. Mason (ed.), *Matthew Boulton: Selling What All the World Desires* (New Haven, CT and London), 63–70.

Anon. (1749), *Essay on the Increase and Decline of Trade* (London).

Anstey, R. (1975), *The Atlantic Slave Trade and British Abolition, 1760–1810* (London).

Ascott, D. E, Lewis, J. E. and Power, M. J. (eds) (2006), *Liverpool 1660–1750: People, Prosperity and Power* (Liverpool).

Ashiagbor, D. (2021), 'Race and Colonialism in the Construction of Labour Markets and Precarity', *Industrial Law Journal* 50, 4: 506–31.

Ashton, T. S. (1945), 'The Bill of Exchange and Private Banks in Lancashire 1790–1830', *Economic History Review* 15, 1: 25–35.

Ashton, T. S. (ed.) (1950), *Letters of a West African Trader, Edward Grace 1767–1770* (London).

Ashworth, W. (2003), *Customs and Excise. Trade, Production and Consumption in England 1649–1845* (Oxford).

Ashworth, W. (2017), *The Industrial Revolution: The State Knowledge and Global Trade* (London).

Atkins, A. (1737), *A Voyage to Guinea, Brasil, and the West-Indies* (London).

Austen, R. A. and Smith W. D. (1990), 'Private Tooth Decay as Public Economic Virtue: The Slave-Sugar Triangle, Consumerism and European Industrialization', *Social Science History* 14, 1: 95–115.

Austin, G. (2008), *Land, Labour and Capital in Ghana: From Slavery to Free Labour in Asante* (London).

Avery, V. (2019), 'Letters from William Perrin's Jamaican Sugar Plantations', in V. Avery and M. Calaresu, *Feast and Fast: the Art of Food in Europe 1500–1800* (Cambridge), 88–91.

Avery, V. and Calaresu, M. (2019), *Feast and Fast: the Art of Food in Europe 1500–1800* (Cambridge).

Bailey, R. W. (1986), 'Africa, the Slave Trade, and the Rise of Industrial Capitalism in Europe and the United States: a Historiographic Review', *American History: A Bibliographic Review* 2: 1–91.

Baker, I. P. (1775), *An Essay on the Art of Making Muscovado Sugar Wherein a New Process Is Proposed* (Kingston, Jamaica).

Baptist, E. E. (2014), *The Half Has Never Been Told: Slavery and the Making of American Capitalism* (Ithaca).

Baptist, E. E. (2016), 'Toward a Political Economy of Slave Labour: Hands, Whipping Machines and Modern Power', in S. Beckert and S. Rockman (eds), *Slavery's Capitalism: A New History of American Economic Development* (Philadelphia), 31–62.

Barczewski, S. (2014), *Country Houses and the British Empire* (Manchester).

Baumgarten, L. (2012), *What Clothes Reveal: The Language of Clothing in Colonial and Federal America* (New Haven, CT).

Beckert, S. (2014), *Empire of Cotton. A New History of Global Capitalism* (New York).

Beckert, S. and Desan, C. (2014), 'Interchange: The History of Capitalism', *Journal of American History* 101, 2: 503–36.

Beckert, S. and Desan, C. (eds) (2018), *American Capitalism: New Histories* (New York).

Beckert, S. and Rockman, S. (2016), 'Introduction', *Slavery's Capitalism: A New History of American Economic Development* (Philadelphia), 1–27.

Beckles, H. M. (2013), *Britain's Black Debt. Reparations for Caribbean Slavery and Native Genocide* (Kingston, Jamaica).

Belgrove, W. and Drax, H. (1755), *A Treatise Upon Husbandry or Planting* (Boston, New England).

Berendt, S. D. (2001), 'Markets, Transaction Cycles and Profits: Merchant Decision Making in the British Slave Trade', *William and Mary Quarterly* 58, 1: 171–204.

Berg, M. (2004), 'In Pursuit of Luxury: Global History and British Consumer Goods in the Eighteenth Century', *Past & Present* 182: 85–142.

Berg, M. (2005), *Luxury and Pleasure in Eighteenth-Century Britain* (Cambridge).

Berg, M. (2013), 'Useful Knowledge, Industrial Enlightenment and the Place of India', *Journal of Global History* 8, 1: 117–41.

Berg, M. and Clifford, H. (eds) (1999), *Consumers and Luxury: Consumer Culture in Europe, 1650–1850* (New York).

Berg, M., Gottman, D., Hodacs, H. and Nierstrasz, C. (eds) (2015), *Goods from the East. Trading Eurasia 1600–1800* (Basingstoke).

Berg, M. and Hudson P. (2021), 'Slavery, Atlantic Trade and Skills: A Response to Mokyr's Holy Land of Industrialism', *Journal of the British Academy* 9: 259–81.

Berg, T. and Berg, P. (trans.), (2001), *R. R. Angerstein's Illustrated Travel Diary, 1753–1755. Industry in England and Wales from a Swedish Perspective* (London).

Berlin, I. (2003), *Generations of Captivity: A History of African-American Slaves* (Cambridge, MA).

Bhattacharyya, G. (2018), *Rethinking Racial Capitalism: Questions of Reproduction and Survival* (Lanham, MD).

Bickham, T. (2008), 'Eating the Empire: Intersections of Food, Cookery and Imperialism in Eighteenth-century Britain', *Past & Present* 198, 1: 71–109.

Birch, A. (1967), *The Economic History of the British Iron and Steel Industry 1784 to 1879* (London).

Bischoff, J. (1842/1968), *A Comprehensive History of the Woollen and Worsted Manufactures, and the Natural and Commercial History of Sheep, from the Earliest Records to the Present Period*, vol. 1 (London).

Blackburn, R. (1997), *The Making of New World Slavery from the Baroque to the Modern 1492–1800* (London).

Blackburn, R. (2015), 'The Scope of Accumulation and the Reach of Moral Perception: Slavery, Market Revolution and Atlantic Capitalism', in C. Hall, N. Draper and K. McClelland (eds), *Emancipation and the Remaking of the British Imperial World* (Manchester), 1–15.

Blake, P. (1798), 'Culture of Sugar in the West Indies', in A.Young (ed.), *Annals of Agriculture* 31 (London), 360–70.

Bogart, D. (2022), 'Transport and Urban Growth in the First Industrial Revolution', unpublished Economic History Seminar Paper 25, Institute of Historical Research.

Boldizzoni, F. and Hudson, P. (eds), (2016), *The Routledge Handbook of Global Economic History* (London).

Bourne, H. R. F. (1866), *English Merchants*, vol. 2 (London).

Bowen, G. A. (2007), 'The Challenges of Poverty and Social Welfare in the Caribbean', *International Journal of Social Welfare* 16, 2: 150–58.

Bowen, H. V. (1998), *War and British Society, 1688–1815* (Cambridge).

Brandon, P. (2017), 'From Williams's Thesis to Williams Thesis: An Anticolonial Trajectory', *International Review of Social History* 62: 305–27.

Brandon, P. and Bosma, U. (2021), 'Slavery and the Dutch Economy, 1750–1800', *Slavery and Abolition* 42, 1: 43–76.

Braudel, F. (1977), *Afterthoughts on Material Civilization and Capitalism* (Baltimore).

Breen, T. (2004), *The Marketplace of Revolution. How Consumer Politics Shaped American Independence* (Oxford).

Brereton, B. (2005), 'Family Strategies, Gender and the Shift to Wage Labor in the British Caribbean', in P. Scully and D. Paton (eds), *Gender and Slave Emancipation in the Atlantic World* (Durham), 143–61.

Brewer, J. (1989), *The Sinews of Power: War and the English State, 1688–1783* (London).

Broadberry, S., Campbell, B. M. S., Klein, A., Overton M. and van Leeuwen, B. (2015), *British Economic Growth 1270–1870* (Cambridge).

Brown, P. and Schwarz, M. H. (1996), *Come Drink the Bowl Dry. Alcoholic Liquors and their Place in 18th Century Society* (York).

Burnard, T. G. (1996), 'European Migration to Jamaica 1655–1780', *William and Mary Quarterly* 53, 4: 769–96.

Burnard, T. G. (2001), 'Prodigious Riches: the Wealth of Jamaica Before the American Revolution', *Economic History Review* 54, 3: 506–24.

Burnard, T. G. (2015), *Planters, Merchants and Slaves: Plantation Societies in British America, 1650–1820* (Chicago).

Burnard, T. G. (2019), 'Plantations and the Great Divergence', in G. Riello and T. Roy (eds), *Global Economic History* (London), 102–17.

Burnard, T. G. (2020a), '"I know I have to Work": The Moral Economy of Labor among Enslaved Women in Berbice, 1819–1834', in S. White and T. G. Burnard (eds), *Hearing Enslaved Voices* (London), chapter 9.

Burnard, T. G. (2020b), *Jamaica in the Age of Revolution* (Philadelphia).

Burnard, T. G. and Garrigus J. (2016), *The Plantation Machine: Atlantic Capitalism in French St Domingue and British Jamaica* (Philadelphia).

Burnard, T. G. and Graham, A. (2020), 'Security, Taxation and the Imperial System in Jamaica, 1721–1782', *Early American Studies* 18, 4: 461–89.

Burnard, T. G. and Riello, G. (2020), 'Slavery and the New History of Capitalism', *Journal of Global History* 15, 5, 2: 225–44.

Butler, K. M. (1995), *Economics of Emancipation: Jamaica and Barbados, 1823–1843* (Chapel Hill, CA).

Butt, D. (2008), *Rectifying International Injustice: Principles of Compensation and Restitution Between Nations* (Oxford).

Cain, P. J. and Hopkins, A. G. (1993a), *British Imperialism, Innovation and Expansion 1688–1914* (London).

Cain, P. J. and Hopkins, A. G. (1993b), *British Imperialism: Crisis and Deconstruction 1914–1990* (London).

Cannadine, D. (1990), *The Decline and Fall of the British Aristocracy* (New York).

Carey, D. and Finlay, C. (eds) (2011), *The Empire of Credit: the Financial Revolution in Britain, Ireland and America, 1688–1815* (Dublin).

Carey, J. (1712), *A Discourse of the Advantage of the African Trade to this Nation* (London).

Carlos, A. M., Fletcher, E. K., Neal, L. and Wandschneider, K. (2013), 'Financing and Refinancing the War of Spanish Succession and Then Refinancing the South Sea Company', in D. Coffman, A. Leonard and L. Neal (eds), *Questioning Credible Commitment: Perspectives on the Rise of Financial Capitalism* (Cambridge), 147–68.

Carlos, A. M., Maguire, K. and Neal, L. (2008), 'Women in the City: Financial Acumen During the South Sea Bubble', in A. Lawrence, J. Maltby and J. Rutterford (eds), *Women and Their Money: Essays on Women and Finance* (London), 33–45.

Carrington, S. H. H. (1987), 'The American Revolution and the British West Indies' Economy', *Journal of Interdisciplinary History* 17, 4: 823–50.

Carrington, S. H. H. (1999), 'Management of Sugar Estates in the British West Indies at the End of the Eighteenth Century', *Journal of Caribbean History* 33, 1: 27–53.

Chandler, A. D. (1969), *Strategy and Structure: Chapters in the History of American Industrial Enterprise* (Cambridge, MA).

Chapman, S. D. (1970), 'Fixed Capital Formation in the British Cotton Industry, 1770–1815', *Economic History Review* 23, 2: 235–66.

Chapman, S. D. (1979), 'Financial Constraints on the Growth of Firms in the Cotton Industry', *Economic History Review* 32, 2: 52–66.

Chapman, S. D. (1984/2010), *The Rise of Merchant Banking* (London).

Chapman, S. D. (2004), Review of Chris Aspin, *The Water Spinners: A New Look at the Early Cotton Trade*, in *Textile History* 35, 2: 229.

Chapman, S. D. (2016), 'The Strettons and the Lowes. Sir Richard Arkwright's Builders and Millrights', in C. Wrigley (ed.), *Industrialisation and Society in Britain: Cromford and Beyond in the Era of the Industrial Revolution* (Cromford), 15–38.

Chater, K. (2011), *Untold Histories: Black People in England and Wales During the Period of the British Slave Trade, c.1660–1807* (Manchester).

Checkland, S. G. (1954), 'The Lancashire Bill System and Its Liverpool Protagonists, 1810–1827', *Economica* 21, 82: 129–42.

Checkland, S. G. (1957), 'Two Scottish West Indian Liquidations After 1793', *Scottish Journal of Political Economy* 4, 2: 127–43.

Checkland, S. G. (1958a), 'Finance for the West Indies, 1780–1815', *Economic History Review* 10, 3: 461–9.

Checkland, S. G. (1958b), 'American Versus West Indian Traders in Liverpool, 1793–1815', *Journal of Economic History* 18: 141–60.

Checkland, S. G. (1975), *Scottish Banking: A History 1695–1793* (Glasgow).

Christophers, B. (2020), *Rentier Capitalism. Who Owns the Economy and Who Pays for It?* (London).

Clapham, J. H. (1945), *The Bank of England: A History*, vol. 1: *1694–1797* (London).

Clemens, P. G. E. (1976), 'The Rise of Liverpool 1665–1750', *Economic History Review* 29: 211–23.

Clifford, H. (1999), 'Concepts of Invention, Identity and Imitation in the London and Provincial Metal-Working Trades, 1750–1800', *Journal of Design History* 12: 241–56.

Clifford, H. (1999) 'A Commerce with Things: the Value of Precious Metalwork in Early Modern England', in M. Berg and H. Clifford (eds), *Consumers and Luxury: Consumer Culture in Europe, 1650–1850* (New York), 147–68.

Clifford, H. (2018), *From Grossers to Grocers: A History of the Grocers' Company*, vol. 1: *From Foundation to 1798* (London).

Coelho, P. R. P. (1973), 'The Profitability of Imperialism: the British Experience in the West Indies 1768–72', *Explorations in Economic History* 10, 3: 252–80.

Coffman, D., Leonard, A. and Neal, L. (eds) (2013), *Questioning Credible Commitment: Perspectives on the Rise of Financial Capitalism* (Cambridge).

Coleman, D. (2018), *Henry Smeathman, the Flycatcher: Natural History, Slavery and Empire in the Late Eighteenth Century* (Liverpool).

Commissioners for Trade and Plantations (1920–38), *Journal of the Commissioners for Trade and Plantations*, 14 vols (London).

Cookson, G. (2018), *The Age of Machinery. Engineering the Industrial Revolution 1770–1850* (Woodbridge).

Court, W. H. B. (1938), *The Rise of the Midland Industries 1600–1838* (Oxford).

Cowan, B. (2005), *The Social Life of Coffee* (New Haven, CT).

Crafts, N. F. R. (1985), *British Economic Growth During the Industrial Revolution* (Oxford).

Crafts, N. F. R. (2004), 'Steam as a General Purpose Technology: A Growth Accounting Perspective', *Economic Journal* 114: 338–51.

Crafts, N. F. R. (2021), 'Understanding Productivity Growth in the Industrial Revolution', *Economic History Review* 74, 2: 309–38.

Crafts, N. F. R. and Harley, C. K. (1992), 'Output Growth and the Industrial Revolution: A Restatement of the Crafts-Harley View', *Economic History Review* 45: 703–30.

Crowley, J. E. (2016), 'Sugar Machines: Picturing Industrialized Slavery', *American Historical Review*: 14–16.

Cuenca-Esteban, J. (1997), 'The Rising Share of British Industrial Exports in Industrial Output, 1700–1851', *Journal of Economic History* 57: 879–906.

Cuenca-Estaban, J. (2004), 'Comparative Patterns of Colonial Trade: Britain and its Rivals', in L. Prados de la Escosura (ed.), *Exceptionalism and Industrialization: Britain and Its European Rivals 1688–1815* (Cambridge), 35–66.

Cuenca-Esteban, J. (2014), 'British "Ghost" Exports, American Middlemen, and the Trade to Spanish America 1790–1819', *William and Mary Quarterly*, 3rd series, 71, 1: 63–98.

Curtin, P. D. (1969), *The Atlantic Slave Trade: A Census* (Madison, WI).

Curtin, P. D. (1998), *The Rise and Fall of the Plantation Complex: Essays in Atlantic History* (Cambridge).

Darity, W. Jr. (1990), 'British Industry and the West Indies Plantations', *Social Science History* 14, 1: 117–49.

Darity, W. Jr., Hamilton, D., Paul, M., Aja, A., Price, A., Moore, A. and Chiopris, C. (2018), *What We Get Wrong About Closing the Racial Wealth Gap*,

Samuel DuBois Cook Center on Social Equity, Insight Center for Community Economic Development Duke University (Durham, NC).

Darwin, J. (2012), *Unfinished Empire: The Global Expansion of Britain* (London).

Daudin, G. (2004), 'The Profitability of Slave and Long-Distance Trading in Context: The Case of Eighteenth-Century France', *Journal of Economic History* 64, 1: 144–71.

Daudin, G. (2021), 'How Important Was the Slavery System to Europe', *Slavery and Abolition* 42, 1: 151–7.

Daunton, M. (1989), '"Gentlemanly Capitalism" and British Industry 1860–1914', *Past & Present* 12: 119–58.

Daunton, M. (1991), 'Reply', *Past & Present*, 132: 170–87.

Daunton, M. and Halpern, R. (eds), (1999), *Empire and Others: British Encounters with Indigenous People 1600–1850* (London).

Davies, K. G. (1958), *The Royal African Company* (London).

Davis, D. B. (2010), 'Foreword', in D. Eltis and D. Richardson (eds), *Atlas of the Transatlantic Slave Trade* (New Haven, CT and London), xvii–xxii.

Davis, R. (1962), 'English Foreign Trade, 1700–1774', *Economic History Review*, 2nd Series, 15: 285–303.

Davis, R. (1973), *The Rise of the Atlantic Economies* (Ithaca).

Davis, R. (1979), *The Industrial Revolution and British Overseas Trade* (Leicester).

Day, I. (2019), 'A Furnished Entertainment', in V. Avery and M. Calaresu (eds), *Feast and Fast: the Art of Food in Europe 1500–1800* (Cambridge), 2–7.

Day, I. (2002), *Royal Sugar Sculpture* (Barnard Castle).

Deane, (1957), 'The Output of the British Woollen Industry in the Eighteenth Century', *Journal of Economic History* 17, 2: 207–23.

Deane, P. and Cole, W. A. (1962/1967), *British Economic Growth 1688–1959* (Cambridge).

Deerr, N. (1949–50), *The History of Sugar,* 2 vols (London).

De Jong, A., Kooijmans, T. and Koudijs, P. (2021), 'Going for Broke: Underwriter Reputation and the Performance of Mortgage-Backed Securities', https://sites.google.com/view/peter-koudijs/research?authuser=0.

Delbourgo, J. (2010), 'Gardens of Life and Death', *British Journal of the History of Science* 43, 113–18.

Delbourgo, J. (2017), *Collecting the World: Hans Sloane and the Origins of the British Museum* (Harvard).

Delbourgo J. and Dew, N. (eds), (2007), *Science and Empire in the Atlantic World* (London).

Delbourgo, J., Schaffer, S., Roberts, L. and Raj, K. (eds), (2009), *The Brokered World: Go-Betweens and Global Intelligence* (Sagamore Beach, MA).

Devine, T. M. (1975), *The Tobacco Lords: a Study of the Tobacco Merchants of Glasgow and Their Trading Activities, c.1740–1790* (Edinburgh).

Devine, T. M. (1976), 'The Colonial Trades and Industrial Investment in Scotland *c.*1700–1815', *Economic History Review* 29, 1: 1–13.

Devine, T. M. (1978), 'An Eighteenth Century Business Elite: Glasgow-West India Merchants *c.*1750–1815', *Scottish Historical Review* 57: 40–67.

Devine, T. M. (1996), 'The Colonial Trades and Industrial Investment in Scotland, *c.*1700–1815', in P. Emmer and F. Gaastra (eds), *The Organization of Inter-Oceanic Trade in European Expansion, 1450–1800* (Aldershot).

Devine, T. M. (2015a), 'Did Slavery Make Scotia Great? A Question Revisited', in T. M. Devine (ed.), *Recovering Scotland's Slavery Past: the Caribbean Connection* (Edinburgh), 225–45.

Devine, T. M. (2015b), 'Scotland and Transatlantic Slavery', in T. M. Devine (ed.), *Recovering Scotland's Slavery Past: the Caribbean Connection* (Edinburgh), 1–20.

Devine, T. M. and Jackson, G. (eds) (1995), *Glasgow*, vol. 1: *Beginnings to 1830* (Manchester).

de Vries, J. (2003), 'Luxury in the Dutch Golden Age in Theory and Practice', in M. Berg and E. Eger (eds), *Luxury in the Eighteenth Century* (London), 41–56.

de Vries, J. (2008), *The Industrious Revolution: Consumer Behavior and Household Behavior 1650 to the Present* (Cambridge).

de Vries, J. (2010), 'The Limits of Globalization in the Early Modern World', *Economic History Review* 63: 710–33.

de Vries, J. (2015), 'Understanding Eurasian Trade in the Era of the Trading Companies', in M. Berg et al. (eds), *Goods from the East* (Basingstoke), 7–39.

de Vries, J. (2018), 'Changing the Narrative: The New History That Was and Is to Come', *Journal of Interdisciplinary History* 48: 313–34.

de Vries, J. (2019), *The Price of Bread: Regulating the Market in the Dutch Republic* (Cambridge).

de Vries, J. and van der Woude, A. (1997), *The First Modern Economy. Success, Failure and Perseverance of the Dutch Economy, 1500–1815* (Cambridge).

Dickson, P. G. M. (1968), *The Financial Revolution in England: The Development of Public Credit, 1688–1756* (London).

Donnan, E. (1931), *Documents Illustrative of the Slave Trade to America*, vols 1, 2 and 3 (Washington).

Donnington, K., Hanley R. and Moody, J. (eds) (2016), *Britain's History and Memory of Transatlantic Slavery* (Liverpool).

Drake, B. K. (1976), 'The Liverpool–African Voyage *c.*1790–1807', in R. Anstey and P. E. H. Hair (eds), *Liverpool, the African Slave Trade and Abolition* (Liverpool), 126–56.

Draper, N. (2010), *The Price of Emancipation: Slave-Ownership, Compensation and British Society at the End of Slavery* (Cambridge).

Draper, N. (2015a), 'Scotland and Colonial Slave Ownership: the Evidence of the Slave Compensation Records', in T. M. Devine (ed.), *Recovering Scotland's Slavery Past* (Edinburgh), 166–86.

Draper, N. (2015b), 'The British State and Slavery: George Baillie, Merchant of London and St Vincent, and the Exchequer Loans of the 1790s', Economic History Society, Working Papers 15029.

Draper, N. (2021), 'The Rise of the New Planter Class? Some Counter Currents from British Guiana and Trinidad 1807–33', *Atlantic Studies* 9, 1: 65–83.

Drayton, R. (2000), *Nature's Government: Science, Imperial Britain, and the 'Improvement' of the World* (New Haven, CT).

Drescher, S. (1977), *Econocide: British Slavery in the Era of Abolition* (Pittsburgh, PA).

Dresser, M. (2001), *Slavery Obscured: The Social History of the Slave Trade in an English Provincial Port* (London).

Dresser, M. (2007), 'Set in Stone? Statues and Slavery in London', *History Workshop Journal* 64: 162–99.

Dresser, M. and Hann, A. (eds) (2013), *Slavery and the British Country House* (London).

Duisenberre, W. (1996), *Them Dark Days. Slavery in the American Rice Swamps* (Oxford).

Dummett, R. E. (1999), *Gentlemanly Capitalism and British Imperialism: the New Debate on Empire* (London).

Dunn, R. S. (2014), *A Tale of Two Plantations. Slave Life and Labor in Jamaica and Virginia* (Cambridge, MA), 75–88.

DuPlessis, R. S. (2016), *The Material Atlantic: Clothing. Commerce and Colonization in the Atlantic World, 1650–1800* (Cambridge).

Durie, A. J. (1979), *The Scottish Linen Industry* (Edinburgh).

Earle, R. (2020), *Feeding the People: The Politics of the Potato* (Cambridge).

Eden, F. (1797/1984), *The State of the Poor* (London).

Edwards, M. M. (1967), *The Growth of the British Cotton Trade, 1780–1815* (Manchester).

Ellis, J. (1770), *Directions for Bringing Over Seeds and Plants, From the East Indies and Other Distant Countries, in a State of Vegetation* (London).

Ellis, M., Coulton, R. and Mauger, M. (2015), *Empire of Tea: The Asian Leaf That Conquered the World* (London).

Eltis, D. (1979), 'The British Contribution to the Nineteenth Century Transatlantic Slave Trade', *Economic History Review* 32, 2: 211–27.

Eltis, D., Emmer, P. C. and Lewis, F. D. (2016), 'More Than Profits? The Contribution of the Slave Trade to the Dutch Economy: Assessing Fatah-Black and van Rossum', *Slavery and Abolition* 37, 4: 724–35.

Eltis, D. and Engerman, S. L. (2000), 'The Importance of Slavery and the Slave Trade to Industrializing Britain', *Journal of Economic History* 60, 1: 123–44.

Eltis, D. and Engerman, S. L. (2011), 'Dependence, Servility, and Coerced Labour in Time and Space', in D. Eltis and S. Engerman, (eds), *The Cambridge World History of Slavery*, vol. 3: *AD 1420–AD 1804* (Cambridge), 1–24.

Eltis, D., Lewis, F. D. and Richardson, D. (2005), 'Slave Prices, the African Slave Trade and Productivity Growth in the Caribbean', *Economic History Review*, 58: 673–700.

Eltis, D. and Richardson, D. (2010), *Atlas of the Transatlantic Slave Trade* (New Haven, CT).

Emmer, P. C. (2005), *The Dutch Slave Trade 1500–1850* (London).

Engerman, S. L. (1972), 'The Slave Trade and British Capital Formation in the 18th Century: a Comment on the Williams Thesis', *Business History Review* 46, 4: 430–3.

Engerman, S. L. and Sokoloff, K. L. (2012), *Economic Development in the Americas since 1500* (Cambridge).

Engineer, U. (2016), 'Sugar Revisited: Sweetness and the Environment in the Early Modern World', in A. Gerritsen and G. Riello (eds), *The Global Lives of Things* (London), 198–220.

Evans, C. (2005), 'The Industrial Revolution in Iron in the British Isles', in C. Evans and G. Rydén (eds), *The Industrial Revolution in Iron: the Impact of British Coal Technology in Nineteenth Century Europe* (Aldershot), 15–28.

Evans, C. (2010), *Slave Wales: the Welsh and Atlantic Slavery 1660–1850* (Cardiff).

Evans, C. (2012), 'The Plantation Hoe: The Rise and Fall of an Atlantic Commodity 1650–1850', *William and Mary Quarterly* 69: 71–100.

Evans, C. (2013), 'Brazilian Gold, Cuban Copper and the Final Frontier of British Antislavery', *Slavery and Abolition* 34, 1: 118–34.

Evans, C. (2014), 'Slavery and Welsh Industry Before and After Emancipation', in C. Hall, N. Draper and K. McClelland (eds), *Emancipation and the Remaking of the British Imperial World* (Manchester), 61–75.

Evans, C. and Miskell, L. (2020), *Swansea Copper: A Global History* (Baltimore).

Evans, C. and Rydén, G. (2007), *Baltic Iron in the Atlantic World in the Eighteenth Century* (Leiden).

Evans, C. and Rydén, G. (2018), '"Voyage Iron": an Atlantic Slave Trade Currency, Its European Origins, and West African Impact', *Past & Present* 239: 41–70.

Fatah-Black, K. and van Rossum, M. (2015), 'Beyond Profitability: the Dutch Trans-Atlantic Slave Trade and Its Economic Impact', *Slavery and Abolition* 36, 1: 63–83.

Feinstein, C. H. (1998), 'Pessimism Perpetuated: Real Wages and the Standard of Living in Britain During and After the Industrial Revolution', *Journal of Economic History* 58: 625–8.

Feinstein, C. H. and Pollard, S. (1988), *Studies in Capital formation in the United Kingdom 1750–1920* (Oxford).

Fergus, C. K. (2013), *Revolutionary Emancipation: Slavery and Abolitionism in the British West Indies* (Baton Rouge).

Findlay, R. and O'Rourke, K. H. (2007), *Power and Plenty: Trade, War, and the World Economy in the Second Millennium* (Princeton).

Findlay, R. and O'Rourke, K. H. (2015), 'The Triangular Trade from a Global Perspective', in C. A. Palmer (ed.), *The Legacy of Eric Williams: Caribbean Scholar, and Statesman* (Kingston), 165–89.

Finlay, R. (2010), *The Pilgrim Art: Cultures of Porcelain in World History* (Berkeley).

Finley, M. (1980), *Ancient Slavery and Modern Ideology* (London).

Fitton, R. S. and Wadsworth, A. P. (1986), *The Strutts and the Arkwrights 1758–1830: A Study of the Early Factory System* (Manchester).

Fleischmann R. K. and Parker L. D. (eds) (1997), *What Is Past Is Prologue: Cost Accounting During the Industrial Revolution* (London).

Floud, R., Humphries, J. and Johnson, P. (eds) (2014), *The Cambridge Economic History of Modern Britain*, vol. 1: *1700–1870* (Cambridge).

Fogel, R. W. and Engerman, S. L. (1974), *Time on the Cross: The Economics of American Negro Slavery* (New York).

French, C. J. (1992), '"Crowded with Traders and a Great Commerce": London's Dominion of English Overseas Trade, 1700–1775', *London Journal* 17: 27–35.

Fuentes, M. J. (2016), *Dispossessed Lives: Enslaved Women, Violence and the Archive* (Philadelphia).

Gallagher J. and Robinson, R. (1953), 'The Imperialism of Free Trade', *Economic History Review* 6, 1, 1–15.

Galpin, W. F. (1925), *The Grain Supply of England During the Napoleonic War Period* (London).

Gardner, L. and Roy, T. (2020), *The Economic History of Colonialism* (Bristol).

Gee, J. (1729), *The Trade and Navigation of Great Britain Consider'd* (London).

Gerritsen, A. (2020), *The City of Blue and White: Chinese Porcelain and the Early Modern World* (Cambridge).

Gerritsen, A. and Riello, G. (eds) (2016), *The Global Lives of Things* (London).

Gifford, A. (2000), 'The Legal Basis of the Claim for Slavery Reparations', *Human Rights Magazine* 27: https://www.americanbar.org/groups/crsj/publications /human_rights_magazine_home/human_rights_vol27_2000/spring2000/hr _spring00_gifford/.

Gifford, A. (2007), *The Passionate Advocate* (Kingston).

Goodall, M. (2020), 'The Rise of the Sugar Trade and Sugar Consumption in Early British America 1650–1720', *Historical Research* 93, 262: 678–91.

Goodall, M. (2022), 'Sugar Consumption in the Early Modern Atlantic World', D. Phil. thesis (Oxford).

Goodfellow, M. (2020), *Hostile Environment: How Immigrants Became Scapegoats* (London).

Graham, A. (2018a), 'The British Financial Revolution and the Empire of Credit in St Kitts and Nevis, 1706–21', *Historical Research* 91, 254: 685–704.

Graham, A. (2018b), 'Technology and the Falmouth Water Company', *Slavery and Abolition* 39: 323–9.

Graham, A. (2020a), 'Patents and Invention in Jamaica and the British Atlantic before 1857', *Economic History Review* 73: 940–63.

Graham, A. (2020b), 'A Descent into Hellshire: Safety, Security and the End of Slavery in Jamaica, 1819–1820', *Atlantic Studies* 17, 2: 184–205.

Graham, A. (2021), 'Slavery, Banks and the Ambivalent Legacies of Compensation in South Africa, Mauritius and the Caribbean', *Journal of Southern African Studies* 47, 3: 473–87.

Graham, A. (2023, forthcoming), *Tropical Leviathan: Slavery, Society and Security in Jamaica, 1770–1840* (Oxford).

Graham, A. and Walsh, P. (eds) (2016), *The British Fiscal Military States 1660–1830* (London).

Grainger, J. (1746), *The Sugar Cane – A Poem* (London).

Green, T. (2020), *A Fistful of Shells: West Africa from the Rise of the Slave Trade to the Age of Revolution* (Harmondsworth).

Greggus, D. P. (1993), 'Sugar and Coffee Cultivation in Saint-Domingue and the Shaping of the Slave Labor Force', in I. Berlin and P. D. Morgan (eds), *Cultivation and Culture: Labor and the Shaping of Slave Life in the Americas* (Charlottesville, VA), 73–98.

Griffin, E. (2018), 'Diets, Hunger and Living Standards During the British Industrial Revolution', *Past & Present* 239: 71–111.

Griffiths, T., Hunt, P. A. and O'Brien, P. K. (1992), 'Inventive Activity in the British Textile Industry, 1700–1800', *Journal of Economic History* 52, 4: 881–906.

Guilding, L. (1825), *An Account of the Botanic Garden in the Island of St. Vincent, From its First Establishment to the Present Time* (Glasgow).

Haggerty, S. (2012), *Merely for Money? Business Culture in the British Atlantic 1750–1815* (Liverpool).

Haggerty, S. (2023, forthcoming), *Ordinary People, Extraordinary Times: Living the British Empire in Jamaica 1756* (Montreal).

Hahn, B. (2020), *Technology in the Industrial Revolution* (Cambridge).

Hall, C., Draper, N. and McClelland, K. (eds) (2014), *Emancipation and the Remaking of the British Imperial World* (Manchester).

Hall, C., Draper, N., McClelland, K. et al. (2014), *Legacies of British Slave-Ownership: Colonial Slavery and the Formation of Victorian Britain* (Cambridge).

Hamilton, D. J. (2005), *Scotland, the Caribbean and the Atlantic World, 1750–1820* (Manchester).

Hamilton, H. (1926), *The English Brass and Copper Industries to 1700* (London).

Hamilton, H. (1963), *An Economic History of Scotland in the Eighteenth Century* (Oxford).

Hancock, D. (1995), *Citizens of the World: London Merchants and the Integration of the British Atlantic Community, 1735–1785* (Cambridge).

Hannah, L. and Bennett, B. (2022), 'Large Scale Victorian Manufacturers: Reconstructing the Lost 1881 UK Employer Census', *Economic History Review* 75, 3: 830–56.

Hannah-Jones, N. (2021), *The 1619 Project* (London).

Harding, T. (2022), *White Debt. The Demerara Uprising and Britain's Legacy of Slavery* (London).

Harley, C. K. (1998), 'Cotton Textile Prices and the Industrial Revolution', *Economic History Review* 51, 1: 49–83.

Harley, C. K. (2015), 'Slavery, the British Atlantic Economy, and the Industrial Revolution', in A. B. Leonard and D. Pretel (eds), *The Caribbean and the Atlantic World Economy: Circuits of Trade, Money and Knowledge* (London), 161–83.

Harris, J. R. (1964/2003), *The Copper King. A Biography of Thomas Williams of Llanidan* (Liverpool).

Harris, J. R. (1988), *The British Iron Industry 1700–1850* (Basingstoke).

Harris, J. R. (1992), 'Copper and Shipping in the Eighteenth Century', in J. R. Harris, *Essays in Industry and Technology in the Eighteenth Century* (Aldershot), 176–94.

Harris, J. R. (1998), *Industrial Espionage and Technology Transfer: Britain and France in the Eighteenth Century* (Aldershot).

Harvey, M. (2019), 'Slavery, Indenture and the Development of British Industrial Capitalism', *History Workshop Journal* 88: 66–88.

Havard, R. (2004), 'Sir Thomas Picton', *Oxford Dictionary of National Biography* (Oxford).

Hay, D. and Craven, P. (eds), (2004), *Masters, Servants and Magistrates in Britain and the Empire, 1562–1955* (Chapel Hill, CA).

Hazareesingh, S. (2021), *Black Spartacus: The Epic Life of Toussaint Louverture* (London).

Hazareesingh, S. and Curry-Machado, J. (2009), 'Editorial: Commodities, Empire and Global History', *Journal of Global History* 4: 1–5.

Hersh, J. and Voth, H.-J. (2009), 'Coffee, Consumer Choice and the Consequences of Columbus', https://cepr.org/voxeu/columns/coffee-consumer-choice-and-consequences-columbus.

Hersh, J. and Voth, H.-J. (2011), 'Sweet Diversity: Colonial Goods and Welfare Gains from Trade after 1492', Working Paper, Chapman University Digital Commons (London), https://digitalcommons.chapman.edu/economics_articles/204/.

Herschtal, E. (2021), *The Science of Abolition: How Slave Holders Became the Enemies of Progress* (New Haven, CT).

Heuman, G. J. (1994), *'The Killing Time': The Morant Bay Rebellion in Jamaica* (Knoxville, TN).

Higman, B. W. (1984/1995), *Slave Populations of the British Caribbean 1807–1834* (Kingston, Jamaica).

Higman, B. W. (2000), 'The Sugar Revolution', *Economic History Review* 53: 213–36.

Higman, B. W. (2008), *Plantation Jamaica, 1750–1850: Capital and Control in a Colonial Economy* (Kingston, Jamaica).

Hilt, E. (2017), 'Economic History, Historical Analysis, and the "New History of Capitalism"', *Journal of Economic History* 77, 2: 511–36.

Hirschman, A. O. (1977), *The Passions and the Interests: Political Arguments for Capitalism Before Its Triumph* (Princeton).

Hodacs, H. (2016), *Silk and Tea in the North. Scandinavian Trade and the Market for Asian Goods in Eighteenth-Century Europe* (Basingstoke).

Hoffman, P. T., Postel-Vinay, G. and Rosenthal, J. L. (2014), 'Capitalism and Financial Development: the Case of Mortgage Markets in France, 1807–1899', *Social Science History* 38, 1 and 2: 13–41.

Honeyman, K. (2007), *Child Workers in England 1780–1820: Parish Apprentices and the Making of the Early Industrial Labour Force* (London),

Hoonhout, B. (2013), 'The Crisis of the Subprime Plantation Mortgages in the Dutch West Indies, 1750–1775', *Leidschrift, Jaagang* 28, 2: 85–99.

Hoppit, J. (2011), 'Compulsion, Compensation and Property Rights in Britain, 1688–1833', *Past & Present* 201: 93–128.

Hoppit, J. (2017), *Britain's Political Economies: Parliament and Economic Life 1660–1800* (Cambridge).

Hoppit, J. (2021), *The Dreadful Monster and Its Poor Relations: Taxing, Spending and the United Kingdom* (London).

Horne, G. (2021), 'The Politician Scholar. Eric Williams and the Tangled History of Capitalism and Slavery', *The Nation*, 5 October 2021, https://www.thenation.com/article/society/eric-williams-capitalism-slavery/.

Howes, A. (2020), *Arts and Minds: How the Royal Society of Arts Changed a Nation* (Princeton).

Hudson, P. (1986), *The Genesis of Industrial Capital: a Study of the West Riding Wool Textile Industry 1750–1850* (Cambridge).

Hudson, P. (ed.) (1989), *Regions and Industries: A Perspective on the Industrial Revolution in Britain* (Cambridge).

Hudson, P. (1992), *The Industrial Revolution* (London).

Hudson, P. (1994) 'Some Aspects of Nineteenth Century Accounting Development in the West Riding Textile Industry', in R. H. Parker and B. S. Yamey (eds), *Accounting History: Some British Contributions* (Oxford), 434–49.

Hudson P. (2009), 'The Limits of Wool and the Potential of Cotton in the Eighteenth and Early Nineteenth Centuries', in P. Parsatharathi and G. Riello, *The Spinning World. A Global History of Cotton Textiles 1200–1850* (Oxford), 327–50.

Hudson, P. (2014), 'Slavery, the Slave Trade and Economic Growth: a Contribution to the Debate', in C. Hall, N. Draper and K. McClelland (eds), *Emancipation and the Remaking of the British Imperial World* (Manchester), 36–59.

Humphries, J. (2010), *Childhood and Child Labour in the British Industrial Revolution* (Cambridge).

Humphries, J. and Schneider, B. (2019), 'Spinning in the Industrial Revolution', *Economic History Review* 72, 1: 126–55.

Hunt, E. H. (1986), 'Industrialisation and Regional Inequality: Wages in Britain, 1760–1914', *Journal of Economic History* 46, 4: 965–6.

Hunt, N. (2013), 'Contraband, Freeports and British Merchants in the Caribbean World, 1739–72', *Diacronie* 13, 1: 1–11.

Hyde, F. E., Parkinson, B. B. and Marriner, S. (1953), 'The Nature and Profitability of the Liverpool Slave Trade', *Economic History Review* 5, 3: 368–77.

Inikori, J. (1977), 'The Import of Firearms into West Africa 1750–1807', *Journal of African History* 28, 3: 339–68.

Inikori, J. (1987), 'Slavery and the Development of Industrial Capitalism in England', in B. L. Solow and S. Engerman (eds), *British Capitalism and Caribbean Slavery* (Cambridge), 79–101.

Inikori, J. E. (1989), 'Slavery and the Revolution in Cotton Textile Production in England', *Social Science History* 13: 343–79.

Inikori, J. E. (2000), 'Africa and the Transatlantic Slave Trade', in T. Falola (ed.), *Africa*, vol. 1: *African History Before 1885* (Durham, NC), 389–412.

Inikori, J. E. (2002), *Africans and the Industrial Revolution: A Study in International Trade and Economic Development* (Cambridge).

Inikori, J. E. (2014), 'Reversal of Fortune and Socio-economic Development in the Atlantic World: a Comparative Examination of West Africa and the Americas, 1400–1850', in E. G. Akeampon, R. H. Bates, N. Nunn and J. Robinson (eds), *Africa's Development in Historical Perspective* (Cambridge).

Inikori, J. E. (2015), 'The Industrial Revolution in Atlantic Perspective: County History and National History', in C. A. Palmer (ed.), *The Legacy of Eric Williams, Caribbean Scholar and Statesman* (Kingston Jamaica), 224–65.

Inikori, J. E. and Engerman, S. L. (eds) (1992), *The Atlantic Slave Trade: Effects on Economies, Societies and Peoples in Africa, the Americas and Europe* (Durham, NC).

Innes, J. (2009), *Inferior Politics: Social Problems and Social Policies in Eighteenth Century Britain* (Oxford).

Ishizu, M. (2013), 'Boom and Crisis in Financing the British Transatlantic Trade: a Case Study of the Bankruptcy of John Leigh and Company in 1811', in T. M. Safley (ed.), *The History of Bankruptcy: Economic, Social and Cultural Implications in Early Modern Europe* (London), 141–54.

James, J. (1857), *History of the Worsted Manufacture in England* (London).

Jenkins, J. G. (1969), *The Welsh Woollen Industry* (Cardiff).

Jenkins, D. and Leroy, J. (eds) (2021), *Histories of Racial Capitalism* (New York).

Jeppesen, C. (2016), 'East Meets West: Exploring the Connections Between Britain, the Caribbean and the East India Company, *c.*1757–1857', in K. Donnington, R. Hanley and J. Moody (eds), *Britain's History and Memory of Transatlantic Slavery* (Liverpool), 102–25.

John, A. H. (1953), 'Insurance Investment and the London Money Market of the Eighteenth Century', *Economica* 20, 78: 137–58.

John, A. H. (1958), 'The London Assurance Company and the Marine Insurance Market of the Eighteenth Century', *Economica* 25, 98: 126–51.

Johnson, W. (2013), *River of Dark Dreams: Slavery and Empire in the Cotton Kingdom* (Cambridge, MA).

Johnston, K. (2020), 'Endangered Plantations: Environmental Change and Slavery in the British Caribbean, 1631–1807', *Early American Studies* 3, 259–86.

Johnstone, G. N. (1976), 'The Growth of the Sugar Trade and Refining Industry', in D. Oddy and D. Miller (eds), *The Making of the Modern British Diet* (London), 58–64.

Jones, G. (2002), *Merchants to Multinationals: British Trading Companies in the Nineteenth and Twentieth Centuries* (Oxford).

Jones, P. (2009), *Industrial Enlightenment: Science, Technology and Culture in Birmingham and the West Midlands, 1760–1820* (Manchester).

Karabell, Z. (2021), *Inside Money: Brown Brothers Harriman and the American Way of Power* (London).

Karaman, K. and Pamuk, Ş. (2013), 'Different Paths to the Modern State in Europe: the Interaction Between Warfare, Economic Structure, and Political Regime', *American Political Science Review* 107, 3: 603–26.

Kaye, A. (2009), 'The Second Slavery: Modernity in the Nineteenth Century Atlantic World', *Journal of Southern History* 75: 627–50.

Kean, S. (2019), 'Science's Debt to the Slave Trade', *Science* 364: 16–20.

Keegan, T. (1996), *Colonial South Africa and the Origins of the Racial Order* (London).

Keibek, S. (2017), 'The Male Occupational Structure of England and Wales, 1600–1850', unpublished Ph.D. dissertation, University of Cambridge.

Keiser, R. G. (2021), 'An Empire of Free Ports: British Commercial Imperialism in the 1766 Free Port Act', *Journal of British Studies* 2: 334–61.

Kelly, M., Mokyr, J. and Ó Gráda, C. (2014), 'Precocious Albion: A New Interpretation of the British Industrial Revolution', *Annual Review of Economics* 6: 363–89.

Kelly, M., Ó Gráda, C. and Solar, P. M. (2021), 'Safety at Sea During the Industrial Revolution', *Journal of Economic History* 81, 1: 239–75.

Kenny, G. L. (2010), *Contentious Liberties: American Abolitionists in Post-Emancipation Jamaica, 1834–1866* (Athens, GA).

Kidd, A. J. (2008), 'Touchet, Samuel (*c*.1705–1773), Merchant and Politician', *Oxford Dictionary of National Biography.*

Kimball, E. (2016), '"What have we to do with slavery?" New Englanders and the Slave Economies of the West Indies', in S. Beckert and S. Rockman (eds), *Slavery's Capitalism: A New History of American Economic Development* (Philadelphia), 181–94.

Klein, H. S. (1990), *The Atlantic Slave Trade* (Cambridge).

Kobayashi, K. (2019), *Indian Cotton Textiles in West Africa. African Agency, Consumer Demand and the Making of the Global Economy, 1750–1850* (London).

Kocka, J. (2016), *Capitalism: A Short History* (Princeton).

Kocka, J. and van der Linden, M. (2016), *Capitalism: The Reemergence of a Historical Concept* (London).

Koram, K. (2022), *Uncommon Wealth. Britain and the Aftermath of Empire* (London).

Koth, K. B. and Serieux, J. E. (2019), 'Sugar, Slavery and Wealth: Jamaica Planter Nathaniel Phillips and the Williams Hypothesis (1761–1813)', *Capitalism: A Journal of History and Economics* 1: 59–91.

Koyama, M. and Rubin, J. (2022), *How the World Became Rich: The Historical Origins of Economic Growth* (Cambridge).

Kriger, C. E. (2009), 'Guinea Cloth: Production and Consumption of Cotton Textiles in West Africa Before and During the Atlantic Slave Trade', in P. Parthasarathi and G. Riello (eds), *The Spinning World. A Global History of Cotton Textiles 1200–1850* (Oxford), 105–26.

Kumar, M. (2020), 'Omission of Data in Wrigley's "Reconsidering the Industrial Revolution"', *Journal of Interdisciplinary History* 51: 297–9.

Kynaston, D. (2017), *Till Times Last Stand: A History of the Bank of England 1694–2013* (London).

Lambert, D. (2005), *White Creole Culture, Politics and Identity During the Age of Abolition* (Cambridge).

Lambert, D. (2018), '"[A] Mere Cloak for their Proud Contempt and Antipathy Towards the African Race": Imagining Britain's West India Regiments in the Caribbean, 1795–1838', *Journal of Imperial and Commonwealth History* 46: 627–50.

Landes, D. S. (1995), *The Wealth and Poverty of Nations* (Boston).

Langton, J. and Laxton, P. (1978), 'Parish Registers and Urban Structure: the Example of Eighteenth Century Liverpool', *Urban History Yearbook* 5: 75–84.

Lascelles, E. et al. (1786), *Instructions for the Management of a Plantation in Barbados, and for the Treatment of Negroes* (London).

Leonard, A. B. (2015), 'From Local to Transatlantic: Insuring Trade in the Caribbean', in A. B. Leonard and D. Pretel (eds), *The Caribbean and the Atlantic World Economy: Circuits of Trade Money and Knowledge 1650–1914* (Basingstoke), 137–60.

Leonard A. B. (2022), *London Marine Insurance 1438–1824: Risk, Trade and the Early Modern State* (Woodbridge).

Levy, J. (2021), *Ages of American Capitalism: A History of the United States* (New York).

Lindert, P. and Williamson, J. (1982), 'Revising England's Social Tables 1688–1812', *Explorations in Economic History* 19: 385–408.

Long, E. (1774), *The History of Jamaica* (London).

Longmore, J. (2006), 'Civic Liverpool: 1660–1800', in J. Belcham (ed.), *Liverpool 800: Culture, Character and History* (Liverpool), 13–170.

Lovejoy, P. E. (2000), *Transformations in Slavery: A History of Slavery in Africa*, 2nd edn (Cambridge).

Lovejoy, P. E. and Richardson, D. (2007), 'African Agency and the Liverpool Slave Trade', in D. Richardson, S. Schwarz and A. Tibbles (eds), *Liverpool and Transatlantic Slavery* (Liverpool), 43–65.

McCants, A. E. C. (2007), 'Exotic Goods, Popular Consumption and the Standard of Living: Thinking about Globalization in the Early Modern World', *Journal of World History* 18: 433–62.

McCants, A. E. C. (2020), 'Economic History and the Historians', *Journal of Interdisciplinary History* 50: 547–66.

McClellan III, J. E. (2010), *Colonialism and Science: Saint-Domingue in the Old Regime* (Chicago).

McCloskey, D. N. (2010), *Bourgeois Dignity: Why Economics Cannot Explain the Modern World* (Chicago).

McCusker, J. (2000), 'The Business of Distillling' in J. J. McCusker and P. Morgan (eds), *The Early Modern Atlantic Economy* (Cambridge), 186–224.

Mackillop, A. (2015), 'A North Europe World of Tea: Scotland and the Tea Trade, *c*.1690–*c*.1790', in M. Berg with F. Gottmann, H. Hodacs and C. Nierstrasz (eds), *Goods from the East 1600–1800. Trading Eurasia* (Basingstoke), 294–308.

MacLeod, C. (2002), *Inventing the Industrial Revolution: The English Patent System 1660–1800* (Cambridge).

McNeill, J. R. (1985), *Atlantic Empires of France and Spain: Louisburg and Havana 1700–1763* (Chapel Hill, CA).

Majewski, J. (2016), 'Why Did Northerners Oppose the Expansion of Slavery? Economic Development and Education in the Limestone South', in S. Beckert and S. Rockman (eds), *Slavery's Capitalism: A New History of American Economic Development* (Philadelphia), 277–98.

Malm, A. (2016), *Fossil Capital: The Rise of Steam Power and the Roots of Global Warming* (London).

Malthus, T. R. (1820), *Principles of Political Economy* (London).

Manchester, A. K. (1933), *British Pre-Eminence in Brazil, Its Rise and Decline* (Chapel Hill, CA).

Mandeville, B. (1714/1924), *The Fable of the Bees. Or Private Vices, Publick Benefits*, 2 vols (Oxford).

Manjapra, K. (2018), 'Plantation Dispossession: the Global Travel of Agricultural Racial Capitalism', in S. Beckert and C. Desan, *American Capitalism: New Histories* (New York), 370–87.

Manning, P. (1990), *Slavery and African Life: Occidental, Oriental and African Slave Trades* (Cambridge).

Manning, P. (1992), 'The Slave Trade: the Formal Demography of a Global System', in J. Inikori and S. L. Engerman (eds), *The Atlantic Slave Trade: Effects on Economies Societies and Peoples in Africa, the Americas and Europe* (Durham, NC), 117–41.

Manton, M. G. (2008), 'The Rise of British Managing Agencies in North Eastern India 1836–1918', M. Phil., SOAS, https://eprints.soas.ac.uk/28816/1/10672984.pdf, chapter 1.

Marryat, J. (1810), *Observations Upon the Report of the Committee of Marine Insurance* (London).

Marshall, P. (1975) *Bristol and the Abolition of Slavery: the Politics of Emancipation* (Bristol).

Martin, S. (1765), *Essay Upon Plantership* 4th edn (London).

Marx, K. (1867/1976), *Capital*, vol. 1 (London).

Mason, S. (ed.) (2009), *Matthew Boulton: Selling What all the World Desires* (New Haven, CT and London).

Massie, J. (1759), *A State of the British Sugar Colony Trade* (London).

Massie, J. (1760), *A Computation on the Money that hath been exorbitantly Raised upon the People of Great Britain by the Sugar Planters, in One Year from January 1759 to January 1760; shewing how much Money a Family of each Rank, Degree or Class hath lost by that rapacious monopoly, after I laid it open.* (London).

Mathias, P. (1959), *The Brewing Industry in England, 1750–1830* (Cambridge).

Mathias, P. (1969), *The First Industrial Nation* (London).

Mathias, P. (1979), *The Transformation of England* (London).

Mathias, P. and O'Brien, P. K. (1976), 'Taxation in Britain and France 1715–1810: a Comparison of the Social and Economic Incidence of Taxes Collected for Central Governments', *Journal of European Economic History* 5, 3: 601–50.

Maw, P. (2010), 'Yorkshire and Lancashire Ascendant: England's Textile Exports to New York and Philadelphia, 1750–1805', *Economic History Review* 63, 3: 734–68.

Meredith, D. and Oxley, D. (2014), 'Food and Fodder: Feeding England 1700–1900', *Past & Present* 222: 163–214.

Minchinton, W. E. (1979), 'The Triangular Trade Revisited', in H. A. Gemery and J. S. Hogendorn (eds), *The Uncommon Market: Essays in the Economic History of the Atlantic Slave Trade* (New York), 331–52.

Mintz, S. W. (1985), *Sweetness and Power: the Place of Sugar in Modern History* (London).

Mintz, S. W. (1993), 'Changing Roles of Food', in J. Brewer and R. Porter (eds), *Consumption and World of Goods* (Cambridge), 261–73.

Misselden, E. (1622), *Free Trade or the Means to Make Trade Flourish* (London).

Mitchell, B. R. (ed.) (1988), *British Historical Statistics* (Cambridge).

Mitchell, B. R. and Deane, P. (1962), *Abstract of British Historical Statistics* (Cambridge).

Mokyr, J. (2009), *The Enlightened Economy: an Economic History of Britain 1700–1850* (New Haven, CT).

Mokyr, J. (2017), *A Culture of Growth: The Origins of the Modern Economy* (Princeton).

Mokyr, J. (2021), 'The Holy Land of Industrialism: Rethinking the Industrial Revolution', *Journal of the British Academy* 9: 223–47.

Monteith, K. E. A. (2019), *Plantation Coffee in Jamaica 1790–1848* (Kingston, Jamaica).

Morgan, K. (1993a), *Bristol and the Atlantic Trade in the Eighteenth Century* (Cambridge).

Morgan, K. (1993b), 'Bristol West India Merchants in the Eighteenth Century', *Transactions of the Royal Historical Society* 3: 185–208.

Morgan, K. (2000), *Slavery, Atlantic Trade and the British Economy, 1660–1800* (Cambridge).

Morgan, K. (2004a), 'Edward Colston', *Oxford Dictionary of National Biography* (Oxford).

Morgan, K. (2004b), 'Thomas Goldney 1696–1768', *Oxford Dictionary of National Biography* (Oxford).

Morgan, K. (2005), 'Remittance Procedures in the Eighteenth-Century British Slave Trade', *Business History Review* 79, 4: 715–49.

Morgan, K. (2007), 'Liverpool's Dominance of the British Slave Trade, 1740–1807', in D. Richardson et al. (eds), *Liverpool and Transatlantic Slavery* (Liverpool), 43–65.

Morgan, K. (2016a), *A Short History of Transatlantic Slavery* (London).

Morgan, K. (2016b), 'Merchant Networks, the Guarantee System and the British Slave Trade to Jamaica in the 1790s', *Slavery and Abolition* 37, 2: 334–52.

Morriss, R. (2004), *Naval Power and British Culture: Public Trust and Government Ideology* (Aldershot).

Mulcahy, M. (2005), *Hurricanes and Society in the British Greater Caribbean 1624–1783* (Baltimore).

Muldrew, C. (2011), *Food, Energy and the Creation of Industriousness* (Cambridge).

Mullen, S. (2015), 'The Great Glasgow West India House of John Campbell Senior and Co', in T. M. Devine (ed.), *Recovering Scotland's Slavery Past: the Caribbean Connection* (Edinburgh), 124–44.

Mullen, S. (2022), *The Glasgow Sugar Aristocracy: Scotland and Caribbean Slavery, 1775–1838* (London).

Munford, C. (1996), *Race and Reparations: A Black Perspective for the Twenty-first Century* (Trenton, NJ).

Murphy, K. (2013), 'Collecting Slave Traders: James Petiver, Natural History, and the British Slave Trade', *William and Mary Quarterly* 70: 637–70.

Naipaul, V. S. (1969), *The Loss of El Dorado* (London).

Nash, R. C. (1985), 'Irish Atlantic Trade in the Seventeenth and Eighteenth Centuries', *William and Mary Quarterly* 42, 3: 329–56.

Neal, L. (1990), *The Rise of Financial Capitalism* (Cambridge).

Nesbit, S. M. (2015), 'Early Scottish Sugar Planters in the Leeward Islands', in T. M. Devine (ed.), *Recovering Scotland's Slavery Past: the Caribbean Connection* (Edinburgh), 62–81.

New York Times (2019), 14.08. and 20.12.

Nierstrasz, C. (2015), *Rivalry for Trade in Tea and Textiles: the English and Dutch East India Companies 1700–1800* (Basingstoke).

North, D. C. and Weingast, B. (1989), 'Constitutions and Commitment: the Evolution of Institutions Governing Public Choice in Seventeenth Century England', *Journal of Economic History* 43, 4: 803–32.

Nunn, N. (2008), 'The Long-term Effects of Africa's Slave Trades', *Quarterly Journal of Economics* 128: 139–76.

Nunn, N. (2010), 'Shackled to the Past: the Causes and Consequences of Africa's Slave Trades', in J. Diamond and J. A. Robinson (eds), *Natural Experiments in History* (Harvard), 142–84.

Nunn, N. (2017), 'Understanding the Long Run Effects of Africa's Slave Trades', https://voxeu.org/article/understanding-long-run-effects-africa-s-slave-trades.

O'Brien, P. K. (1988), 'The Political Economy of British Taxation, 1660–1815', *Economic History Review* 41, 1: 1–32.

O'Brien, P. K. (1998), 'Inseparable Connections: Trade, Economy, Fiscal State, and the Expansion of Empire, 1688–1815', in P. J. Marshall (ed.), *The Oxford History of the British Empire*, vol. 2: *The Eighteenth Century* (Oxford), 53–77.

O'Brien P. K. (2011), 'The Nature and Historical Evolution of an Exceptional Fiscal State and Its Possible Significance for the Precocious Commercialization and Industrialization of the British Economy from Cromwell to Nelson', *Economic History Review* 64: 408–46.

O'Brien P. K. (2021), 'Britain's Wars with France 1793–1815, and Their Contribution to the Consolidation of Its Industrial Revolution', in P. K. O'Brien (ed.), *The Crucible of Revolutionary and Napoleonic Warfare and European Transitions to Modern Economic Growth* (Leiden), 22–49.

O'Brien, P. K. and Engerman, S. L. (1991), 'Exports and the Growth of the British Economy from the Glorious Revolution to the Peace of Amiens', in

B. L. Solow (ed.), *Slavery and the Rise of the Atlantic System* (Cambridge), 177–209.

O'Brien, P. K., Griffiths, T. and Hunt, P. (1991), 'Political Components of the Industrial Revolution: Parliament and the English Cotton Textile Industry', *Economic History Review* 44, 199: 395–423.

O'Brien, P. K., Griffiths, T. and Hunt, P. A. (1996), 'Technological Change During the First Industrial Revolution: the Paradigm Case of Textiles, 1688–1851', in R. Fox (ed.), *Technological Change: Methods and Themes in the History of Technology* (Amsterdam), 155–76.

O'Brien, P. K. and Hunt, P. (1999), 'Excises and the Rise of the Fiscal State in England', in M. Ormrod, M. Bonney and R. Bonney (eds), *Crises, Revolutions and Self-sustained Growth: Essays in European Fiscal History* (Stanford).

O'Brien, P. K. and Palma, N. (2020a), 'Not an Ordinary Bank but a Great Engine of State: the Bank of England and the British Economy, 1694–1844', *European Association for Banking and Financial History*, Paper 3, https://bankinghistory.org/wp-content/uploads/eabhPaper_202003.pdf.

O'Brien, P. K. and Palma, N. (2020b), 'Danger to the Old Lady of Threadneedle Street? The Bank Restriction Act and the Regime Shift to Paper Money, 1797–1821', *European Review of Economic History* 24, 2: 390–426.

Ogborn, M. (2013), 'Talking Plants: Botany and Speech in Eighteenth-Century Jamaica', *History of Science*, 51: 251–82.

Ogle, V (2020), '"Funk Money": the End of Empires, the Expansion of Tax Havens and Decolonization as an Economic and Financial Event', *Past & Present* 249: 213–49.

Olmstead, A. L. and Rhode, P. W. (2008), 'Biological Innovation and Productivity Growth in the Antebellum Cotton Economy', *Journal of Economic History* 68, 4: 1, 123–71.

Olmstead, A. L. and Rhode, P. W. (2018), 'Cotton, Slavery, and the New History of Capitalism', *Explorations in Economic History* 67: 1–17.

Olusoga, D. (2016/2017), *Black and British: a Forgotten History* (London).

Olusoga, D. (2022a), 'Britain's Shameful Slavery History Matters – That's Why a Jury Acquitted the Colston Four', *The Guardian*, 6 January.

Olusoga, D. (2022b), 'This Verdict Puts Bristol on the Right Side of History at Last', *The Guardian*, 7 January.

Onnekink, D. and Rommelse, G. (2019), *The Dutch in the Early Modern World: a History of Global Power* (Cambridge).

Orbell, J. (2004), 'Sir Francis Baring', *Oxford Dictionary of National Biography* (Oxford).

Ormrod, P. (2003), *The Rise of Commercial Empires: England and the Netherlands in the Age of Mercantilism, 1650–1770* (Cambridge).

Ormrod, D. and Rommelse, G. (2020), *War, Trade and the State: Anglo-Dutch Conflict, 1652–89* (Woodbridge).

O'Shaughnessy, A. J. (2000), *An Empire Divided: The American Revolution and the British Caribbean* (Philadelphia).

O'Sullivan, M. (2018), 'An Intelligent Woman's Guide to Capitalism', *Enterprise and Society* 19: 751–802.

O'Sullivan, M. (2023, forthcoming), 'Power and Profit: Copper Mines on the "Eve of a Revolution" in Late Eighteenth Century Cornwall', *Past & Present*.

Otele, O. (2020), *African Europeans: an Untold History* (London).

Overton, M. (1996), *Agricultural Revolution in England: the Transformation of the Agrarian Economy 1500–1850* (New York).

Palmer, C. A. (1994), 'Introduction', in E. Williams, *Capitalism & Slavery* (Chapel Hill, CA), xi–xxi.

Pares, R. (1936), *War and Trade in the West Indies, 1739–1763* (Oxford).

Pares, R. (1950), *A West India Fortune* (New York).

Pares, R. (1956), 'The London Sugar Market 1740–1769', *Economic History Review* 9, 2: 254–70.

Pares, R. (1960), *Merchants and Planters* (Cambridge).

Parker, R. H. and Yamey, B. S. (eds) (1994), *Accounting History: Some British Contributions* (Oxford).

Paul, H. J. (2011), *The South Sea Bubble: an Economic History of Its Origins and Consequences* (London).

Pearce, A. (2007), *British Trade with Spanish America, 1763–1808* (Liverpool).

Pearson, R. (2004), *Insuring the Industrial Revolution: Fire Insurance in Great Britain, 1700–1850* (London).

Pearson, R. and Richardson, D. (2008), 'Social Capital, Institutional Innovation and Atlantic Trade Before 1800', *Business History* 50, 6: 765–80.

Pearson, R. and Richardson, D. (2019), 'Insuring the Transatlantic Slave Trade', *Journal of Economic History* 79, 2: 417–46.

Pellizzari, P. (2020), 'Supplying Slavery: Jamaica, North America, and British Intra-Imperial Trade, 1752–69', *Slavery and Abolition* 41, 3: 528–54.

Pereira, T. A. Z. (2018), *The Rise of the Brazilian Cotton Trade in Britain During the Industrial Revolution* (Cambridge).

Pettigrew, W. (2013), *Freedom's Debt: The Royal African Company and the Politics of the Atlantic Slave Trade 1672–1752* (Chapel Hill, CA).

Phillips, A. and Sharman, J. C. (2020), *Outsourcing Empire: How Company-States Made the Modern World* (Princeton).

Phillips, J. (1805/1970), *A General History of Inland Navigation, Foreign and Domestic*, 5th edn (1805), reprinted as *Phillips' Inland Navigation* (Newton Abbot).

Piketty, T. (2014), *Capital in the Twenty-first Century* (Cambridge, MA).

Piketty, T. (2020), *Capital and Ideology* (Cambridge, MA).

Pincus, S. (2009), *1688: the First Modern Revolution* (New Haven, CT).

Pincus, S. (2012), 'Rethinking Mercantilism: Political Economy, the British

Empire, and the Atlantic World in the Seventeenth and Eighteenth Centuries', *William and Mary Quarterly* 69, 1: 3–34.

Pincus, S. and Robinson, J. (2016), 'Challenging the Fiscal-Military Hegemony: the British Case', in A. Graham and P. Walsh (eds), *The British Fiscal Military States 1660–1783* (London), 229–61.

Pincus, S. and Robinson, J. (2017), 'Wars and State-making Reconsidered: The Rise of the Developmental State', *Annales: Histoire, Sciences Sociale*, English edn, 71, 1: 9–34.

Platt, V. B. (1969), 'The East India Company and the Madagascar Slave Trade', *William and Mary Quarterly* 26: 548–71.

Polanyi, K. (1944), *The Great Transformation: the Political and Economic Origins of Our Time* (New York).

Polanyi, K. (1966/2022), *Dahomey and the Slave Trade: an Analysis of an Archaic Economy* (Washington).

Pollard, S. (1965), *The Genesis of Modern Management: a Study of the Industrial Revolution in Great Britain* (Cambridge, MA).

Pollard, S. (1981), *Peaceful Conquest: the Industrialisation of Europe 1760–1970* (Oxford).

Pomeranz, K. (2000), *The Great Divergence: China, Europe and the Making of the Modern World Economy* (Princeton).

Pons, F. M. (2007), *History of the Caribbean: Plantations Trade and War in the Atlantic World* (Princeton).

Poskett, J. (2022), *Horizons: A Global History of Science* (Harmondsworth).

Post, C. (2012), *The American Road to Capitalism: Studies in Class-Structure, Economic Development and Political Conflict 1620–1877* (London).

Post, C. (2015), 'Review of Sven Beckert, *Empire of Cotton: A Global History*', *Journal of the Civil War Era* 5: 581–3.

Postlethwayt, M. (1745), *The Africa Trade the Great Pillar and Support of the British Plantation Trade in America* (London).

Postlethwayt, M. (1757), *The Universal Dictionary of Trade and Commerce. Translated from the French of . . . Monsieur Savary . . . with Large Additions and Improvements*, 2nd edn, 2 vols. (London).

Postlethwayt, M. (1766), *The Universal Dictionary of Trade and Commerce*, 3rd edn, 2 vols. (London).

Potofsky, A. (2011), 'Paris on-the-Atlantic from the Old Regime to the Revolution', *French History* 25: 89–107.

Pressnell, L. S. (1956), *Country Banking in the Industrial Revolution* (Oxford).

Price, J. M. (1980), *Capital and Credit in British Overseas Trade: the View from the Chesapeake, 1700–1776* (Harvard).

Price, J. M. (1991), 'Credit in the Slave Trade and Plantation Economies', in B. L. Solow (ed.), *Slavery and the Rise of the Atlantic Trading System* (Cambridge), 293–339.

Price, J. M. (1995), *Tobacco in Atlantic Trade: the Chesapeake, London and Glasgow, 1675–1775* (Brookfield, VT).

Price, J. M. (1998), 'The Imperial Economy, 1700–1776', in P. J. Marshall (ed.), *The Oxford History of the British Empire,* vol. 2 (Oxford), 78–101.

Quinn, S. (2008), 'Securitization of Sovereign Debt: Corporations as a Sovereign Debt Restructuring Mechanism in Britain 1694–1720', SSRN, https://ssrn.com/abstract=991941 or http://dx.doi.org/10.2139/ssrn.991941.

Radburn, N. J. (2009), 'William Davenport, the Slave Trade and Merchant Enterprise in Eighteenth Century Liverpool', MA, Victoria University, Wellington, https://researcharchive.vuw.ac.nz/xmlui/handle/10063/1187.

Radburn, N. J. (2015a), 'Guinea Factors, Slave Sales, and the Profits of the Transatlantic Slave Trade in Late Eighteenth-century Jamaica: the Case of John Tailyour', *William and Mary Quarterly* 72, 2: 243–86.

Radburn, N. J. (2015b), 'Keeping "the wheels in motion": Transatlantic Credit Terms, Slave Prices and the Geography of Slavery in the British Americas, 1755–1807', *Journal of Economic History* 75, 3: 660–89.

Radburn, N. J. (2021), '"Managed at first as if they were beasts": The Seasoning of Enslaved Africans in Eighteenth Century Jamaica', *Journal of Global History* 6, 1: 11–30.

Radburn, N.J. (forthcoming), 'The British Gunpowder Industry and the Slave Trade', *Business History.*

Radburn, N. and Roberts J. (2019), 'Gold Versus Life: Jobbing Gangs and British Caribbean Slavery', *William and Mary Quarterly* 76, 2: 223–56.

Ragatz, L. G. (1931), 'Absentee Landlordism in the British Caribbean, 1750–1833', *Agricultural History* 5, 1: 7–24.

Rawley, J. A. (1981), *The Transatlantic Slave Trade: a History* (New York).

Rawley, J. A. (2003), *London: Metropolis of the Slave Trade* (Columbia).

Rawlinson, K. (2020), 'Lloyds of London and Greene King to Make Slave Trade Reparations', *The Guardian*, 18 June.

Read, C. (2023), *Calming the Storms: the Carry Trade, the Banking School and British Financial Crises since 1825* (London).

Reddiker, M. (2007), *The Slave Ship: a Human History* (London).

Reed, M. C. (1975), *Investment in Railways in Britain 1820–1844: a Study in the Development of the Capital Market* (Oxford).

Rees, G. (1972), 'Copper Sheathing: an Example of Technological Diffusion in the English Merchant Fleet', *Journal of Transport History* 2: 85–94.

Richards, W. A. (1980), 'The Import of Firearms into West Africa in the Eighteenth Century', *Journal of African History* 21, 1: 43–59.

Richardson, D. (1975), 'Profitability in the Bristol–Liverpool Slave Trade', *Outre-Mers: Revue d'histoire,* 226–7: 301–8.

Richardson, D. (1976), 'Profits in the Liverpool Slave Trade: the Accounts of

William Davenport 1757–1784', in R. Anstey and P. E. H. Hair (eds), *Liverpool, the African Slave Trade and Abolition* (Liverpool), 60–90.

Richardson, D. (1979), 'West African Consumption Patterns and Their Influence on the Eighteenth Century Slave Trade', in H. A. Gemery and J. S. Hogendorn (eds), *The Uncommon Market: Essays in the Economic History of the Atlantic Slave Trade* (New York), 49–51.

Richardson, D. (1985), *The Bristol Slave Traders: a Collective Portrait* (Bristol).

Richardson, D. (1987), 'The Slave Trade, Sugar and British Economic Growth 1748–1756', *Journal of Interdisciplinary History* 17, 4: 739–69.

Richardson, D. (1998), 'The British Empire and the Atlantic Slave Trade 1660–1807', in P. J. Marshall (ed.), *The Oxford History of the British Empire*, vol. 2: *The Eighteenth Century* (Oxford), 430–64.

Richardson, D. (2005) 'Slavery and Bristol's "Golden Age"', *Slavery and Abolition* 26, 35–54.

Richardson, D. (2022), *Principles and Agents: the British Slave Trade and Its Abolition* (New Haven, CT and London).

Richardson, D., Schwarz, S. and Tibbles, A. (2007), *Liverpool and Transatlantic Slavery* (Liverpool).

Riello, G. (2013), *Cotton: the Fabric That Made the Modern World* (Cambridge).

Riello, G. (2022), 'Cotton Textiles and the Industrial Revolution in Global Context', *Past & Present* 255: 87–139.

Roberts, C. E. (2017), 'To Heal and to Harm: Medicine, Knowledge, and Power in the British Slave Trade', unpublished Harvard University thesis.

Roberts, J. (2013), *Slavery and the Enlightenment in the British Atlantic, 1750–1807* (Cambridge).

Robinson C. J. (1983), *Black Marxism: the Making of the Black Radical Tradition* (London).

Robinson, C. J. (1987), 'Capitalism, Slavery and Bourgeois Historiography', *History Workshop Journal* 23, 1: 122–40.

Robinson, R. (2000), *The Debt: What America Owes Blacks* (New York).

Rockman, S. (2018), 'Negro Cloth: Mastering the Market for Slave Clothing in Antebellum America', in S. Beckert and C. Desan (eds), *American Capitalism: New Histories* (New York), 170–94.

Rodger, N. A. M. (1986), *The Wooden World: an Anatomy of the Georgian Navy* (London).

Rodger, N. A. M. (1998), 'Sea Power and Empire, 1688–1793', in P. J. Marshall (ed.), *The Oxford History of the British Empire*, vol 2: *The Eighteenth Century* (Oxford, 1998), 169–71.

Rodger, N. A. M. (2004), *The Command of the Ocean: a Naval History of Britain*, vol. 2: *1649–1815* (2004).

Rodger, N. A. M. (2010), 'War as an Economic Activity in the "Long" Eighteenth Century', *International Journal of Maritime History* 22, 2: 1–18.

Rodney, W. (1972/2018), *How Europe Underdeveloped Africa* (London).

Rönnbäck, K. (2010), 'New and Old Peripheries: Britain, the Baltic, and the Americas in the Great Divergence', *Journal of Global History* 5, 3: 373–94.

Rönnbäck, K. (2014), 'Sweet Business: Quantifying the Value Added in the British Colonial Sugar Trade in the Eighteenth Century', *Revista de Història Economica, Journal of Iberian and Latin American History* 32, 2: 223–45.

Rönnbäck, K. (2018), 'On the Economic Importance of the Slave Plantation Complex to the British Economy During the Eighteenth Century: a Value-Added Approach', *Journal of Global History* 13: 309–27.

Rose, J. H. (1929), 'British West India Commerce as a Factor in the Napoleonic War', *Cambridge Historical Journal* 3, 1: 34–46.

Rose, M. (1986), *The Gregs of Quarry Bank Mill: The Rise and Decline of a Family Firm* (Cambridge).

Rosenthal, C. (2016), 'Slavery's Scientific Management: Masters and Management', in S. Beckert and S. Rockman (eds), *Slavery's Capitalism: a New History of American Economic Development* (Philadelphia), 62–86.

Rosenthal, C. (2018), *Accounting for Slavery: Masters and Management* (Cambridge, MA).

Rössner, P. R. (2020), *Freedom and Capitalism in Early Modern Europe: Mercantilism and the Making of the Modern Economic Mind* (London).

Rostow, W. W. (1960), *The Stages of Economic Growth: a Non-Communist Manifesto* (Cambridge).

Rowlands, M. (1975), *Masters and Men in the West Midlands Metalware Trades Before the Industrial Revolution* (Manchester).

Royal Commission of Ancient and Historical Monuments of Wales (2000), *Coppperopolis: Landscapes of the Early Industrial Period in Swansea* (Aberystwyth).

Rubinstein, W. D. (2006), *Men of Property. the Very Wealthy in Britain since the Industrial Revolution* (London).

Russell, E. (2011), *Evolutionary History: Uniting History and Biology to Understand Life on Earth* (Cambridge).

Rustin, M. and Massey, D. (2014), 'Whose Economy? Reframing the Debate', *Soundings* 57: 170–91.

Rustin, M. and Massey, D. (2015), 'Rethinking the Neo-Liberal World Order', *Soundings* 58: 110–29.

Rydén, D. B. (2009), *West Indian Slavery and British Abolition 1783–1807* (Cambridge).

Rydén, D. B. (2013), '"One of the Finest and Most Fruitful Spots in America": an Analysis of Eighteenth-Century Carriacou', *Journal of Interdisciplinary History* 43, 4: 539–70.

Sanghera, S. (2021), *Empireland: How Imperialism Has Shaped Modern Britain* (London).

Satchell, V. (2010), *Sugar, Slavery and Technological Change: Jamaica 1760–1830* (Saarbrücken).

Satia, P. (2018), *Empire of Guns: the Violent Making of the Industrial Revolution* (New York).

Schermerhorn, C. (2016), 'A Coastwise Slave Trade and a Mercantile Community of Interest', in S. Beckert and S. Rockman (eds), *Slavery's Capitalism: a New History of American Economic Development* (Philadelphia), 209–24.

Schiebinger, L. (2017), *Secret Cures of Slaves: People, Plants and Medicine in the Eighteenth-Century Atlantic World* (Stanford).

Schneider, E. B. (2013), 'Inescapable Hunger? Energy Cost Accounting and the Costs of Digestion, Pregnancy, and Lactation', *European Review of Economic History* 17: 340–63.

Schofield, R. (1963), *The Lunar Society of Birmingham: a Social History of Provincial Science and Industry in Eighteenth-century England* (Oxford).

Schumpeter, E. B. (1960), *English Overseas Trade Statistics 1697–1808* (London).

Scully, P. and Paton, D. (eds) (2005), *Gender and Slave Emancipation in the Atlantic World* (Durham, NC).

Shammas, C. (1983), 'Food Expenditures and Economic Well-Being in Early Modern England', *Journal of Economic History* 43: 89–100.

Shammas, C. (1984), 'The Eighteenth-century Diet and Economic Change', *Explorations in Economic History* 21, 3: 254–69.

Shammas, C. (1990), *The Pre-industrial Consumer in England and America* (Oxford).

Shammas, C. (1993), 'Changes in English and Anglo-American Consumption from 1550 to 1800', in J. Brewer and R. Porter (eds), *Consumption and the World of Goods* (London), 177–205.

Shammas, C. (2000), 'The Revolutionary Impact of European Demand for Tropical Goods', in J. McCusker and K. Morgan (eds), *The Early Modern Atlantic Economy* (Cambridge), 163–85.

Shaw-Taylor, L. and Wrigley, E. A. (2014), 'Occupational Structure and Population Change', in R. Floud, J. Humphries and P. Johnson (eds), *The Cambridge Economic History of Modern Britain*, vol. 1: *1700–1870* (Cambridge), 53–88.

Shepherd, V. A. (1991), 'Livestock and Sugar: Aspects of Jamaica's Agricultural Development from the Late Seventeenth to the Early Nineteenth Century', *Historical Journal* 34: 627–43.

Sheridan, R. B. (1957), 'The Molasses Act and the Market Strategy of the British Sugar Planters', *Journal of Economic History* 17: 62–83.

Sheridan, R. B. (1958), 'Commercial and Financial Organisation of the British Slave Trade, 1750–1807', *Economic History Review* 11, 2: 249–63.

Sheridan, R. B. (1960), 'The British Credit Crisis of 1772 and the American Colonies', *Journal of Economic History* 20, 2: 161–86.

Sheridan, R. B. (1961), 'The Rise of the Colonial Gentry: A Case Study of Antigua, 1730–75', *Economic History Review* 13, 3: 342–57.

Sheridan, R. B. (1965), 'The Wealth of Jamaica in the Eighteenth Century', *Economic History Review* 18: 292–311.

Sheridan, R. B. (1969), 'The Plantation Revolution and the Industrial Revolution', *Caribbean Studies* 9: 5–25.

Sheridan, R. B. (1971), 'Simon Taylor, Sugar Tycoon of Jamaica, 1740–1813', *Agricultural History* 45, 4: 285–96.

Sheridan, R. B. (1974), *Sugar and Slavery: an Economic History of the British West Indies 1623–1775* (Baltimore).

Sheridan, R. B. (1976), 'The Crisis of Slave Subsistence in the British West Indies During and After the American Revolution', *William and Mary Quarterly* 33, 4: 615–41.

Shumway, R. (2011), *The Fante and the Transatlantic Slave Trade* (Rochester, NY).

Sissoko, C. (2022), 'Becoming a Central Bank: the Development of the Bank of England's Private Sector Lending Policies During the Restriction', *Economic History Review* 75: 601–32.

Sissoko, C. and Ishizu, M. (2023), 'How the West India Trade Fostered Innovations in Bank of England Lending Techniques', *Economic History Review*, forthcoming.

Slare, F. (1715), *A Vindication of Sugars Against the Charge of Dr. Willis, other Physicians, and Common Prejudices. Dedicated to the Ladies. Together with Further Discoveries and Remarks* (London).

Smail, J. (1999), *Merchants, Markets and Manufacture: The English Wool Textile Industry in the Eighteenth Century* (Basingstoke).

Smith, A. (1776), *The Wealth of Nations,* 2 vols (Oxford).

Smith, M. J. (2014), *Liberty, Fraternity, Exile: Haiti and Jamaica After Emancipation* (Chapel Hill, CA).

Smith, S. D. (1996), 'Accounting for Taste: British Coffee Consumption in Historical Perspective', *Journal of Interdisciplinary History* 27: 183–214.

Smith, S. D. (1998), 'The Market for Manufactures in the Thirteen Continental Colonies, 1698–1776', *Economic History Review* 51, 4: 676–708.

Smith, S. D. (2002), 'Merchants and Planters Revisited', *Economic History Review* 55, 3: 434–65.

Smith, S. D. (2006), *Slavery, Family, and Gentry Capitalism in the British Atlantic: The World of the Lascelles, 1648–1834* (Cambridge).

Smith, S. D. (2008), 'Sugar's Poor Relation: Coffee Planting in the British West Indies 1720–1833', *Slavery and Abolition* 19: 68–89.

Smith, S. D. (2011), 'Volcanic Hazard in a Slave Society: the 1812 Eruption of Mt Soufrière in St Vincent', *Journal of Historical Geography* 37, 1: 56–67.

Smith, S. D. (2012), 'Storm Hazard and Slavery: the Impact of the 1831 Great Caribbean Hurricane on St Vincent', *Environment and History* 18, 1: 97–123.

Solar, P. M. and Rönnbäck, K. (2015), 'Copper Sheathing and the British Slave Trade', *Economic History Review* 68, 3: 806–29.

Solow, B. L. (1985), 'Caribbean Slavery and British Growth: the Eric Williams Hypothesis', *Journal of Development Economics* 17: 99–115.

Solow, B. L. (1987), 'Capitalism and Slavery in the Exceedingly Long Run', in B. L. Solow and S. Engerman (eds), *British Capitalism and Caribbean Slavery: the Legacy of Eric Williams* (Cambridge), 51–78.

Solow, B. L. (ed.) (1991), *Slavery and the Rise of the Atlantic System* (Cambridge).

Solow, B. L. and Engerman, S. (eds) (1987), *British Capitalism and Caribbean Slavery: the Legacy of Eric Williams* (Cambridge).

Sraffa, P. and Dobb, M. H. (eds) (1966), *The Works and Correspondence of David Ricardo*, vol. 2 (Cambridge).

Stanziani, A. (2014), *Bondage, Labour and Rights in Eurasia from the Sixteenth to the Early Twentieth Centuries* (Oxford).

Stein, R. L. (1980), 'The French Sugar Business in the Eighteenth Century: A Quantitative Study', *Business History* 22, 1: 3–17.

Stein, R. L. (1988), *The French Sugar Business in the Eighteenth Century* (Baton Rouge).

Stephens, S. G. (1976), 'The Origin of Sea Island Cotton', *Agricultural History* 50, 2: 391–9.

Stobart, J. (2004), *The First Industrial Region: North-west England, c.1700–60* (Manchester).

Stobart, J. (2013), *Sugar and Spice: Grocers and Groceries in Provincial England 1650–1830* (Oxford).

Stuart, S. E. (2008), *Gillows of Lancaster and London 1730–1840* (London).

Sturmey, S. G. (1962), *British Shipping and World Competition* (Oxford).

Styles, J. (2000), 'Product Innovation in Early Modern London', *Past & Present* 168: 124–69.

Styles, J. (2020), 'The Rise and Fall of the Spinning Jenny: Domestic Mechanisation in Eighteenth Century Cotton Spinning', *Textile History* 51: 195–236.

Styles, J. (2022a), 'Transformations in Textiles, 1500–1760', forthcoming in P. Hohti (ed.), *Refashioning the Renaissance: Everyday Dress and the Reconstruction of Early Modern Material Culture* (Manchester).

Styles, J. (2022b), 'Refashioning the Industrial Revolution: Fibres, Fashion and Technical Innovation in British Cotton Textiles, 1600–1780', in G. Nigro (ed.), *Fashion as an Economic Engine*, Datini Studies in Economic History ebook, https://books.fupress.com/chapter/re-fashioning-industrial-revolution-fibres-fashion-and-technical-innovation-in-british-cotton-textil/11714.

Sugden, K., Keibek, S. and Shaw-Taylor, L. (2023), 'Adam Smith Revisited: Coal and the Location of the Woollen Manufacture in England Before Mechanisation, c.1500–1820', *Continuity and Change*, forthcoming.

Tadman, M. (1989), *Speculators and Slaves: Masters, Traders and Slaves in the Old South* (Maddison, WI).

Tate, W. E. (1944), 'The Five English Statutory Registries of Deeds', *Bulletin of the Institute of Historical Research* 20, 60: 97–105.

Taylor, B. (1983/2016), *Eve and the New Jerusalem: Socialism and Feminism in the Nineteenth Century* (London).

Taylor, M. (2020), *The Interest: How the British Establishment Resisted the Abolition of Slavery* (London).

Teso, E. (2019), 'The Long Term Effect of Demographic Shocks on the Evolution of Gender Roles: the Evidence from the Trans-Atlantic Slave Trade', *Journal of the European Economic Association* 17, 2: 497–534.

Thirsk, J. (2014), *Food in Early Modern England: Phases, Fads, Fashions 1500–1760* (Totnes, Devon).

Thomas, D. (1690), *An Historical Account of the Rise and Growth of the West-India Colonies and of the Great Advantages they are to England in Respect of Trade* (London).

Thomas, R. P. (1968), 'Sugar Colonies of the Old Empire: Profit or Loss for Great Britain?', *Economic History Review* 21, 1: 30–45.

Thompson, P. (2009), 'Henry Drax's Instructions on the Management of a Seventeenth Century Barbadian Sugar Plantation', *William and Mary Quarterly* 66, 3: 565–604.

Thornton, J. K. (1999), *Warfare in Atlantic Africa 1500–1800* (London).

Tilly, C. (1990), *Coercion, Capital and European States AD 990–1990* (Cambridge, MA).

Timmins, G. (1993), *The Last Shift: the Decline of Handloom Weaving in Nineteenth Century Lancashire* (Manchester).

Tinker, H. (1974), *A New System of Slavery: the Export of Indian Labour Overseas 1830–1920* (London).

Tomich, D. W. (2004), *Through the Prism of Slavery: Labour, Capital and the World Economy* (Lanham, MA).

Turnbull, G. (1987), 'Canals, Coal and Regional Growth During the Industrial Revolution', *Economic History Review* 40: 537–60.

Turner, M. (ed.) (1995), *From Chattel Slaves to Wage Slaves: the Dynamics of Labour Bargaining in the Americas* (Kingston, Jamaica).

Turner, M. (2004), 'The British Caribbean: the Transition from Slave to Free Legal Status', in D. Hay and P. Craven (eds), *Masters, Servants and Magistrates in Britain and the Empire, 1562–1955* (Chapel Hill, CA), 303–22.

Unwin, G. (1968), *Samuel Oldknow and the Arkwrights: the Industrial Revolution at Stockport and Marple* (Manchester).

Van der Voort, J. P. (1981), 'Dutch Capital in the West Indies During the Eighteenth Century', *Acta Historiae Needlandica* (Low Countries History Yearbook) 14: 85–105.

Van Zanden, J. L. and Prak, M. (eds.) (2013), *Technology, Skills and the Pre-Modern Economy* (Leiden).

Von Tunzelmann, G. N. (1978), *Steam Power and British Industrialization to 1860* (Oxford).

Vries, P. (2015), *State, Economy and the Great Divergence: Great Britain and China, 1680–1850s* (London).

Vries, P. (2017), 'Cotton, Capitalism, and Coercion: Some Comments on Sven Beckert's Empire of Cotton', *Journal of World History* 28, 1, 20: 131–40.

Wadsworth, A. P. and Mann, J. De L. (1931/1968), *The Cotton Trade and Industrial Lancashire 1600–1780* (New York).

Walton, J. K. (1989), 'Proto-industrialisation in Lancashire', in P. Hudson (ed.), *Regions and Industries: a Perspective on the Industrial Revolution in Britain* (Cambridge), 41–68.

Walvin, J. (1993), *Black Ivory: a History of British Slavery* (London).

Walvin J. (2008), *The Trader, the Owner, the Slave: Parallel Lives in the Age of Slavery* (London).

Walvin, J. (2011), *The Zong: a Massacre, the Law and the End of Slavery* (New Haven, CT).

Walvin, J. (2017), *Slavery in Small Things: Slavery and Modern Cultural Habits* (London).

Ward, J. R. (1978), 'The Profitability of Sugar Planting in the British West Indies', 1650–1834', *Economic History Review* 31, 2: 197–213.

Watts, S. D. (1987), *The West Indies: Patterns of Development, Culture and Environmental Change Since 1492* (Cambridge).

Weatherill, L. (1971), *The Pottery Trade of North Staffordshire 1660–1760* (Manchester).

Weatherill, L. (1988), *Consumer Behaviour and Material Culture in Britain 1660–1760* (London).

Weatherill, L. (1990), *The Account Book of Richard Latham 1724–1767* (Oxford).

Webster, A. (2008), 'Liverpool and the Asian Trade 1800–1850: Some Insights into a Provincial British Commercial Network', in S. Haggerty, A. Webster and N. White (eds), *The Empire in One City: Liverpool's Inconvenient Imperial Past* (Manchester), 35–54.

Wilentz, S. (2019), 'American Slavery and "the Relentless Unforeseen"', *The New York Review of Books*, 19 November.

Williams, A. R. (1753), *The Liverpool Memorandum Book or Gentleman's, Merchant's and Tradesman's Daily Pocket Journal for the Year 1753* (London).

Williams, E. (1938/2014), *The Economic Aspect of the Abolition of the West Indian Slave Trade and Slavery* (Lanham, MA).

Williams, E. (1944/1994), *Capitalism & Slavery* (Durham, NC).

Williams, E. (2022), *Capitalism and Slavery* (London).

Williams, G. (1897, 1966), *History of the Liverpool Privateers and Letters of Marque With An Account of the Liverpool Slave Trade* (Liverpool).

Williams, M. W. (2016), *A Brief History of the Royal Navy* (London).

Williamson, O. E. (1985), *The Economic Institutions of Capitalism* (New York).

Wilson, C. (1941), *Anglo-Dutch Commerce and Finance in the Eighteenth Century* (Cambridge).

Wilson, R. G. (1971), *Gentleman Merchants: the Merchant Community of Leeds, 1700–1830* (Manchester).

Wilson, R. G. (1973), 'The Supremacy of the Yorkshire Cloth Industry in the Eighteenth Century', in N. B. Harte and K. G. Ponting (eds), *Textile History and Economic History: Essays in Honour of Miss Julia De Lacy Mann* (Manchester), 228–30.

Wilson, R. G. and Mackley, A. L. (1999), 'How Much Did the English Country House Cost to Build 1660–1880', *Economic History Review* 52: 436–68.

Withington, P. (2020), 'Where Was the Coffee in Early Modern England', *Journal of Modern History* 92: 40–75.

Wood, W. (1718), *A Survey of Trade together with Considerations on Our Money, Bullion etc. In Four Parts* (London).

Wright, C. and Fayle, C. E. (1928), *A History of Lloyds* (London).

Wright, G. (2020), 'Slavery and Anglo American Capitalism Revisited', *Economic History Review* 73: 353–83.

Wrigley, E. A. (1985), 'Urban Growth and Agricutural Change: England and the Continent in the Early Modern Period', *Journal of Interdisciplinary History* 15: 683–728.

Wrigley E. A. (1988), *Continuity, Chance and Change: the Character of the Industrial Revolution in England* (Cambridge).

Wrigley, E. A. (2009), 'Rickman Revisited: The Population Growth Rates of English Counties in the Early Modern Period', *Economic History Review* 62, 3: 711–35.

Wrigley, E. A. (2016), *The Path to Sustained Growth: England's Transition from an Organic Economy to an Industrial Revolution* (Cambridge).

Wrigley, E. A. (2018), 'Reconsidering the Industrial Revolution: England and Wales', *Journal of Interdisciplinary History* 49, 1: 9–42.

Wrigley, E. A. (2020), 'A Reply to Kumar's "Omission of Data in Wrigley's Reconsidering the Industrial Revolution"', *Journal of Interdisciplinary History* 51, 2: 301–2.

Zahedieh, N. (1999), 'Making Mercantilism Work: London Merchants and Atlantic Trade in the Late Seventeenth Century', *Transactions of the Royal Historical Society* 9: 143–58.

Zahedieh, N. (2009), 'Economy', in D. Armitage and M. Braddick (eds), *The British Atlantic World, 1500–1800*, 2nd edn (Basingstoke), 53–70.

Zahedieh, N. (2010), *The Capital and the Colonies: London and the Atlantic Economy 1660–1700* (Cambridge).

Zahedieh, N. (2013), 'Colonies, Copper and the Market for Inventive Activity in England and Wales 1680–1730', *Economic History Review* 66: 805–25.

Zahedieh, N. (2014), 'Overseas Trade and Empire', in R. Floud, J. Humphries and P. Johnson (eds), *The Cambridge Economic History of Modern Britain*, vol. 1: *1700–1870* (Cambridge), 392–420.

Zahedieh, N. (2018), 'Defying Mercantilism. Illicit Trade, Trust and the Jamaican Sephardim, 1660–1730', *Historical Journal* 61: 77–102.

Zahedieh, N. (2021), 'Eric Williams and William Forbes: Copper, Colonial Markets and Commercial Capitalism', *Economic History Review* 74: 784–808.

Zahedieh, N. (2022), 'A Copper Still and the Making of Rum in the Eighteenth-century Atlantic World', *The Historical Journal* 65: 149–66.

Zahedieh, N. (2023), 'The Rise of "King Sugar" and Enslaved Labour in Early English Jamaica', *Early American Studies* (forthcoming).

Ziegler, P. (1988), *The Sixth Great Power: Barings 1762–1929* (London).

Zylberberg, D. (2015), 'Fuel Prices, Regional Diets and Cooking Habits in the English Industrial Revolution (1750–1830)', *Past & Present*, 229, 1: 91–122.

Index